MYTHS & LEGENDS!

Senior Editor Sam Atkinson
Project Art Editor Joe Lawrence
Senior US Editor Megan Douglass
Editors Zaina Budaly, Abi Maxwell, Kelsie Besaw
Designers Tory Gordon-Harris, Rosie Burnett
Senior Jacket Designer Rashika Kachroo
DTP Designer Mohd Rizwan, Vikram Singh
DK Media Archive Kaylee Wisternoff
Picture Research Geetam Biswas, Manpreet Kaur
Production Editor Gillian Reid
Production Controller Ena Matagic
Managing Editor Rachel Fox
Managing Art Editor Owen Peyton Jones
Publisher Andrew Macintyre
Art Director Mabel Chan

Written by Andrea Mills, Philip Parker, Phil Hunt,
Sam Atkinson, Zaina Budaly

Consultant Dr. Jean Menzies

Illustrators Peter Bull; Mark Clifton; Jason Harding;
Stuart Jackson-Carter; Arran Lewis; Sofian Moumene; KJA Artists

First American Edition, 2025
Published in the United States by DK Publishing,
a division of Penguin Random House LLC
1745 Broadway, 20th Floor, New York, NY 10019

Copyright © 2025 Dorling Kindersley Limited
25 26 27 28 29 10 9 8 7 6 5 4 3 2 1
001–342551–Aug/2025

All rights reserved.
Without limiting the rights under the copyright reserved above, no part of this publication may be reproduced, stored in or introduced into a retrieval system, or transmitted, in any form, or by any means (electronic, mechanical, photocopying, recording, or otherwise), without the prior written permission of the copyright owner.

DK values and supports copyright. Copyright fuels creativity, encourages diverse voices, promotes free speech, and creates a vibrant culture. Thank you for buying an authorized edition of this publication and for complying with copyright laws by not reproducing, scanning, or distributing any part of it in any form without permission. You are supporting writers and artists and allowing DK to continue to publish books that inform and inspire readers. No part of this publication may be used or reproduced in any manner for the purpose of training artificial intelligence technologies or systems.
Published in Great Britain by Dorling Kindersley Limited

ISBN 978-0-5939-6562-7

DK books are available at special discounts when purchased in bulk for sales promotions, premiums, fund-raising, or educational use.
For details, contact: DK Publishing Special Markets,
1745 Broadway, 20th Floor, New York, NY 10019
SpecialSales@dk.com

Printed and bound in China
www.dk.com

This book was made with Forest Stewardship Council™ certified paper—one small step in DK's commitment to a sustainable future.
Learn more at
www.dk.com/uk/information/sustainability

MYTHS & LEGENDS!

DK

CONTENTS

EUROPE

ANCIENT GREECE AND ROME — 8
- Greek creation and the early universe — 10
- War against the Titans — 12
- The creation of humans — 14
- Hades and Persephone — 16
- The Greek underworld — 18
- Athena — 20
- Perseus, slayer of Medusa — 22
- Apollo and Artemis — 24
- Jason and the Argonauts — 26
- Theseus and the Minotaur — 28
- The mistakes of mortals — 30
- The labors of Hercules — 32
- Aphrodite — 34
- The Trojan War — 36
- The return of Odysseus — 38
- The beginnings of Rome — 40
- Gods of the home — 42
- Psyche and Cupid — 44

NORTHERN EUROPE — 46
- Norse creation stories — 48
- The World Tree — 50
- Odin, the Allfather — 52
- Thor and Loki — 54
- Twilight of the gods — 56
- The Kalevala — 58
- Beowulf — 60
- Sigurd the dragon slayer — 62

WESTERN EUROPE — 64
- The Island of Destiny — 66
- The Tuatha Dé Danann — 68
- The Hound of Chulainn — 70
- Fionn mac Cumhaill — 72
- The Mabinogi — 74
- The legend of King Arthur — 76

EASTERN EUROPE — 78
- Early Slavic gods — 80
- Bába Yagá — 82
- Koschei the Deathless — 84
- The firebird — 86

AFRICA

ANCIENT EGYPT — 90
- The Egyptian story of creation — 92
- Journey of the sun — 94
- Osiris and the underworld — 96
- The Hall of Two Truths — 98

SOUTH OF THE SAHARA — 100
- Yoruba sacred stories — 102
- Mawu-Lisa — 104
- Tales of Ananse — 106
- The black and red gods — 108
- The adventures of Mwindo — 110
- Stories of the San — 112

ASIA

WEST ASIA	**116**
Marduk and Tiamat	118
Inanna, Queen of Heaven	120
The Epic of Gilgamesh	122
Baal and Anat	124
The struggle of good and evil	126

SOUTH ASIA	**128**
The Trimurti	130
The ten avatars of Vishnu	132
The Great Goddess	134
The Mahabharata	136
The Ramayana	138

EAST ASIA	**140**
Pangu and Nüwa	142
Yi, the Heavenly Archer	144
Adventures of the Monkey King	146
The Jade Emperor's court	148
Izanami and Izanagi	150
The Three Noble Children	152
Descendants of the kami	154
Kintaro, the golden boy	156
The creation and foundation of Korea	158

What is a myth?

There are different types of stories in this book: myths, legends, and sacred stories. A myth often tells the story of a powerful being, such as a god or supernatural creature. Most creation stories are myths because they describe the deeds of a god or many gods. A legend, on the other hand, may be a story based on a real person or event, and magical elements have been added to it over time. Other stories in this book are sacred because they form part of a religion still practiced today, and are therefore highly valued.

THE AMERICAS

NORTH AMERICA	**162**
Turtle Island	164
Spider Grandmother	166
Stories of Raven	168
Sedna, Mother of the Deep	170

MESOAMERICA	**172**
The Hero Twins	174
The Legend of the Five Suns	176
Aztec gods of nature	178

SOUTH AMERICA	**180**
Viracocha the creator	182
Inca gods of earth and sky	184
Tales of the Taino	186

OCEANIA

AUSTRALIA AND THE PACIFIC	**190**
The Rainbow Serpent	192
Tales from the Dreaming	194
Ta'aroa creates the world	196
Maui of a Thousand Tricks	198
Myths of the Pacific	200

Glossary	202
Index	204
Acknowledgments	208

EUROPE

The myths and legends of Europe are famous throughout the world. Though no longer a part of any active set of beliefs, larger-than-life characters such as Zeus, Loki, and Bába Yagá are some of the most enduring figures in storytelling.

ANCIENT GREECE AND ROME

The Greeks were not a single nation or empire, but a collection of city-states, and their gods came from many different traditions. But Greeks everywhere came to worship a large pantheon of gods who bickered, fell in love, and went to war with each other. When the Romans overtook the Greeks as the leading power in the Mediterranean, they combined these deities with their own to create new versions of the gods that fitted their ideas of empire.

SOURCES OF THE MYTHS

Some of the earliest Greek tellings of the myths were poems, originally performed by storytellers and later written down. When the Greeks developed the art of theater in the 5th century BCE, mythology became a popular subject for drama. The Romans produced many collections of tales, as well as an origin myth of the Roman people themselves.

Greek poets
The two greatest epic poems of Greek myth, the *Iliad* and the *Odyssey*, are attributed to the 8th century BCE poet Homer. These epics tell of the last days of the Trojan War and the eventful journey home of the hero Odysseus (see pages 36-39).

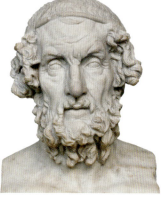

HOMER

Greek theater
The Greeks produced both tragedies and comedies based on mythological stories. The three greatest Greek playwrights were Euripides and Aeschylus, who wrote tragedies, and Aristophanes, who is known for his comic drama.

GREEK THEATER REBUILT BY ROMANS AT KOS, GREECE

Roman poets
Some Greek myths are known to us today from their Roman tellings. The poet Ovid wrote down many tales of different kinds of love, such as that of Narcissus who fell in love with his own reflection. The Roman poet Virgil also produced an epic origin story for Rome (see pages 40-41).

NARCISSUS

HOME OF THE GODS

The major deities of Greek myth were known as the Olympians because they lived at the top of a great mountain, Mount Olympus. These were the most powerful generation of Greek gods, who banished the Titans to Tartarus (see pages 12-13). From Olympus they ruled the universe, watching over the world below.

Mount Olympus
The Greeks had always thought of a mountain called Olympus as the home of the gods. But it was only around c.600 CE that a particular mountain in central Greece was given the name.

Fit for the gods
Mount Olympus is the highest mountain in Greece, with 52 peaks.

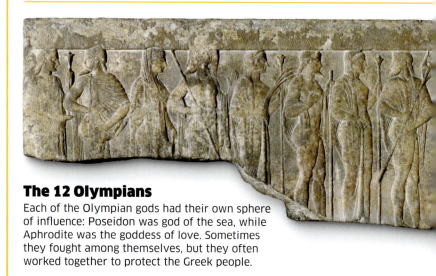

The 12 Olympians
Each of the Olympian gods had their own sphere of influence: Poseidon was god of the sea, while Aphrodite was the goddess of love. Sometimes they fought among themselves, but they often worked together to protect the Greek people.

PLACES OF WORSHIP

The Greeks and Romans both built temples to create a house for the statue of a god. Small offerings would be left at the statue, but most of the ceremonies were held outside. The exteriors of these temples might be highly decorated, while the insides were more restrained.

Oracle at Delphi
At Apollo's temple in Delphi, Greece, the high priestess was known as the Pythia. She was also the oracle of Delphi, offering advice based on her prophetic visions. Many myths include a prophecy told by Delphi's oracle.

RUINS OF THE TEMPLE OF APOLLO, DELPHI

Serving the gods
Some Greek gods had duties to perform for the Olympian gods. Hermes was one of the Olympians himself, but took his role as guider of human souls very seriously.

Hebe
The goddess of youth was also the cupbearer to the gods at their feasts.

Hermes
The herald of the gods, Hermes was a messenger and also guided souls to the underworld.

Iris
Also a messenger, Iris traveled on either her wings or a rainbow to deliver messages to humans.

Roll call
This marble relief shows the Olympians from left to right: Hestia, Hermes, Aphrodite, Ares, Demeter, Hephaestus, Hera, Poseidon, Athena, Zeus, Artemis, and Apollo.

THE PANTHEON, ROME

The Pantheon
The temple known as the Pantheon in Rome is one of the finest examples of Roman temple architecture. But which god or gods the temple was dedicated to is unclear.

FESTIVALS
The Greeks and Romans held various festivals throughout the year to honor the gods. Sporting events held significance for the Greeks, who believed that athletic competition was a way to worship the gods. The Roman calendar was filled with festival days that celebrated a particular deity.

Olympic Games
Held every four years at Olympia in honor of Zeus, the Olympic Games saw athletes from the various city-states competing for laurel wreath crowns.

Panathenaia
This Athenian festival was held every four years in honor of the city's patron goddess, Athena. Athletic games were held in the Panathenaic Stadium.

Saturnalia
On the feast of Saturnalia, in honor of the god Saturn, Romans gave each other small gifts and roles were reversed as masters waited on their servants.

ROME'S ADOPTED GODS
As the Romans expanded from a city-state into an empire, they adopted the local deities of the people they conquered. Most famously the Romans took aspects of the Greek gods and combined them with their own, but they also took gods from other cultures.

Greek name	Roman name	Role
Aphrodite	Venus	Goddess of love and beauty
Ares	Mars	God of war
Artemis	Diana	Goddess of the hunt
Athena	Minerva	Goddess of wisdom and war
Demeter	Ceres	Fertility and mother goddess
Hades	Pluto	God of the underworld
Hephaestus	Vulcan	Blacksmith god
Hermes	Mercury	Messenger of the gods
Hera	Juno	Wife of Zeus/Jupiter
Cronus	Saturn	Father of Zeus/Jupiter
Poseidon	Neptune	Sea god
Zeus	Jupiter	Sky and thunder god

Mithras
The Roman god Mithras was based on an Iranian deity called Mithra. His worship is shrouded in mystery, but his temples were often built underground. The cult of Mithras was popular throughout the western Roman Empire.

Mithras and the bull
Many sculptures show Mithras killing a bull.

SUPERNATURAL CREATURES
Many of the most common magical beings from fantasy stories and Western folklore have their origin in the myths and legends of Greece and Rome.

Centaur
Half-human, half-horse, the centaurs combined the wildness of nature with wisdom. The wisest centaur, Chiron, was the tutor to heroes such as Achilles.

Satyr
With the upper body of a man and the lower parts, ears, and horns of a goat, satyrs were noisy and hot-blooded followers of the god of wine, Dionysus.

Nymph
Tied to a specific location, nymphs were female nature deities. A dryad was a type of nymph who was the spirit of an oak tree. The dryad and tree lived and died together.

Hippocampus
A wild sea creature, the hippocampus had the front parts of a horse and the tail of a fish. The chariot of the sea god Poseidon was drawn by hippocampi.

Phoenix
The bird that is reborn again after burning to ash appears in some Asian myths, but the original phoenix was a creature of the ancient Greeks.

Cyclopes means "Round-eyes" in Ancient Greek.

Greek creation and the early universe

To the ancient Greeks, the forces of nature, such as the Earth and sky, took the form of gods. The first gods, known as primordials, sprung out of Chaos and went on to create the giants and the Titan gods.

According to the Greek poet Hesiod, there was nothing but a formless and infinite void called Chaos at the beginning of time. From this unstable force, the goddess Nyx and her brother Erebus emerged as dark entities, and later came the goddess Gaia, who married the god Ouranos. Together, these gods created the universe, monstrous beings, and the first generation of gods known as the Titans.

BIRTHED FROM CHAOS

When Chaos created Nyx, goddess of the night, she merged with it to create Erebus, the god of darkness. Later, the goddess Gaia (Earth) emerged from the dark abyss of Chaos.

Goddess of the night

When Nyx joined with Erebus, they produced Aither ("Air") and Hemera ("Day"). On her own Nyx gave birth to darker forces. These included Ker ("Doom"), Thanatos ("Death"), Hypnos ("Sleep"), Oizys ("Misery"), Nemesis ("Revenge"), Eris ("Strife"), and Geras ("Old Age"). The goddess of the night was much feared, and was described as living at the farthest end of the Earth.

Riding in the night
In Classical Greek art, Nyx was shown riding through the sky in a chariot drawn by dark horses.

OURANOS

GAIA

Earth and sky

Gaia rose out of Chaos and gave birth to Ouranos alone. The two joined together to have 12 sons and 6 daughters. Ouranos was the supreme ruler of the sky, and his realm was imagined to be a starry brass dome arching over the Earth. Gaia's body was the Earth itself, which was covered in forests and oceans.

GAIA'S CHILDREN

Gaia had three sets of children by Ouranos. The Hecatoncheires, Cyclopes, and Titans were all immensely powerful beings.

The Hundred-Handed Giants

The Hecatoncheires were three mighty beings with fifty heads and a hundred arms. They were called Briareus ("The Sea Goat"), Cottus ("The Furious"), and Gyges ("The Long-Limbed"). Ouranos hated them, so he pushed them back into the Earth, Gaia, where they came from.

The major Titans

The first generation of Titans were the children of Ouranos and Gaia, and were thought to reign over a Golden Age of the universe. They represented the basic elements of nature, such as time.

Kronos	Rhea	Mnemosyne	Oceanus
Kronos was the god of time, and monitored the seasons.	Wife of Kronos, Rhea was the goddess of fertility.	This goddess created language and was the mother of the nine Muses.	The eldest Titan, Oceanus was the river surrounding the Earth.
Theia	**Hyperion**	**Phoebe**	**Coeus**
This goddess's name means "sight," and she represented light and vision.	Married to his sister Theia, Hyperion was the god of light and wisdom.	Grandmother of Apollo and Artemis, Phoebe was the goddess of prophecy.	Married to Phoebe, Coeus was the god of intellect and wisdom.

In some stories, the **goddess Nyx** had the power to control **people's dreams**, and even sent **prophetic visions**.

3,000 The number of **Oceanid nymphs**, daughters of the **god Oceanus** and **goddess Tethys**.

One-eyed giants
Gaia gave birth to the three Cyclopes: Arges ("Bright"), Brontes ("Thunderer"), and Steropes ("Lightener"), who were also imprisoned in Gaia's body by their cruel father. These skilled beings forged the gods Zeus's lightning bolts, Poseidon's trident, and Hades' helmet.

CHILDREN OF THE TITANS
The children of the major Titans were also called Titans, apart from Zeus and his siblings who were known as the Olympians.

Helios
Son of the Titans Hyperion and Theia, the sun god Helios drove his fiery chariot across the sky each day.

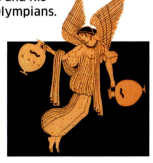
Eos
Sister of Helios and goddess of the dawn, Eos was the mother of the winds and the stars.

Selene
Goddess of the moon, Selene's chariot was pulled by winged horses. Her children included the Horae, goddesses of the seasons and hours.

The Fates
Also known as the Moirai, the Fates were three sisters who were in charge of everyone's destinies.

Oceanid nymphs
Daughters of Oceanus and Tethys, the Oceanids were the nymphs of springs.

The nine Muses
The daughters of Mnemosyne, each of the Muses ruled over a discipline in the arts, such as Calliope for epic poetry, Terpsichore for dance, and Thalia for comedy.

Strong allies
The Cyclopes, along with the Hecatoncheires, allied with Zeus in the war to end the rule of Kronos (see pages 12–13).

> "AND BEYOND, AWAY FROM **ALL THE GODS,** LIVE THE TITANS, BEYOND GLOOMY CHAOS AND AIR."
> Hesiod, *Theogony*, c.730–700 BCE

Tethys
A sea goddess, she was depicted in mosaics in the baths of ancient Greece.

Themis
As the goddess of justice, she made the laws that governed the universe.

Crius
This god was the constellations and is associated with the season of spring.

Iapetus
Married to the Oceanid nymph Clymene, Iapetus was the god of mortality.

KRONOS TAKES OVER
Gaia was furious that Ouranos had imprisoned her children in her body, and so she persuaded her son Kronos to kill his father and then take over from him as ruler of the universe. To help Kronos in his task, Gaia carved a sickle for him to use as a weapon.

> "GAIA MADE THE ELEMENT OF **GRAY FLINT AND SHAPED A GREAT SICKLE,** AND TOLD HER PLAN **TO HER DEAR SONS.**"
> Hesiod, *Theogony*, c.730–700 BCE

Death of Ouranos
Ouranos was too strong for Kronos to kill by himself, so the god of time asked his brothers to help him. Hyperion, Iapetus, Crius, and Coeus all agreed, but Oceanus refused to join in. When they found their father, Kronos's four brothers held the struggling Ouranos down, leaving Kronos free to fatally wound him with the sickle.

Dying curse
With his dying breath, Ouranos cursed Kronos, saying he, too, would be killed by his own sons.

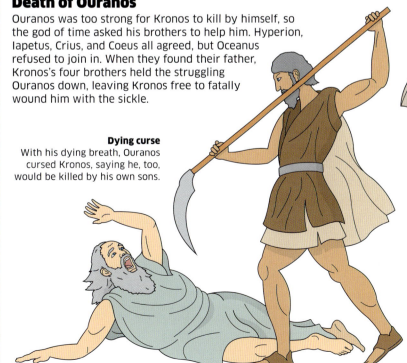

Ouranos's last children
The blood that flowed from Ouranos's body created his last children. Among them were the Erinyes, also known as the Furies. They were three evil sisters who punished those who committed crimes against their families, and cursed them with madness. Aphrodite, the most beautiful goddess, was born when Ouranos's blood flowed into the sea (see pages 32–33).

9 The number of **Kronos's siblings** who fought **on the side of the Titans**.

War against the Titans

The Titans, under their leader Kronos, were once the rulers of the universe. But Zeus, son of Kronos, waged a war against his father and his allies. In the end, Zeus emerged victorious.

The god Kronos murdered his father Ouranos, the god of the sky, and seized control of the universe. But, as he lay dying, Ouranos foretold that Kronos too would be defeated by one of his children.

To prevent this prophecy from coming true, Kronos swallowed each of his children soon after they were born. His wife Rhea wanted to put an end to this cruelty. When Zeus was born, she fooled Kronos by wrapping a stone in swaddling and giving it to Kronos to swallow instead. She then sent Zeus away to be hidden in a cave and raised by the nymph Amalthea.

Later, when Zeus grew up, Amalthea told him that he was a god and that his father had swallowed his siblings. In a plan to get revenge, Zeus, in disguise as a cupbearer, gave Kronos a potion. This made him first vomit up the stone, and then his children Hera, Demeter, Hestia, Hades, and Poseidon, who had grown up in their father's body. They allied with Zeus to fight in the battle against the Titans.

The long war between the Titans and the six children of Kronos, who were later known as Olympians, caused major devastation on Earth. To gain the advantage, Zeus snuck into the underworld and released the Cyclopes and the Hecatoncheires (see pages 10–11) from their prisons. They joined the Olympians' cause, with the Cyclopes also crafting new weapons for the gods. With these new allies, the Olympians managed to trap the Titans in Tartarus. The Olympians now ruled over the world, with Zeus as their supreme leader and king of the gods.

Banished to the underworld
In the final battle, the Earth shook under the mighty Olympians as they defeated the Titans, who were pushed into the gloomy underworld realm of Tartarus.

Supreme spear
When it struck the ground, Poseidon's trident could cause destructive earthquakes.

Powerful opponent
The god Poseidon, along with Hades and Zeus, fought in the war from beginning to end.

Defeated Titan
Fighting on the losing side, this Titan's powers were no match against the Olympians.

Battling Typhon
Gaia was furious at Zeus for imprisoning her children the Titans in Tartarus, so she sent the fearsome monster Typhon to attack the Olympians. Zeus defeated him by crushing him with a mountain, which became the volcano Mount Etna.

Terrifying monster
Typhon was human from the waist up but had two serpents for legs. He was so tall that his head could touch the stars.

During the war, **some Titans fought** on the side of the Olympians, such as the **goddess Themis** and her **son Prometheus**.

Atlas, who led the Titans in battle, was given the **harsh punishment** of holding **the sky on his shoulders**.

13

Terrifying lightning
The lightning bolts of Zeus inspired much fear among the gods.

King of the gods
When Zeus defeated Kronos in the war, the other gods regarded him as their ruler.

The weapons of the gods
The Cyclopes were expert blacksmiths who made weapons for the Olympian gods that helped them secure their victory against the Titans.

Lightning bolts
With a flash of lightning, Zeus killed his enemies.

Trident
Poseidon's trident could summon great floods.

Helmet
The helm of darkness made Hades invisible.

Helmet of invisibility
The helmet not only protected Hades but allowed him to deliver a surprise attack on his enemies.

europe ○ **THE CREATION OF HUMANS**

*Some legends claim that **people aged backward** during the **Golden Age** and **grew younger over time**.*

THE FIVE AGES OF HUMANS
According to Hesiod, the gods went through a process of trial and error in creating the ideal race of human beings, one that would obey and worship them. There were five ages of humans, the first one existing when the god Cronus ruled the cosmos. With each age, the quality of life gradually worsened.

1 THE GOLDEN AGE
Under the god Cronus's rule, people enjoyed life like the gods, and did not grow old or suffer diseases. They died out when Zeus won the war against the Titans.

2 THE SILVER AGE
Zeus ruled the world in this age. He made this race less intelligent than the gods. These humans refused to be obedient, so the gods destroyed them.

3 THE BRONZE AGE
These people were created from wood and their armor was forged from bronze. They were violent warriors who fought until their race was wiped out.

4 THE AGE OF HEROES
This age produced powerful demigods who went to war and fought courageously. Many of them died on the battlefield and were remembered as heroes.

5 THE IRON AGE
The people of this age were selfish and greedy. Hesiod lived in this age and it is the age we live in now. Hesiod predicted that wars will bring this age to an end.

PROMETHEUS AND EPIMETHEUS
The Greek writer Apollodorus claimed that Zeus tasked Prometheus ("Thinking Ahead") and his brother Epimetheus ("Thinking After") to populate the Earth. The brothers made the animals out of clay. Prometheus was more intelligent than Epimetheus and molded the clay into the first humans, using the appearance of the gods as his inspiration.

Assembling the animals
Epimetheus crafted the first animals by hand, and decided on their traits, such as their strength, speed, and intelligence.

Offerings to Zeus
When Zeus saw Prometheus's creation, he demanded that the humans show gratitude by offering him a gift. Prometheus tricked him by getting the humans to sacrifice an ox and have Zeus choose from two offerings. As Prometheus expected, Zeus picked the offering wrapped in meat, not knowing that it was concealing the bones. Zeus was furious.

Meat in the ox's skin
One offering was the finest cut of beef hidden inside the unappealing skin.

Bones hidden in meat
The attractive option was a thin layer of meat, but with the bones hidden inside it.

The Creation of Humans

The stories of human creation told by the ancient Greek writers Hesiod and Apollodorus depict a troubled relationship between the gods and humans. The Olympian Zeus was enraged with humans, but the Titan Prometheus came to their rescue.

There were various ages of humans that were created and destroyed by the gods. When the Olympians won the war against the Titans (see pages 12-13), they took charge of the cosmos. Zeus tasked Prometheus with creating another age of humankind. The Titan made men from clay and water, and Zeus expected them to worship and make special offerings to the gods, but instead people were unruly and fought each other. Prometheus took many risks to help humanity survive, such as stealing fire from the gods. Zeus punished humanity severely for using fire and sent curses with the first woman, Pandora.

CREATING THE FIRST WOMAN
In Hesiod's story of creation, women were created many years after men. Zeus was jealous when he saw how people prospered with the gift of fire that Prometheus had stolen from him, and decided to curse them. The first part of his plan involved creating the first woman. The gods gave her many traits and skills, and named her Pandora, which means "all gifts." Unfortunately, the gift of curiosity would get the better of her.

Beauty
The goddess of beauty, Aphrodite, made Pandora beautiful, so she was always attractive to others.

Curiosity
The goddess of women and children, Hera, made Pandora curious, which would later prove to be her downfall.

Sewing skills
The goddess of wisdom and crafts, Athena, shared her sewing skills with Pandora and dressed her in fine clothes.

Speech
The messenger god, Hermes, gave Pandora the power to communicate, so she could speak her mind, and even tell lies.

The Age of Heroes is the only one not named after a metal. The blacksmith god Hephaestus forged the first woman Pandora. **700** The Greek writer Hesiod wrote the story of Pandora in 700 BCE. 15

Gift from a god
Zeus decided to punish humanity for their trick. The god kept the gift of fire from them so people lived without warmth and heat. Prometheus felt responsible for their suffering, so he risked the wrath of Zeus by stealing fire from Mount Olympus and giving it to humans. This gift transformed the lives of people for the better.

Fire thief
Prometheus stole a tiny flame from the gods and disguised it with a fennel plant. He went down to Earth and lit fires in the encampments where people lived.

> "AFTER HE HAD **FASHIONED MEN** FROM WATER AND EARTH, PROMETHEUS ALSO **GAVE THEM FIRE.**"
> Apollodorus, *Library*, c. 2nd century BCE

Prometheus and the eagle
Infuriated with Prometheus for sharing the gift of fire with humans, Zeus sentenced him to a horrific punishment. The god had Prometheus chained to a rock, where every day an eagle would peck out his liver. Prometheus was immortal, so the wound healed, allowing the eagle to return the next day and do the same again.

Punished and freed
Prometheus was chained to a rock and attacked by an eagle daily until one day the hero Hercules freed him.

Pandora's box
Zeus sent Pandora to Earth with a special box, but warned her not to open it. The god Hermes presented her to Epimetheus who now looked after the world of men instead of Prometheus. He was not as wise as his brother and accepted Pandora as a gift from Zeus. Although Pandora tried to leave the box alone, she was curious. One day Pandora opened the box and released Zeus's curse that included hunger, sickness, and loss. Pandora quickly closed the box, stopping hope from escaping.

Unleashing misery
Pandora accidentally unleashed many evils into the world from a box. Hope stayed in the box, however, meaning no matter how hard life became, people had the power to overcome their suffering.

DEUCALION AND PYRRHA
During the Bronze Age of Humans, Zeus sent a great flood to destroy humanity for their evil deeds. Once again Prometheus outwitted Zeus by building his mortal son Deucalion and his wife Pyrrha a chest to carry them to safety. When they survived, Deucalion thanked Zeus. In return for their gratitude, Zeus told them how to repopulate the Earth—by picking up stones and throwing them over their heads. When the stones landed, they transformed into humans.

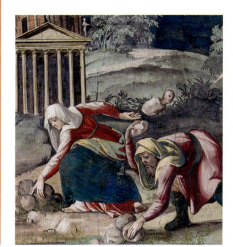

Stone throwers
Deucalion and Pyrrha threw stones over their heads to populate the world. Deucalion's stones turned into men and Pyrrha's transformed into women when they hit the ground.

europe ○ HADES AND PERSEPHONE

Pluto was the Roman equivalent of Hades, and Proserpine was the Roman Persephone.

In charge of the seasons
The ancient Greeks and Romans relied on the changing seasons for food. To ensure a good harvest, they worshipped the gods and goddesses of nature.

The Horae (Hours)
Each member of this group of goddesses represented a season, and together they symbolized the passing of time and the cycle of nature.

Cybele's chariot was pulled by two lions to represent her ability to tame wild creatures.

Maternal goddess
A goddess adopted from the region of Phrygia by the Greeks, Cybele was responsible for farming and fertility. She was known to the Romans as Magna Mater ("Great Mother").

Among the flowers
Chloris is more popularly known by her Roman name, Flora. She was the goddess of flowers, spring, and youth. She is often depicted wearing a long, flowing dress.

Caring for nature
The orchards of ancient Rome were cared for by the goddess Pomona. She tended to the flowers and fruits, and banned men from entering her domain and distracting her.

Flower in hand
Before Kore left Earth, she picked a daffodil and carried it with her on the journey.

Lonely king
Hades fell in love with Kore, and kidnapped her to keep him company and make her a queen.

9 Demeter mourned the loss of Kore for nine days before Zeus intervened.

When Demeter was searching for Kore, it was the sun god Helios who told her that Kore had been abducted by Hades.

The earth goddess
The goddess Demeter and her daughter Kore were worshipped as deities of agriculture. They made the fields grow, creating abundant harvests. Demeter was fiercely protective of her only daughter.

TERRA-COTTA BUST OF DEMETER FROM TUNISIA, NORTH AFRICA

Hades and Persephone

When the goddess Persephone was captured by Hades, the lord of the underworld, her mother's despair covered the world in darkness. This tragic tale of innocence lost explains how the seasons came to be.

The earth goddess Demeter and the supreme god Zeus had a daughter named Kore ("maiden"), who enjoyed playing in the meadow every day. At that time, it was summer all year long. The underworld god Hades fell in love with her and one day, when she had wandered far from her mother's watchful gaze, he caught her and took her to the underworld.

Alone in the realm of the dead, Kore missed her old life on Earth. In her grief, Demeter dressed herself in black, mourning the loss of her daughter, and searched high and low for her. She neglected her duties as the goddess of the harvest, and crops failed.

Zeus stepped in to stop the chaos, and insisted that Kore be brought back immediately, as long as she hadn't eaten the food of the dead. Unaware of this condition, Kore swallowed six seeds from a pomegranate growing in the gardens of Hades—an act which would seal her fate forever, and she became known as Persephone ("bringer of destruction").

Since Persephone had eaten the fruit of the dead, Zeus offered a compromise. Persephone could return to her mother for six months of the year. But she would have to live in the underworld for the remaining six months—the number of seeds she had eaten. Hades agreed, and the goddess was reunited, briefly, with her mother.

When Persephone was with Demeter, the earth goddess was happy and she brought the seasons of spring and summer. When Persephone was in the underworld, fall and winter were signs of Demeter's mourning.

Black as death
The horses and chariot belonging to Hades were black to represent his role as god of the dark and eerie underworld.

Dark entrance
The ground cracked open beneath the chariot to reveal the underworld.

Persephone's abduction
When Kore, who came to be known as Persephone, was out picking beautiful flowers in the glorious sunshine, her uncle Hades rode in on his dark chariot and whisked her away to the underworld.

europe ○ THE GREEK UNDERWORLD

3 The **three heads** of the **goddess Hecate** were a **young woman**, a mother, and a **very old lady**.

○ JOURNEY OF THE DEAD

Always dark and bleak, Hades was the opposite of the sunlit Earth. There were murky waters to cross and ferocious monsters to face. Judges gathered to decide the final fate of the shades and allocate them a suitable realm for all eternity.

Sailing in dark waters

Five rivers ran through and around Hades. When a person died, their shade reached the entrance to the underworld at the river of sadness, called Acheron. There, the shade would be taken through the river of hatred, Styx, by the ferryman Charon. Other rivers in the underworld included Cocytus the river of mourning, Phlegethon the river of fire, and Lethe the river of forgetfulness.

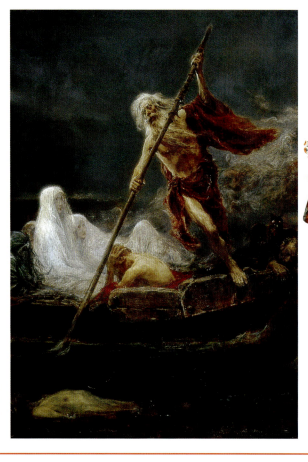

A ferryman's fare
The deceased were often buried with an obol coin in their mouths to use as payment for Charon's ferrying service in the underworld.

Judgment time

The fate of the dead was decided by a trio of judges. These were once mortal men who had encouraged law and order on Earth. Aeacus was the keeper of the keys and judge of shades from the west, Rhadamanthys was the judge of shades from the east, and Minos cast the deciding vote.

The decision-makers
The three judges created the underworld's laws and had great power over a shade's fate.

The realms of Hades

Once the judges made their verdict, the dead souls went to either Elysium, Asphodel, or Tartarus. The paradise of Elysium welcomed fallen heroes and those chosen by the gods. The Asphodel Fields were where ordinary people spent eternity, and Tartarus was reserved for the wicked.

Elysium
The idyllic islands of Elysium, also known as the Isles of the Blessed, lay above ground at the western edge of the world.

The Asphodel Fields
Gray flowers and eerie silence filled the fields of Asphodel, offering a joyless afterlife for people who led normal lives.

Tartarus
The dungeons of Tartarus were the most terrifying of all because endless torture was in store for the worst wrongdoers.

Monsters and gods

Many kinds of frightening creatures and deities lurked in Hades. On arrival, the souls of the dead faced the three-headed, snake-tailed beast Cerberus who guarded the gates to Hades. Shades could also encounter the night goddess Nyx, the witch-goddess Hecate, and the flesh-eating demon Eurynomos.

Three-headed goddess
The goddess Hecate used her torches to guide shades on their underworld journeys.

The Greek underworld

Named after its ruler Hades, the underworld was where souls of the dead, known as shades, spent eternity. Mostly a gloomy place, it could be a paradise for the blessed, or a prison for those who displeased the gods.

The god Hades ruled the underworld alongside his wife, the goddess Persephone. In this subterranean realm, the souls of mortals were judged and led to their final destination. With the monstrous creature Cerberus guarding the gates, no one could escape the underworld, although many tried.

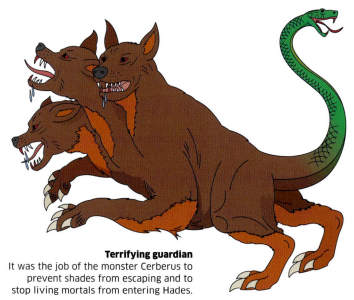

Terrifying guardian
It was the job of the monster Cerberus to prevent shades from escaping and to stop living mortals from entering Hades.

CRIME AND PUNISHMENT

Evildoers were punished for their crimes after death. Attempts to deceive the gods were judged particularly harshly. The guilty often suffered repetitive tortures in the dark realm of Tartarus. Such punishments were given to teach a lesson and make the culprits humble before the gods.

"THOSE WHO APPEAR TO BE INCURABLE ... ARE CAST BY THEIR FITTING DESTINY INTO TARTARUS, WHENCE THEY NEVER EMERGE."
Plato, *Phaedo*, c. 360 BCE

Sisyphus and the rock
When Sisyphus died, he tricked the goddess Persephone into releasing him from Hades by complaining that his wife had not given him a proper burial. Back on Earth, Sisyphus enjoyed his life, but when he died again, he was forced to spend eternity lifting a great boulder up a hill.

Ixion's wheel
Ixion was King of the Lapiths, an ancient tribe from Thessaly, but he was better known for his selfishness and arrogance. When Ixion tried to seduce the god Zeus's wife Hera, he paid the price. Zeus took Ixion to Hades and bound him to a fiery wheel that never stopped spinning.

The greed of Tantalus
The evil Tantalus murdered his son Pelops and served him for dinner at a feast with the gods. The gods resurrected Pelops and Zeus sent Tantalus to Hades, where he was forced to spend eternity craving food and water, which were always beyond his reach.

Lasting labor
Whenever Sisyphus lifted the great boulder to the top of the hill, it fell back down, and he had to start all over again.

Spinning around
In one version of the myth, the messenger god Hermes bound Ixion to a winged fiery wheel and it spun across the heavens.

Eternally tantalized
Every time Tantalus reached out for a fruit from the tree, the branch moved away, so he remained forever hungry.

HEROES IN HADES

Some of the greatest heroes bravely ventured into Hades. Odysseus entered Hades to get advice from a dead prophet. The Roman hero Aeneas went there to be reunited with his father one last time. And the musician Orpheus took the risky journey to bring back the love of his life, Eurydice.

Orpheus's challenge
Orpheus mourned the untimely death of his wife Eurydice. He begged Hades to release her from the underworld. Hades agreed, but on one condition—Orpheus could not turn back to look at her on their way out. As Orpheus approached the exit, he could not stop himself from turning around. On seeing Eurydice, she vanished from his sight.

"ANXIOUS FOR ANOTHER LOOK AT HER, HE TURNED HIS EYES SO HE COULD GAZE UPON HER. INSTANTLY SHE SLIPPED AWAY."
Ovid, *Metamorphoses*, 8 CE

europe o ATHENA

According to legend, the **ruler** of Athens, **King Erichthonius**, was raised **in secret** by the goddess.

Helmet
Athena's protective helmet was made of bronze.

The aegis
Her shield shone like a mirror and was charged with divine power.

Ready to attack
The spear was her weapon, although she sometimes used Zeus's lightning bolts.

Standing strong
Daughter of Zeus and Metis, Athena was a fierce warrior from the moment she was born, one whom many heroes could count on.

Athena

The Olympian Athena was the goddess of wisdom, war, and weaving. She was highly regarded as a protector of the people and the mightiest heroes, using her strength and intellect to win wars. The goddess was honored as the patron of the city of Athens.

Athena was born a warrior, ready for her first battle. Out of Zeus's children, Athena was his favorite and she did not challenge his supremacy. She was wise like her mother Metis, who was the Titan goddess of wisdom, and came to the aid of many Greek heroes in their adventures. To defeat the Gorgon Medusa, she gave the demigod Perseus her reflective shield (see pages 22–23), but she favored the hero Odysseus the most, defending him in battle and offering him life-saving advice. Although Athena could be sympathetic to people, she did not hesitate to punish them for their mistakes.

> "... **goddess Athena,**
> gray eyes gleaming ... beautiful, tall, and skilled at weaving lovely things"
>
> Homer, *The Odyssey*, c. 7th century BCE

THE WISE WARRIOR

Athena was not only known for her military strength but for having the best tactics in a fight. She wore a loose tunic, a helmet, and always carried her shield (aegis), which bore the terrifying head of Medusa. Her weapon of choice was a spear that she raised in battle.

Birth of Athena

To prevent the goddess Metis from giving birth to a child potentially more powerful than himself, Zeus swallowed her while she was still pregnant. He developed an unbearable headache and asked the Titan god Prometheus for help. He resolved the problem by splitting Zeus's head open with an ax. From Zeus's skull Athena sprang forth, fully grown, and letting out a war cry.

Zeus's head wound
Athena stepped out of the wound in Zeus's head wearing a full suit of armor.

Athena's sacred symbols

Owl
The owl was associated with Athena because it represented wisdom, and was seen as a good omen.

Olive tree
The olive tree symbolized the goddess's victory over Poseidon in the contest to become the patron of Athens.

Spear and aegis
Athena's weapon was her spear, and her aegis (shield) had the head of Medusa on it to scare her enemies in battle.

Distaff
Since Athena was the goddess of weaving, the distaff—a tool used for spinning yarn—was one of her symbols.

The goddess **Minerva** was the **Roman** equivalent of Athena.

Athena is the **female counterpart** to **Ares**—the **god of war**.

3 Athena helped **Hercules** in **3** of his **12 labors**.

21

ANCIENT ATHENS

Ancient Greece reached its height from around 500 BCE to 336 BCE, a period known as The Classical Age. Athens was one of its most powerful city-states, serving as a cultural hub for writers, politicians, and artists. The city-state was named after its patron, Athena.

Competing for the city

In a contest to become the patron of Athens, Athena and the sea god Poseidon were tasked to present the city and its people with a gift. Poseidon struck the earth with his trident and drew forth a spring, but its waters were salty. Athena poked the ground with her spear and from the earth an olive tree grew with valuable fruit. Athena was named the winner.

The Acropolis of Athens

On a hill overlooking ancient Athens was a fortress known as the Acropolis. It was a religious site, with some of its sanctuaries dedicated to the goddess. Ruins of its most prominent temple, the Parthenon, still stand today.

> **OF ATHENA, GUARDIAN** OF THE CITY, I SING
>
> *Homeric Hymn*, c. 7th century BCE

THE PARTHENON

Worshipped at the Parthenon
Built between 447 BCE and 438 BCE, the Parthenon was a temple where Athena was worshipped. Inside, a statue of the goddess towered over people and was referred to as Athena Parthenos.

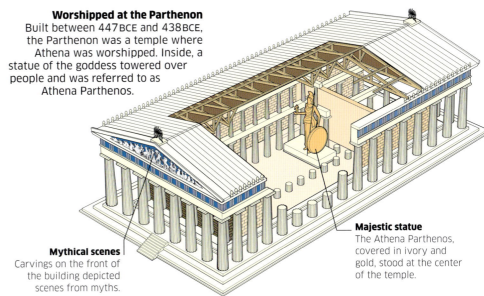

Mythical scenes
Carvings on the front of the building depicted scenes from myths.

Majestic statue
The Athena Parthenos, covered in ivory and gold, stood at the center of the temple.

ATHENA'S FURY

Athena was wise, but she could easily get jealous and be quick to anger. She punished mortals who thought they were equal to the gods, and those who went against her wishes.

Arachne's downfall

Arachne was a fine weaver who claimed that her talent was her own and had nothing to do with Athena. This angered the goddess, so she held a contest to see who was better. When Athena saw the quality of Arachne's weaving, she tore up her work. Arachne tried to kill herself, but Athena stopped her and transformed her rival into a spider.

Turned into a spider
In a fit of rage, Athena destroyed Arachne's tapestry, but transformed her into nature's best weaver—a spider.

The blinding of Tiresias

Tiresias was a man who spied on Athena while she bathed at a sacred spring. When she caught Tiresias watching her, she hit him in the eyes, causing him to go blind. Realizing it was a severe punishment, Athena gave him the gift of prophecy to compensate him for the loss of his sight.

Perseus, slayer of Medusa

One of the greatest heroes in Greek mythology was Perseus, son of the god Zeus and a mortal princess, Danaë. Perseus fought many monsters, but he faced his greatest challenge against the terrifying, snake-haired Medusa, who turned anyone who looked upon her to stone.

Danaë was the daughter of King Acrisius of Argos. A prophecy said that one day the king would be killed by his own grandson. So when Danaë had a son, Acrisius threw mother and baby into the sea inside a wooden chest. The pair were rescued by fisherfolk from the island of Seriphos, where Perseus grew up to become a young man.

The King of Seriphos was Polydectes, who developed an affection for Danaë. To get her son out of the way, the king set Perseus the task of killing the dreaded Medusa. He was sure this challenge would destroy the young man, but he underestimated Perseus.

Before setting out, Perseus called on the gods, who gave him gifts to aid him on his quest. First, he flew to the remote island home of Medusa and her Gorgon sisters, using his gift of a pair of winged sandals. Once on the island, Perseus avoided Medusa's death stare by only looking at her reflection in the reflective shield he had been given, then he sliced off her head using another gift, the harpë sword. To escape the island, he wore a helmet of invisibility borrowed from the god Hades to hide from the other Gorgons.

The blood dripping from Medusa's neck turned into a magical winged horse, named Pegasus, that Perseus rode home. He kept Medusa's still powerful head in a bag, and upon his return to the court of Polydectes, he revealed it to the king, turning him to stone.

Later, Perseus was invited to compete in an athletics event. At the games, he threw a discus that veered into the crowd, accidentally killing a spectator. This turned out to be Acrisius, Perseus's grandfather. The prophecy had been fulfilled.

*Perseus was the **mythical founder** of the great **Greek city-state of Mycenae**.*

Gifts of the gods
Perseus prayed to the gods for help with slaying Medusa. They responded by giving him a collection of special gifts to ensure he succeeded in his quest.

WINGED SANDALS   **REFLECTIVE SHIELD**

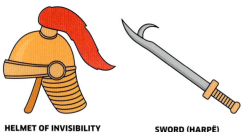

HELMET OF INVISIBILITY   **SWORD (HARPË)**

The Gorgons
The Gorgon sisters were a terrible trio named Stheno, Euryale, and Medusa. Only Medusa, the youngest, could turn people to stone by looking at them. She was also the only Gorgon who could die, because her sisters were immortal.

Snake sisters
Instead of hair, the head of each Gorgon sister was covered in writhing snakes.

Andromeda
On his way home to Seriphos, Perseus rescued Andromeda of Aethiopia, a princess who had been chained to a rock to feed the sea monster Cetus. Perseus revealed Medusa's head to stun the creature before killing it.

To the rescue
Wearing his winged sandals, Perseus flew in to save Andromeda from certain death, and the couple were later married.

Petrified warrior
The island of the Gorgons was full of statues of people Medusa had turned to stone.

3 The number of Gorgon sisters

Perseus gave **Medusa's head** to Athena, who placed it on her shield, **the aegis**, for protection.

Terrifying appearance
According to some myths, Medusa had once been a beautiful woman, but was cursed to have a monstrous face by Athena for her vanity.

He looked with averted gaze on a brazen shield, in which he beheld the image of the Gorgon

Pseudo-Apollodorus, *The Library*, 2nd century CE

Powerful weapon
Hermes gave Perseus an unbreakable harpë sword.

Perseus's plan
Perseus made sure he never looked at Medusa directly during their confrontation.

Shiny shield
The shield given to Perseus by Athena had been polished so well that it reflected the surroundings.

Hideous reflection
Though still hideous to look at, the reflection of Medusa could not turn Perseus to stone.

The murder of Medusa
In films and modern depictions of the Perseus story, the slaying of Medusa is shown like this, with the hero hiding from the monster until a final battle in which he cuts of her head. But in ancient Greek texts and art, Perseus, with the help of the gods, was able to slay Medusa as she awoke from a sleep.

Winged sandals
Perseus flew to Medusa's cave wearing special sandals given by the messenger god Hermes.

europe ○ APOLLO AND ARTEMIS

The **Roman** equivalent of Artemis was the goddess **Diana**.

Apollo and Artemis

The divine twins Apollo and Artemis were powerful gods who represented day and night respectively. When they aligned for the same cause, they became an even greater force to be reckoned with.

Apollo was a sun god, representing the sun's light and its life-giving properties. Artemis was a goddess of the moon and the wild animals that roamed the night. Though they had influence over opposite areas of Greek life, the twins had a strong connection. They shared many similarities, such as a love of hunting, and always looked out for each other.

STRONGER TOGETHER
The twins could not exist without each other, because without Apollo, there was no day, and without Artemis, there was no night. They always defended their family, especially their mother, the Titan goddess Leto. Their expertise with a bow and arrow made them fearless hunters ever ready to destroy their enemies.

Leto gives birth
When Leto fell pregnant by the god Zeus, his furious wife Hera cursed her so she could not give birth on any solid ground on Earth. Leto searched desperately for a place to have her children, but could not find one, so Zeus raised the island of Delos from under the sea especially for her.

Looking out for Leto
After all the trouble Leto went through to give birth, the twins grew up to be fiercely protective of their mother.

Slaying the dragon
Soon after Leto had given birth, the goddess Hera sent the deadly dragon Python to kill her. Little did she know that Apollo had eaten divine ambrosia and nectar, and was fully grown. Apollo shot Python dead when he was just four days old.

Revenge on Niobe
Niobe was an arrogant mortal woman who boasted about having 14 children. When she mocked Leto for only giving birth to two children, the Titan goddess sought revenge and sent her twins to slay all of her sons and daughters.

Deadly shots
Armed with bows and arrows, Apollo killed Niobe's seven sons, while Artemis killed her seven daughters.

THE HEALER
Apollo had many areas of influence in Greek life. As well as being a sun god, Apollo was also the god of music and poetry. In mythical tales, he came to the aid of the ancient Greeks, using his golden arrows to shoot their enemies. The ancient Greeks also regarded him as a god of healing who could banish disease, and a prophet who could see into the future.

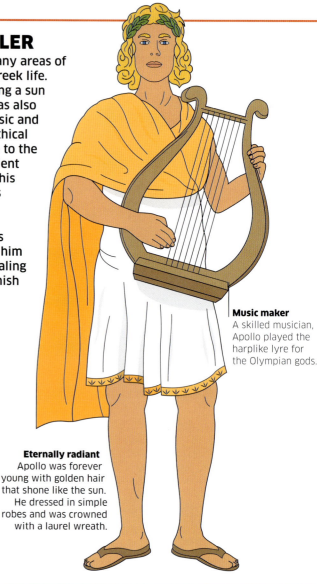

Music maker
A skilled musician, Apollo played the harplike lyre for the Olympian gods.

Eternally radiant
Apollo was forever young with golden hair that shone like the sun. He dressed in simple robes and was crowned with a laurel wreath.

Unrequited love
The god Eros punished Apollo for making fun of him and fired two shots—one at Apollo to make him fall in love with the next person he laid eyes on, and one at a nymph named Daphne to make her reject his love. Apollo was lovestruck, and when he chased after her, Daphne cried out to her father, a river god, who turned her into a tree.

Transformed into a tree
Just as Apollo was about to lean in and kiss Daphne, she was transformed into a laurel tree by the river god Peneus.

Apollo's sacred symbols

Golden bow
Skilled shooter Apollo carried a golden bow that was given to him by the god Hephaestus when he was a child.

Raven
This bird was once white, but was burned by the god for telling him bad news. It has remained black ever since.

Laurel
Apollo wore a wreath of laurel to symbolize his eternal devotion to Daphne, who was turned into the laurel tree.

Lyre
As the god of music, Apollo could play a variety of musical instruments, but his favorite was the lyre.

7 The nature god **Pan** gave Artemis seven **hunting dogs**.

1969 NASA's Apollo **space program**, including the **1969 moon landing**, took its name from the sun god.

Death of Hyacinthus
Apollo struck up a relationship with a young prince and athlete named Hyacinthus. The pair loved playing sports together. One day they were throwing a discus when Apollo sent it high into the clouds. The wind god Zephyrus was jealous of the relationship between the two and sent the discus in the wrong direction, hitting Hyacinthus. The blow killed him instantly.

Floral tribute
Apollo was distraught with grief when Hyacinthus died of a head injury. The sun god made hyacinths grow where his blood had spilled.

Asclepius the healer
Asclepius was the son of Apollo and the princess Coronis. The sun god cut Asclepius out of his mother's womb after her death. Like his father, Asclepius had a gift for healing the sick, and he was taught medicine by Chiron the centaur. He was so good at healing that he began to bring people back from the dead, so Zeus killed him with a thunderbolt for disturbing the natural order.

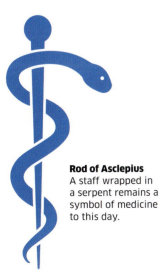

Rod of Asclepius
A staff wrapped in a serpent remains a symbol of medicine to this day.

GODDESS OF THE HUNT
Artemis was a huntress, who rode a chariot pulled by four deer. She was always surrounded by woodland creatures and nymphs. As soon as she was born, she helped her mother deliver her twin brother Apollo, because Hera had cursed Leto with a painful labor. As a result, Artemis became the goddess of birth, although she never had any children of her own.

Powerful bow
Arrows shot from the bow of Artemis could take down any god.

Forever the huntress
Artemis was a young, agile goddess dressed in a tunic and cloak. She was always armed with a quiver of arrows on her back and a bow in her hand.

The Calydonian Boar
To punish King Oeneus for refusing to make offerings to her in his rituals, Artemis released a monstrous boar to ravage his land of Calydon. The king gathered the best hunters around to kill the boar at the Calydonian Boar Hunt. Artemis's female friend and legendary huntress Atalanta wounded the boar before the king's son Meleager delivered the killer shot.

A heroine's reward
Atalanta was first to draw blood from the boar, so Prince Meleager rewarded her with the boar's hide.

From hunter to hunted
Among Artemis's many followers was fellow hunter Actaeon. One day he stumbled across Artemis bathing in a forest pool and stopped to look at her. Angry at this invasion of privacy, she splashed water at him. Soon, antlers began sprouting from his head as he was transformed into a stag. His hounds hunted him as they would a wild animal and tore him apart.

Cursed by Artemis
When Artemis caught Actaeon watching her bathing, she warned him not to speak, but Actaeon called out to his hunting party and was transformed into a stag.

Artemis's sacred symbols

Deer
This animal was close to Artemis's heart—she wore a deerskin cloak and her chariot was pulled by deer.

Cypress
A symbol of immortality, the cypress tree was sacred to the moon goddess because it grew where she was born.

Bear
Bears care deeply for their cubs and represented Artemis's maternal traits as the goddess of childbirth.

Bow & Arrow
The trusty bow and arrow belonging to the hunter goddess were made for her by the one-eyed Cyclopes.

Jason and the Argonauts

Jason was the rightful heir of an ancient city-state known as Iolcos. To claim the throne he was set the challenge of stealing the Golden Fleece from the distant land of Colchis. Jason recruited the greatest heroes to accompany him on his voyage, and together they set sail on the legendary ship, the *Argo*.

The Golden Fleece
The fleece belonged to a ram that once carried the child Phrixus over the Black Sea. Landing in Colchis, Phrixus sacrificed the ram to the gods, hanging its fleece in a grove sacred to the god Ares.

Newly married
Medea joined Jason on the return journey as his wife.

Taking charge
Jason, the daring leader of the Argonauts, kept the Golden Fleece close to him.

Master builder
The *Argo* was named after its builder, Argus, who joined Jason on his quest.

When Jason was a baby, his uncle Pelias captured his father, King Aeson, and made himself king of Iolcos. As an adult, Jason laid claim to the throne, but his uncle insisted that he bring back the Golden Fleece from Colchis first.

Jason took on the challenge and ordered the construction of a great ship, the *Argo*, from a sacred oak tree. He then called on some of the greatest Greek heroes to join him on the adventure, calling them the "Argonauts."

As the expedition neared Colchis, the *Argo* had to pass through the Clashing Rocks, which crushed any vessel that came between them. The Argonauts managed to sail quickly through the obstacle by letting a dove fly between the rocks first to see how fast they would have to sail.

In Colchis, King Aeëtes refused to hand over the famous fleece, which was protected by a giant serpent. He set Jason the task of harnessing two fire-breathing bulls and using them to plow serpents' teeth into the soil. The king's daughter Medea fell in love with Jason and gave him a potion to protect him from the bulls' fiery breath.

The king still refused to give up the fleece so Medea hatched a plan to get it—by sending the giant serpent into a peaceful sleep with a potion.

Now holding the Fleece, Jason set sail for home. On the way, the Argonauts came across the Sirens, as well as the giant bronze man Talos, who hurled rocks at the ship. The crew returned home safely, but the quest did not end well for Jason. Pelias still refused to give up the throne, so in revenge Medea poisoned him, and Jason and Medea were exiled.

A sorceress in love
Medea was a sorceress who had a special talent for brewing deadly potions. Struck by the golden arrow of the god Eros, she fell in love with Jason and helped him steal the Golden Fleece, betraying her father in the process. When her marriage with Jason ended, she went to Athens and married King Aegeus (see page 28).

Escaping Colchis
When Medea helped Jason secure the Golden Fleece, she murdered her brother to delay her father from finding her.

> "The heroes shone like gleaming stars among the clouds"
>
> Apollonius of Rhodes, *Argonautica I*, 3rd century BCE

50 The **Argonauts** was made up of 50 heroes altogether.

In a cruel twist of fate, **Jason died** years later after a **wooden beam** from the *Argo* fell on his head.

Siren
The half-woman, half-bird creature was known to send sailors overboard with its haunting harmonies.

Music in the sea
Turbulent waves and the persuasive song of Sirens caused problems for the Argonauts on their journey. Luckily, the *Argo* was a strong ship and Orpheus's music suppressed the Sirens' song.

Atalanta
The only female member of the Argonauts was also the world's fastest human.

The finest musician
Orpheus played his lyre to drown out the Sirens' deadly song.

Helpless victim
Butes was a foolish Argonaut who gave in to the Sirens' song and jumped off the ship.

A fine vessel
The ship was made from the timbers of a magic oak.

europe ○ THESEUS AND THE MINOTAUR

Aegeus's wife is the same **Medea** who helped the hero **Jason** in his quest (see pages 26–27).

The Six Labors
Theseus grew up in the city of Troezen with his mother, Aethra. As a young man he found out that Aegeus was his father, and traveled to Athens to meet him. He chose a route passing by six gates to the Underworld. At each of these places, he defeated a terrible beast or ferocious bandit terrorizing the surrounding countryside.

THESEUS FIGHTS THE CROMMYONIAN SOW

At the court of Aegeus
Theseus arrived at Athens in disguise, but the king's wife Medea realized who he was. Afraid that Theseus would replace her son as heir of Athens, she tasked him to kill the Marathonian Bull, hoping he would be killed by the wild beast. When Theseus returned triumphant, she put poison in his wine, but then Aegeus recognized his son, threw the wine to the floor, and Medea fled.

Theseus and the Minotaur

One of the greatest heroes of Athens was Theseus, son of King Aegeus. His most famous feat was the slaying of the Minotaur, a flesh-eating, bull-headed man imprisoned within a maze called the Labyrinth beneath the palace of King Minos of Crete.

The son of King Minos had been killed while traveling in Athenian lands. In revenge, Minos waged war with Athens, and the gods sent plagues and droughts to the city. An oracle advised Aegeus to agree to a cruel treaty to return peace to Athens. Every nine years, the city was to send seven young men and seven young women to Crete in a black-sailed ship, to be fed to the Minotaur in the Labyrinth.

When Theseus arrived at his father's court as a young man, it was almost time for the third set of youths to be sent to Crete. Theseus was determined to end this cruel tradition, and decided to go to Crete in place of one of the young men. Before leaving, he promised Aegeus that if he was successful, the black sails of the ship would be replaced with sails of white.

Entering the Labyrinth alone at night with the help of Ariadne, the daughter of King Minos, Theseus was able to fight and kill the Minotaur. He escaped from the Labyrinth and fled Crete with Ariadne and the young Athenians.

But tragedy struck on the way home. Theseus forgot his promise, and when Aegeus saw the black sails of the ship on the horizon, he threw himself from a cliff into the sea below.

Labyrinth
There are not many details given about the Labyrinth at the palace of King Minos, but it is often described as a maze. However, some ancient artifacts, such as this coin, show a single path that leads to the center.

2 Theseus had **two fathers**—King Aegeus of Athens and the **sea god Poseidon**.

The body of water that Aegeus **threw himself into** is called the **Aegean Sea** in his honor.

29

Human remains
The Minotaur fed on human flesh, discarding the bones of its victims.

Part man, part bull
The Minotaur was the result of a curse laid on the wife of King Minos, Pasiphaë, by the god Poseidon. When the queen gave birth to the hideous bull-headed creature, Minos was ashamed of it. He hid it away at the center of the Labyrinth, which was created to imprison the beast.

Theseus
Some stories tell of Theseus killing the Minotaur with his bare hands, while in others he has a hidden sword.

Ariadne
In love with Theseus, Ariadne gave him a ball of string to unravel as he walked the Labyrinth so he could easily follow the thread back to the entrance. Ariadne fled Crete with Theseus, but he left her on the island of Naxos on the way home.

europe o THE MISTAKES OF MORTALS

Dionysus is the Greek **god of wine, festivals,** and **pleasure**.

The mistakes of mortals

Calling on the Greek gods did not always work out well for mortals. Many stories illustrate that it was dangerous for humans to have dealings with the immortals.

When mortals asked favors of the gods, it often ended in disaster. Those who asked for divine powers, or thought they could act like gods, suffered the worst consequences. Sometimes, a mistake could be undone, but most gods weren't forgiving. Some mortals, such as Semele, were tricked by the gods and paid with their lives.

DEATH OF SEMELE

Semele was a princess who the supreme god Zeus had fallen in love with. When Zeus's wife and goddess Hera found out that Semele was pregnant, she tricked Semele into making a fatal request to the god.

The glory of Zeus

When he fell in love with her, Zeus promised to give Semele anything that she wanted. Hera was so jealous of Semele, she disguised herself, befriended her, and made her doubt Zeus's love for her. One day, Semele asked Zeus to reveal himself to her in all his glory. Forced to keep his promise, Zeus unleashed his lightning and Semele burned to death from the flames.

Saving Dionysus

Zeus managed to save Semele's unborn child by removing it from her womb before she died. He then stitched it into his thigh until it was ready to be born. When the time was right, the god Dionysus, whose name means "twice born," emerged from Zeus's thigh.

THE BIRTH OF DIONYSUS

KING MIDAS

Midas, the king of Phrygia, one day found the satyr Silenus passed out in his garden. He took the satyr into his palace and brought him back to health. Silenus was a companion of the god Dionysus, who wondered where the satyr had gone. When Midas returned Silenus to him, Dionysus granted the king a wish.

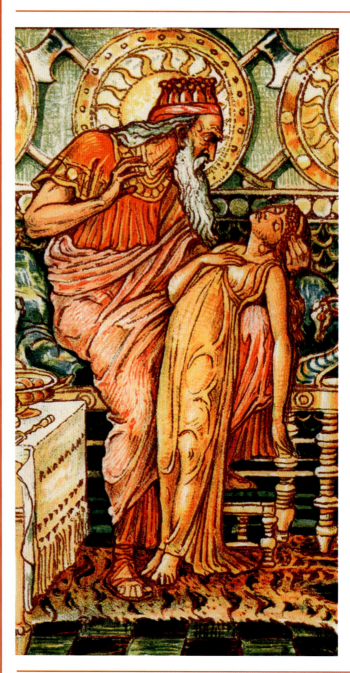

Golden touch

Midas asked to have the ability to turn anything he touched into gold, and Dionysus gave him what he desired. A greedy man, the king touched tree branches, stones, and apples: all turned to gold. But when Midas tried to eat, he turned his food to gold. Anyone he touched turned to gold as well. In desperation and afraid that he would starve or kill more people, Midas pleaded with Dionysus to take away his gift.

A curse in disguise

One version of the story tells of how Midas touched his own daughter, turning her into a golden statue. It was then that he realized his gift was a curse.

Sacred river

To bring an end to his golden "gift," Dionysus advised Midas to bathe in the Pactolus River, not far from the palace. When Midas did so, gold flowed in shimmering flecks from his hands. He was cured from that day on. It was believed that the Pactolus River was a source of gold because of King Midas.

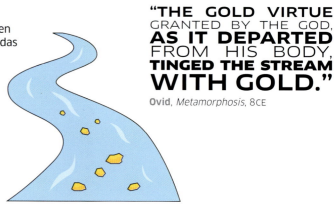

"THE GOLD VIRTUE GRANTED BY THE GOD, **AS IT DEPARTED** FROM HIS BODY, **TINGED THE STREAM WITH GOLD."**

Ovid, *Metamorphosis*, 8CE

7 Phaethon had **seven sisters, known as the Heliades,** and their tears **turned to amber** when he died.

Daedalus named the sea in which Icarus drowned the **Icarian Sea**.

BELLEROPHON'S PUNISHMENT

Once favored by the goddess Athena, Bellerophon was given the magnificent flying horse Pegasus to help him defeat the monstrous chimera—a task thought to be impossible. After his victory, the hero's excessive pride led to his downfall.

Battling the chimera
King Iobates tasked Bellerophon with killing the chimera, which was part lion, part goat, and part snake. The goddess Athena, who favored young heroes, gave him Pegasus so he could fly above the monster and strike it dead.

Flying to Olympus
After killing the chimera, Bellerophon became so proud, he decided to use Pegasus to fly to Olympus, the home of the gods. Angered by Bellerophon's arrogance, Zeus sent a gadfly to sting Pegasus, causing his rider to fall back down to Earth.

"AND RIDING ON THAT STEED, HE ASSAILED ... AND EVEN SLEW THE FIRE-BREATHING CHIMERA."
Pindar, *Olympian Odes*, 464 BCE

THE CHIMERA

Wild Pegasus
Bellerophon used a golden girdle Athena gave him to tame Pegasus, which made the wild winged horse obedient to his commands.

PHAETHON'S WISH

The sun god Helios once promised to give his son Phaethon whatever he desired. Seeking adventure, Phaethon asked to drive his father's chariot, but he drove it dangerously close to the Earth, scorching it. To end the chaos, Zeus struck the chariot with a lightning bolt, killing Phaeton.

Careless charioteer
Phaethon lost control of Helios's immortal horses and burned the plains of Africa, turning them into deserts.

THE FALL OF ICARUS

Daedalus was the most skilled of mortal craftsmen. He worked for King Minos and designed the labyrinth to imprison the Minotaur (see pages 28–29). To keep the route of the labyrinth a secret, the king held Daedalus and his son Icarus captive in a tower, so the craftsman devised a plan of escape.

Clever craftsman
Working for King Minos, Daedalus was a craftsman, architect, and inventor. Along with the Labyrinth, he created many things, including the potter's wheel and the first dance floor. To escape from the tower, he made wings out of wax and feathers for himself and his son Icarus.

Too close to the sun
Before flying out of the window of the prison, Daedalus warned Icarus not to fly too close to the sun, which would melt the wax. But once in the air, Icarus was overcome with the joy of flying and soared higher. His wings melted and he fell into the sea. A distraught Daedalus flew on alone to Sicily, whose king gave him refuge.

DAEDALUS

Death of a son
When Icarus's wings fell apart, he plummeted into the sea and drowned. Daedalus wept bitterly for his son and cursed his own skills.

europe • THE LABORS OF HERCULES

30 The stables in Hercules' fifth labor had not been cleaned for 30 years.

The Labors of Hercules

Known as Heracles to the Greeks, the hero Hercules performed great feats of incredible strength. After being cursed to commit terrible crimes, he was given 12 apparently impossible feats to accomplish.

The son of the god Zeus and a mortal woman, Alcmene, Hercules was persecuted by Zeus's jealous wife Hera from the moment he was born. When he was just a baby, Hera sent two snakes to attack him, but he strangled them using his exceptional strength.

As an adult, Hercules married and had several children. Hera was angered by his success and cursed him with a madness that caused him to kill his family. As punishment Hercules had to serve King Eurystheus of Mycenae for 12 years. During this time he was given 12 labors (difficult tasks) to complete. At the end of this servitude, Hercules was forgiven.

Hercules later married the Calydonian princess Deianira. After many years, she worried she was losing the love of her husband. So she rubbed his clothes with the blood of the centaur Nessus, who had told her it would reignite the spark between them. The garment, however, burned Hercules instead, and he died in agony.

As a reward for all he had suffered, Zeus made Hercules a god, raising him up to Mount Olympus, where Hera at last gave up her feud against him.

> **The Hydra** had a gigantic body, with nine huge heads—eight of them mortal.
>
> Pseudo-Apollodorus, *Library*, c.100CE

Multiplying heads
A dangerous monster, the Hydra grew two heads when Hercules sliced one off.

Poisonous monster
The Hydra had venomous breath—it hissed and spat poison.

The first labor
King Eurystheus ordered Hercules to track down and kill the Nemean lion. Hercules found it impossible to pierce the lion's tough hide with his arrows, so he cornered the beast in its cave, knocked it down with his club, and strangled it.

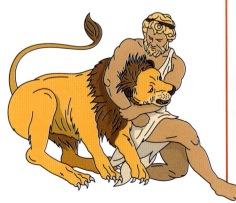

Skin of the lion
Hercules wore the pelt of the Nemean lion that he killed in the first labor.

*The **club of Hercules** was so **heavy** that only he could pick it up and **wield it with ease.***

*Hercules' first wife was **Megara** and together they had **several sons.***

The second labor
After killing the Nemean lion, Hercules moved on to his second labor—slaying the giant water snake Hydra in Lake Lerna. With the help of his nephew Iolaus, Hercules defeated the monster by cutting off its nine heads and having Iolaus cauterize (burn) the stumps to stop new heads from growing back.

Last to go
Hercules cut off the Hydra's one immortal head last and buried it.

Nephew's help
Iolaus quickly cauterized the stump with a flaming torch.

Precious poison
Hercules dipped the tips of his arrows in the monster's blood to make them poisonous.

The remaining labors
Hercules worked hard to finish off the rest of his labors, killing monsters, stealing treasures, and even cleaning up some messy stables along the way.

The long chase
To complete his third labor, Hercules had to capture the Ceryneian hind—a deer with golden antlers. After chasing the beast across the whole of Greece, he caught it in a net.

Hunting a wild boar
Hercules had to hunt the ferocious boar of Mount Erymanthos in his fourth labor. He chased the boar, drove it into a mountain snowdrift, tied it up, and flung it into the sea.

Cleaning up
In his fifth labor, Hercules had a single day to clean King Augeas's filthy stables that housed 1,000 cattle. Hercules diverted two rivers through the site to flush it clean. He was accused of cheating because he didn't do the work himself.

Shooting the birds
Hercules was tasked with killing the human-eating Stymphalian birds in his sixth labor. He found their swamp, startled them with a rattle, and then shot them with his bow and arrows.

Wrestling the Cretan bull
In his seventh labor, Hercules had to capture the bull that was running rampant across the island of Crete. He strangled the bull into submission before taking it to King Eurystheus.

Stealing human-eating mares
To steal the uncontrollable mares of King Diomedes as part of his eighth labor, Hercules killed the king and fed his flesh to the mares. They calmed down shortly after, making it easy for Hercules to harness them.

The simplest task
Hercules's ninth labor proved to be the easiest—to steal Queen Hippolyta's belt. She was so charmed by Hercules that she handed over her belt to him.

The giant's cattle
Next, Hercules traveled to the island of Erytheia, near Libya, to complete his tenth labor. He had to get the red cattle of Geryon, the three-headed giant. After killing Geryon's herdsman Eurytion and his two-headed dog Orthrus, Hercules drove Geryon's cattle to Greece.

Atlas helps out
In his eleventh labor, Hercules had to steal the golden apples of the Hesperides (nymphs of the setting sun). While the Titan god Atlas went to get them, Hercules held up the heavens in his place.

A visit to the Underworld
Hercules's twelfth and final labor was to capture the three-headed watchdog Cerberus from the Underworld without using a weapon. He succeeded by trapping the monster in his lion-skin cloak.

europe · APHRODITE

Aphrodite was called **"the Cypriot,"**–she was believed to have come from the **island of Cyprus**.

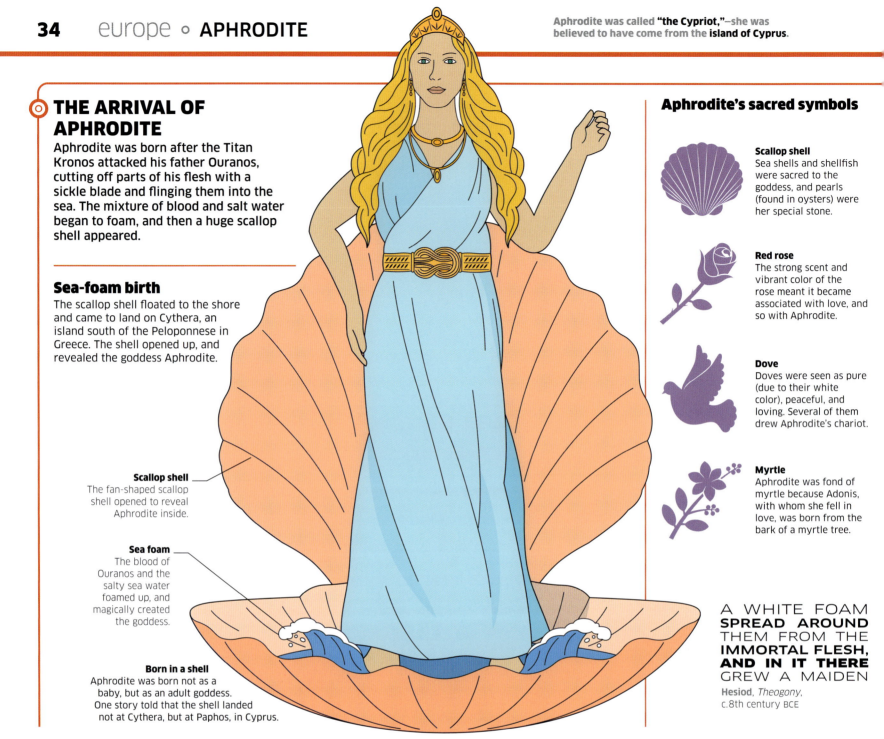

THE ARRIVAL OF APHRODITE
Aphrodite was born after the Titan Kronos attacked his father Ouranos, cutting off parts of his flesh with a sickle blade and flinging them into the sea. The mixture of blood and salt water began to foam, and then a huge scallop shell appeared.

Sea-foam birth
The scallop shell floated to the shore and came to land on Cythera, an island south of the Peloponnese in Greece. The shell opened up, and revealed the goddess Aphrodite.

Scallop shell
The fan-shaped scallop shell opened to reveal Aphrodite inside.

Sea foam
The blood of Ouranos and the salty sea water foamed up, and magically created the goddess.

Born in a shell
Aphrodite was born not as a baby, but as an adult goddess. One story told that the shell landed not at Cythera, but at Paphos, in Cyprus.

Aphrodite's sacred symbols

Scallop shell
Sea shells and shellfish were sacred to the goddess, and pearls (found in oysters) were her special stone.

Red rose
The strong scent and vibrant color of the rose meant it became associated with love, and so with Aphrodite.

Dove
Doves were seen as pure (due to their white color), peaceful, and loving. Several of them drew Aphrodite's chariot.

Myrtle
Aphrodite was fond of myrtle because Adonis, with whom she fell in love, was born from the bark of a myrtle tree.

> A WHITE FOAM SPREAD AROUND THEM FROM THE IMMORTAL FLESH, AND IN IT THERE GREW A MAIDEN
>
> Hesiod, *Theogony*, c.8th century BCE

Aphrodite

The most beautiful of the gods, Aphrodite was the goddess of love, and was known as Venus to the Romans. She lived on Mount Olympus and could inflict helpless love upon anyone. She had many suitors herself, and punished any mortal who dared to reject her.

Aphrodite was the guardian of women, especially those engaged to be married, and bestowed upon them both fertility and passionate love. Her companions, including deities such as Eros, could also cause mortals to fall in love. She was also the goddess of navigation, and sailors prayed to her for safe journeys at sea.

LOVES AND LOSSES
Aphrodite was not faithful to Hephaestus, because she had not wanted to marry him. Her many romances included the gods Ares, Dionysus, Poseidon, and Hermes, and many mortals, such as the huntsman Adonis.

Love and war
Aphrodite had a relationship with Ares, the war god. Hephaestus made a special net with golden chains, which snapped shut and trapped them. The other gods came and laughed at the couple, and only then did Hephaestus set them free.

A deep passion
Aphrodite's affair with Ares was the greatest of all her romances, and resulted in the birth of many children.

Aphrodite and Hephaestus

Hephaestus, the god of fire and metalworking, was thrown from the top of Olympus by his mother, Hera. In revenge he made a golden throne which, when Hera sat on it, trapped her there. Other gods tried and failed to set her free. Hephaestus only agreed to release her when he was allowed to return to Olympus and marry Aphrodite.

The forge of Hephaestus
Hephaestus was believed to create metal objects with magical powers in the intense heat of a volcano, where he lived after being flung down from Olympus.

Venus and Adonis

One day, an arrow from Eros accidentally touched Aphrodite. This meant she fell in love with the next person she saw, Adonis, a mortal prince from Cyprus. Adonis returned Aphrodite's love, which made Ares jealous. He disguised himself as a boar, which gored Adonis to death when he next went hunting. The blood of Adonis dripped onto an anemone flower, which remained a deep red color for ever after.

GODDESS OF LOVE AND BEAUTY

Aphrodite was the goddess of love mainly between unmarried partners (Hera was the goddess of love within marriage). She inspired passion in others, often causing them to act unwisely. As the goddess of beauty, her looks also sometimes caused trouble.

Magic belt

Aphrodite had a magic girdle, or belt, which could cause mortals or immortals to fall in love with whoever was wearing it. She sometimes allowed Hera to borrow it, to stop quarrels between married couples.

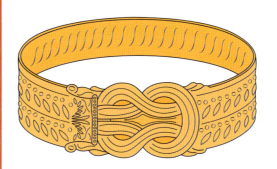

HELPING LOVERS

Aphrodite often granted favors to mortals who fell in love with her, but she was also known to heavily support the romances of others. By helpfully manipulating those in pursuit of love, Aphrodite aided many in finding their happiness.

Atalanta and the Golden Apples

Princess Atalanta swore she would only marry a man who beat her in a race. Everyone who tried lost. Aphrodite gave the mortal Hippomenes three golden apples. As he ran, he threw them down. Atalanta slowed to pick them up, and he beat her, winning her hand in marriage.

Winged gods

Aphrodite was always accompanied by several winged gods, known as the Erotes. Each god symbolized a different type of love. Himeros was the god of desire, Eros of strong and uncontrollable love, Hymenaios of marriage, Pothos of passion, Hedylogos of flattery, and Anteros of love that was returned.

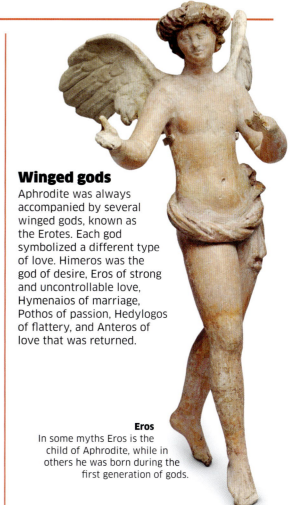

Eros
In some myths Eros is the child of Aphrodite, while in others he was born during the first generation of gods.

Pygmalion

The sculptor Pygmalion, who had vowed never to marry, carved a life-size, ivory statue of a woman so perfect that he fell in love. He then prayed to Aphrodite for a wife just as beautiful as the statue. The goddess granted his wish, transforming the statue into a living woman.

Transformation
As Pygmalion slept, Aphrodite granted his wish and brought the statue to life. He woke to discover the real woman, Galatea, who he married.

> **HE CARVED HIS SNOW-WHITE IVORY WITH MARVELOUS TRIUMPHANT ARTISTRY AND GAVE IT PERFECT SHAPE, MORE BEAUTIFUL THAN EVER WOMAN BORN**
> Ovid, *Metamorphoses*, 8CE

europe • THE TROJAN WAR

The **Greek hero Hercules** and his army had previously tried to **capture Troy**.

Homer's *Iliad* only covers **two or three weeks** of the war.

The Trojan War

One of the most famous conflicts in all of myth, the Trojan War began after the Trojan prince Paris abducted Helen, wife of the Greek king Menelaus. The Greek army sailed to Troy and laid siege to the city for 10 years. The war, part of which is told in Homer's epic poem the *Iliad*, finally ended when the Greeks tricked their way into Troy by hiding themselves inside a wooden horse.

> **Trust not the horse, O Trojans. Be it what it may, I fear the Greeks when they offer gifts.**
>
> Virgil, *Aeneid*, 1st century BCE

After Paris kidnapped Helen from Sparta, Menelaus asked his brother Agamemnon, King of Mycenae, to raise an army to go to Troy to take her back. Heroes came from all over Greece to join the expedition, which sailed in a great fleet to Troy.

Each time one side looked close to winning the conflict, the gods would help the losing side. Athena, Hera, or Hermes would aid the Greeks, or Aphrodite, Apollo, or Ares would aid the Trojans.

After nine years of fighting, Achilles, the greatest Greek hero, argued with Agamemnon and refused to fight any more. Afraid that the Trojans would take advantage of this refusal, Patroclus impersonated his companion Achilles by borrowing his armor, and led their army into battle. But Patroclus was killed by Hector, son of the Trojan king Priam.

Achilles returned to the battle to gain revenge for the death of Patroclus. He killed Hector in single combat, dragging his dead body around the walls of Troy afterward to taunt the Trojans. But the Trojans still did not surrender, and the war dragged on, with many heroes dying on both sides of the conflict. Achilles was ultimately killed by an arrow shot by Paris, which hit his heel—the only vulnerable part of his body.

Finally, the Greek hero Odysseus, known for his cunning, concocted a plan to enter the city. The Greeks pretended to abandon the siege, and left behind a wooden horse as an offering to the gods. Some Greek warriors, including Odysseus, hid inside. A Greek spy, Sinon, persuaded the Trojans it would bring them luck to drag the horse inside the city. That night, the Greeks climbed out, opened Troy's gates, and let the rest of the Greek army inside. They ransacked the city, killing almost all of its people, including King Priam, and Menelaus seized Helen to take her back to Sparta.

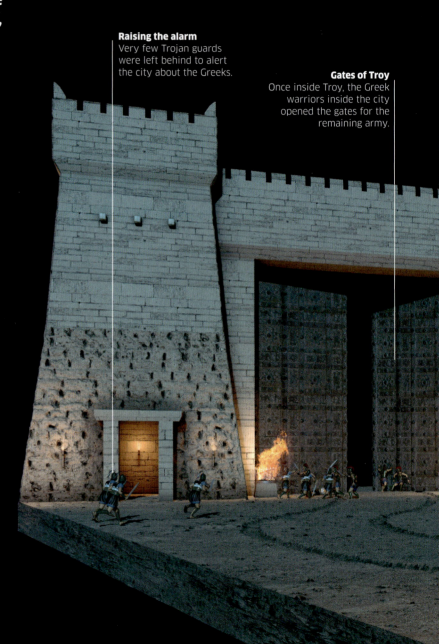

Raising the alarm
Very few Trojan guards were left behind to alert the city about the Greeks.

Gates of Troy
Once inside Troy, the Greek warriors inside the city opened the gates for the remaining army.

The Judgment of Paris

Eris, goddess of strife, was not invited to the wedding of Thetis and Peleus. Offended, she threw a golden apple inscribed with the words "to the fairest" among the guests. Zeus asked Paris to judge which goddess deserved the apple—Aphrodite, Hera, or Athena. Paris chose Aphrodite, who promised that in return he could marry the world's most beautiful woman.

Goddesses scorned
Because of Paris's decision, the goddesses Hera and Athena later supported the Greeks in the war.

The Abduction of Helen

The woman who Aphrodite had promised to Paris was Helen of Sparta, but she was already married to King Menelaus. So Paris pretended to go on a diplomatic mission to Sparta, always intending to kidnap her. To help him, Aphrodite had the love god Eros shoot an arrow at Helen, which caused her to fall in love with Paris and agree to go with him back to Troy. When Menelaus realized his wife had been taken, he asked his brother Agamemnon to raise an army and bring her home.

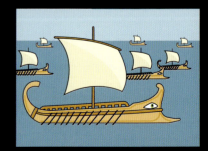

Sailing to Troy
The fleet that Agamemnon gathered to bring Helen back from Troy had more than 1,000 ships.

1,186 The number of **ships** that carried the **Greek army to Troy**

The war lasted **10 years** and it took **10 more years** for Odysseus to **return home**.

37

Fake offering
The Greeks pretended to leave the horse as an offering to Athena to bless their return journey to Greece. Not knowing it was a trick, the Trojans dragged the horse—packed with Greek warriors—into their city.

No guards
The walls had no guards because the Trojans believed the Greeks had left.

A sneaky exit
Greek warriors climbed out of a trapdoor hidden under the horse's hollow belly.

Horse wheels
The Greeks gave the wooden horse wheels, to entice the Trojans to move it inside.

Greek heroes

 **Achilles**
The Greeks' best warrior. He was invulnerable all over, apart from his heel.

 Odysseus
Known for his clever tricks, the hero Odysseus tried to avoid going to Troy by faking insanity.

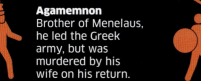 **Agamemnon**
Brother of Menelaus, he led the Greek army, but was murdered by his wife on his return.

 Ajax
The strongest Greek warrior, never wounded by the Trojans. He took his own life after a quarrel with Odysseus.

Trojan heroes

 Hector
Heir to the Trojan throne and devoted to his family, he almost defeated the Greeks on his own.

 Paris
He shot the arrow that killed Achilles, but was in turn killed by the Greeks' best archer, Philoctetes.

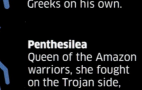 **Penthesilea**
Queen of the Amazon warriors, she fought on the Trojan side, but was killed in battle by Achilles.

 Aeneas
He fled Troy with his father on his back, becoming one of the few Trojans to escape.

12 Odysseus set out on his **journey from Troy** with **12 ships**, none of which survived the journey.

3 In some stories, **Charybdis** was a **monster** living under the sea that caused **whirlpools three times a day**.

The return of Odysseus

After a decade of fighting in the Trojan War, the hero Odysseus longed to return home to be with his wife Penelope and his son Telemachus, but the journey was full of setbacks and tragedies. The famous ancient Greek epic *The Odyssey* recounts Odysseus's incredible adventure and is one of the greatest stories ever told.

When the Greeks won the Trojan War (see pages 34–35), Odysseus was finally free to return to his kingdom. With a crew of more than 600 men, the fleet of ships set sail from Troy to his home in Ithaca.

What should have been a straightforward journey turned into a long series of catastrophes. The crew faced the wrath of the gods, terrible storms, ravenous monsters, and a treacherous whirlpool.

Members of the crew drowned or were devoured during the long voyage until Odysseus remained the sole survivor. Still eager to get home, Odysseus accepted the help of a Phoenician sailor who took him on the last stretch to Ithaca.

Twenty years after the war ended, Odysseus arrived in Ithaca an old man. Even then he had to fight off Penelope's suitors before he could reclaim his throne.

The Trojan War ends
Odysseus and his crew set sail for home after the end of the Trojan War and the destruction of the city of Troy.

Penelope's tapestry
During the 20 years that Odysseus had been missing, many men of Ithaca had been competing to marry Penelope. She insisted she would only remarry once her tapestry was complete. Every night she unraveled her needlework, but in the end her trick was revealed.

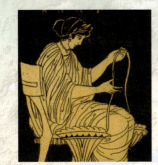

Home of Odysseus
Ithaca was the beloved home and kingdom of Odysseus, who returned as an old man and without his crew.

A god's wrath
The sea god Poseidon, who had sided with Troy in the war, was angry with Odysseus. He stirred up violent storms to drive the ships off course.

Home at last
Odysseus disguised himself as a beggar when he returned home, unsure of how his people would welcome him. Penelope's suitors had forced her to choose a new husband. She declared that she would marry the man who could string Odysseus's bow. Only Odysseus, still in disguise, had the strength to string the bow. He revealed himself, and was reunited with Penelope at last.

On target
Successfully stringing the bow, Odysseus killed all the suitors who had tried to force Penelope to marry.

39

40 europe · THE BEGINNINGS OF ROME

Aeneas was the son of the mortal Anchises and **Venus, goddess of love**.

The harpies
On his voyage to Italy, Aeneas encountered half-female, half-bird wind spirits called harpies. One placed a curse on Aeneas, correctly predicting that his destination would only be reached after a period of extreme hunger.

Fierce fliers
In Roman artwork, harpies were depicted with large wings and sharp faces.

Dido of Carthage
When Aeneas fell in love with Dido, he was distracted from his quest. But the gods told Aeneas to focus on his mission, so he left without telling Dido goodbye. Heartbroken, the devastated queen took her own life.

Queen and warrior
The noble queen and the hero displayed deep affection for each other until Aeneas abruptly departed.

> Huge Cerberus sets these **regions echoing** with his triple-throated howling
>
> Virgil, *Aeneid*, 1st century BCE

Aeneas the warrior
A heroic soldier who fought against the Greeks at Troy, Aeneas was usually shown in his military armor.

The ferryman
Charon, the ferryman of the underworld, carried the souls of the deceased across the river.

Aeneas enters the underworld
Ahead of his visit to his father, Aeneas was told by the Sybil of Cumae to bring a golden branch for Proserpina, the queen of the underworld. The branch would ensure his safe passage across the river.

River crossing
The Acheron River was one of many that flowed through the underworld.

Romulus and Remus were the **sons of Mars, the god of war,** who cast them down the Tiber River at birth.

753BCE Rome was established on **Palatine Hill** in the year **753BCE**.

The underworld
The entrance to the underworld was represented as the mouth of a cave.

Guard dog
Cerberus, a vicious three-headed dog, guarded the entrance to the underworld.

Loaded cake
The Sybil of Cumae fed the hound some honey cake laced with a drug that put it to sleep.

The beginnings of Rome

According to Roman myth, the Trojan hero Aeneas laid the foundations for the Roman state. After Troy was destroyed, he traveled to Greece, Africa, and finally Italy, where he established a home for his people.

Aeneas was a Trojan prince, and a relative of King Priam of Troy. When the Greeks conquered Troy (see pages 34–35), he fled with his father Anchises. Aeneas was then tasked by the gods to find a new home for the Trojans.

Their journey first took them to Greece, but the gods told Aeneas in a vision that Italy was the place he would create a new home. They sailed on to Sicily, where Anchises tragically died from exhaustion. A storm then blew Aeneas off course, and he found himself in Carthage, on the North African coast.

Here, Aeneas fell in love with the Carthaginian queen, Dido. But the god Jupiter ordered Aeneas to continue his mission and journey onward to Italy.

Aeneas returned to Sicily where a priestess, the Sybil of Cumae, took Aeneas to the underworld. There he met with the spirit of his father, who predicted the birth of the great city of Rome. Aeneas and his army then sailed to Latium in Italy, where he was welcomed by the region's king, Latinus.

Aeneas fell in love with Lavinia, the king's daughter. This sparked a war with Turnus, the king of the Rutuli, who had been promised Lavinia's hand. Aeneas killed Turnus in a duel and married Lavinia. He then established a settlement in the region that would become home to Rome.

Romulus and Remus
Aeneas built the first settlement in the area of Rome, but many years later his descendants—the twins Romulus and Remus—founded the city itself. Nursed by a she-wolf after being cast aside at birth, the twins grew up to establish a new city, as the gods foretold. An argument about its location led to Romulus killing Remus and founding Rome on Palatine Hill.

Bronze sculpture
The Capitoline Wolf sculpture depicts the twins suckling on the she-wolf.

europe ○ **GODS OF THE HOME**

More frequently portrayed by the flame of her temple's sacred fire, Vesta was less often depicted in human form.

VESTA
Vesta was the Roman equivalent of Hestia, the Greek goddess of hearth and home, and was seen as the purest of all gods. She was often worshipped in households as well as in a temple bearing her name. This was located in the Forum area of Rome, where an annual festival was held to celebrate the goddess.

Protector of the home
One of Saturn's six children, and the sister of Jupiter (the Roman Zeus), Vesta was devoted to her role. She once begged Jupiter to allow her not to marry, so she could instead focus on being a protector of the home.

On the throne
Some portrayals of Vesta in human form show her standing up, but most depict the goddess seated on a throne.

Vesta's sacred symbols

Torch or fireplace
Fire was vital to many aspects of life in Ancient Rome, so Vesta was sometimes represented by a torch or flame.

Cooking pot
The cooking pot was an important symbol which combined Vesta's roles as a being of plenty and protector of the fireplace.

Wheat
In addition to her role as goddess of the hearth, Vesta was also the patron deity of bakers. Wheat was another one of her symbols.

Donkey
A donkey was used to drive the mill wheel that ground the wheat to make bread. It was also a donkey that saved Vesta from Priapus (see right).

Gods of the home
In Ancient Rome, the home was an important part of everyday life. Gods were worshipped to protect households and bring good fortune to their residents. The most important of these domestic gods was Vesta, goddess of the hearth (fireplace).

Fire was central to the home, providing warmth, light, and heat for cooking. This is why Vesta was such a respected god. Other parts of running a household, including providing food and protection, were also worshipped. These were represented by gods such as the Penates and the Lares. All were honored in the form of prayers to statues, and offerings left at small household shrines.

HOUSEHOLD GODS
The ancient Romans worshipped other gods associated with the home, such as the Penates and the Lares. The Penates were originally gods of household food, while the Lares were associated with crop growth in the fields. But over time, the two groups of deities overlapped. People prayed to them for prosperity and safe-keeping, and they were often honored together alongside Vesta.

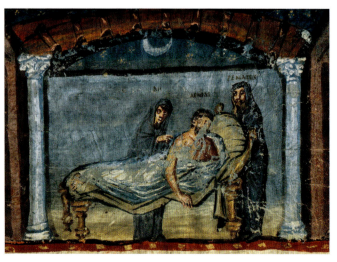

The Penates
The Penates were two gods who arrived in Italy with the Trojan hero Aeneas, after he brought them with him from Troy. They soon came to represent the protectors of the city in general, and of the most central part of a home in particular—household meals. The Penates were often portrayed as two young men, and at mealtimes their statues were moved from the household shrine to the dinner table.

The Penates with Aeneas
Aeneas valued the protection of the Penates, and is sometimes depicted with the two gods by his side.

> **6** There were always **six priestesses** who tended to the Temple of Vesta.

> It was believed that the Lares not only protected their households, but could also **influence their surroundings**.

The Temple of Vesta in Rome
In the Roman capital, a sacred fire was kept continually alight by six priestesses at the Temple of Vesta. This eternal flame was said to represent the everlasting Roman state. The fire was only ever officially extinguished and relit at the time of the Roman new year. If the flame went out at any other time, it was a bad omen for the Roman Empire.

Grand design
The temple's circular architecture and high pillars can still be seen in the ruins of the building in modern-day Rome.

> WHEN THE MULE LET OUT AN UNTIMELY BRAY, **FRIGHTENED BY THE RAUCOUS NOISE,** THE GODDESS LEAPT UP: THE WHOLE TROOP GATHERED, **AND PRIAPUS FLED** THROUGH THEIR HANDS.
>
> Ovid, *Fasti*, 1st century CE

Vestalia
Held for a week in June each year, Vestalia was a public festival in honor of Vesta. It was the only time of the year when the inner sanctuary of the Temple of Vesta was open, and when women could enter. The festival period was marked by sacrifices, offerings, and an official sweeping of the temple building on the last day of festivities.

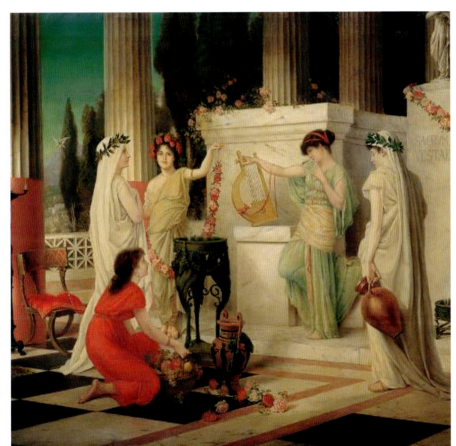

Priestesses of Vesta
The priestesses in charge of the Temple of Vesta tended to the sacred fire, prepared food, and carried out other official duties during Vestalia.

Vesta and Priapus
One myth tells the story of how Vesta had a close encounter with Priapus, the god of fertility who mistreated females. At a party thrown by Cybele, the mother goddess, Vesta fell asleep by a stream after a night of celebrations. When Priapus saw the goddess, he made to approach her, but Vesta was saved by the sound of a braying donkey. It woke Vesta up, and attracted the attention of other gods who drove Priapus away.

The Lares
The Lares were the twin sons of the gods Mercury and Mania. Their role as protectors of the home came from the myth of them using the dogs of Diana, the goddess of hunting, to ward off thieves and others who might threaten a peaceful household. Prayers were said and offerings were made to the Lares, who were depicted as young men with a drinking horn in one hand and a cup in the other.

Household shrine
Roman homes featured small shrines, where tokens including food, wine, and incense were left for household gods.

Household genius
Every man in ancient Rome was given guidance and protection by a mythical personal spirit called a genius. The female equivalent was known as the iuno, and together these spirits were worshipped in the same way as the gods.

Personal gods
A genius protected a Roman for their entire life, and was sometimes carved into their resting place even in death.

europe · PSYCHE AND CUPID

Psyche's name means "soul" or "breath of life" in Ancient Greek.

Psyche and Cupid

The story of Psyche and Cupid is one of jealousy, longing, and ultimately of love conquering all. One of the earliest versions of the story was told by the Roman writer Apuleius.

Cupid was the son of Venus, goddess of love, and he could make anyone fall in love with the next being they saw by shooting them with one of his arrows. When Venus saw that a beautiful mortal princess called Psyche was attracting more attention than her, she commanded Cupid to punish the princess by making her fall in love with a monster.

Cupid readied his bow, but clumsily scratched himself with his own arrow of passion, accidentally falling in love with Psyche. He carried her away to his palace, but to conceal the truth from his mother, Cupid hid himself from Psyche and only visited her in the darkness of night. He told her that if she were to see what he looked like, she'd lose him forever.

Psyche's envious sisters convinced her that Cupid might actually be some kind of terrible serpent, so she set out to kill him while he slept. When she approached her unseen captor holding a light, she was shocked to see it was the god of love. She accidentally scratched herself on one of his arrows and fell deeply in love with him. Hands trembling, she dripped hot oil on him—and Cupid woke up and fled.

Psyche began a quest to find him, which led her to the palace of Venus. The goddess set her a series of difficult missions, the last of which resulted in Psyche falling into a deep sleep. Cupid flew to Psyche to revive her, and the lovers were reunited. Upon finally being accepted by Venus, Psyche was made immortal by the gods and the pair were united for all eternity.

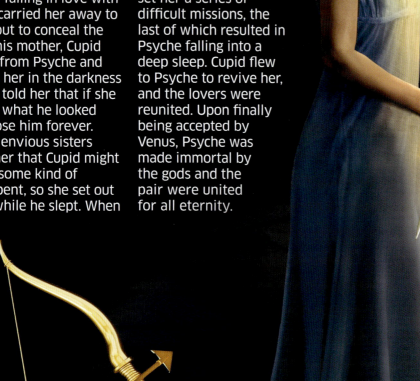

Burning love
A drop of hot oil from Psyche's lamp fell on Cupid, waking him from his sleep.

Heaven on Earth
Psyche possessed such beauty that some believed she was the human form of Venus.

Deadly intentions
Psyche took a dagger to kill Cupid, believing him to be a dangerous serpent.

Cupid's bow
The goddess Venus sent Cupid to shoot many mortals with arrows from his bow to make them fall in love. Even the gods themselves were not immune to the power of the bow and arrows, proven when Cupid himself fell in love with Psyche.

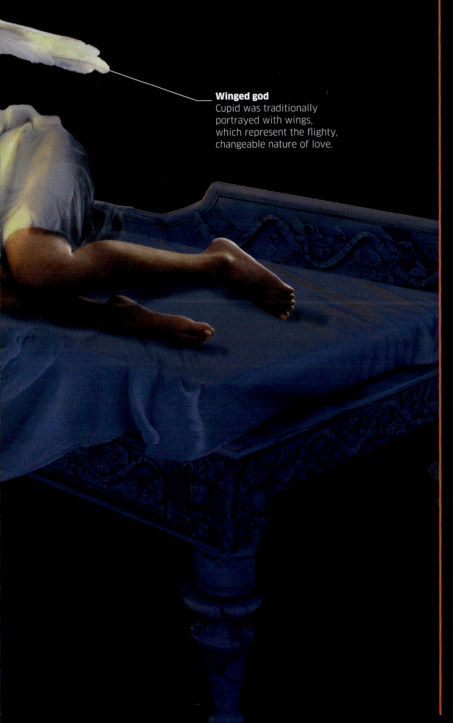

"Punish mercilessly that arrogant beauty ... let this girl be seized with a burning passion for the lowest of mankind"

Apuleius, *Metamorphoses*, 2nd century CE

The discovery
Psyche approached the sleeping Cupid with an oil lamp and a dagger. In shock at discovering her husband was the handsome god, she spilled hot oil from the lamp on to him and he woke up. The god of love felt betrayed that Psyche would disobey his instructions, and fled from her.

Winged god
Cupid was traditionally portrayed with wings, which represent the flighty, changeable nature of love.

Tasks from Venus
Venus was both protective over her son and jealous of Psyche's beauty. As a result, when Psyche approached Venus at her palace to ask for help finding Cupid, the goddess enslaved her and set the mortal princess a series of supposedly impossible challenges. But Psyche got help to complete each task.

Sort the grains
Psyche was given a mixed heap of grains, and told to separate them into individual piles.

Find the fleece
She was ordered to obtain some fleece from a flock of aggressive, golden rams.

Fill a jug
The next task was retrieving water from the River Styx that flowed past the underworld.

Collect beauty
The final task was to collect a jar of beauty from Proserpina, queen of the underworld.

Ant relief
A horde of friendly ants divided the many grains into piles for Psyche.

Reed speak
A reed by the river told Psyche that the wool could be taken as the sheep slept.

Eagle aid
A royal eagle completed the task by filling the jug with river water.

Tower talk
One of the turrets in the palace tower told Psyche how to retrieve the jar.

Deathly sleep
After completing the tasks, Psyche was overcome with curiosity and unsealed the jar from Proserpina. But she discovered that instead of beauty, the jar contained a deadly sleep, and Psyche fell unconscious.

CUPID AWAKENS PSYCHE

Lovers reunited
After Cupid revived Psyche, he took her to Mount Olympus where Jupiter, king of the gods, formally blessed the marriage. Jupiter made Psyche immortal, and Venus finally accepted the union. A wedding ceremony was held in the presence of several other gods.

NORTHERN EUROPE

Between the 8th and 11th centuries, Vikings from Scandinavia became famous maritime raiders and explorers. Their voyages brought their fascinating stories about the creation of the universe and their colorful gods to the rest of northern Europe. In particular, tales of Odin, Thor, and Loki spread far and wide, and they became characters in more local stories.

SOURCES OF MYTHS

The early Vikings did not write down their myths. Instead their stories were passed on by word of mouth. Most of the myths were not recorded on paper until the 13th century, when Icelandic writers began to write down the stories of the Norse people.

The Prose Edda
This set of four books, compiled in Iceland in the 13th-century, is the most detailed source of Norse myth that we know today, and tells stories from the beginning of creation to the end of the world. Much of it was compiled by historian Snorri Sturluson.

Odin illustrated
Medieval Icelandic manuscripts of the *Prose Edda* contain many illustrations showing the gods and scenes from the Norse myths.

SNORRI STURLUSON

The Poetic Edda
The largest part of this collection of poetry is the *Codex Regius*, which contains stories of the gods and giants such as Loki and Thrym. Snorri Sturluson used many of these poems in the construction of his *Prose Edda*.

DETAIL OF RAMSUND CARVING

Icelandic sagas
These medieval tales contain stories of important families, and are a mixture of mythology and history. The most important is the *Saga of the Volsungs*, a tale that is also shown on the Ramsund carving.

ELIAS LÖNNROT

The Kalevala
Finland had a very separate tradition of myth and legend from the Norse. The Finnish stories were combined into a vast epic known as the *Kalevala* in the 19th century by the scholar Elias Lönnrot.

NORSE INFLUENCE
The stories and culture of the Vikings had an influence that lasted for centuries. Some tales that are told in Germany and the British Isles are tales also told in Scandinavia.

SIEGFRIED AND BRÜNHILD

Germanic legend
The epic German story of Siegfried and Brünhild is probably older than the very similar story of Sigurd, which incorporates many elements of Norse myth (see pages 62–63).

GOSFORTH FISHING STONE

The British Isles
The Anglo-Saxons brought tales of Norse gods to Britain, as can be seen on the Gosforth fishing stone that shows Thor's fishing trip with Hymir. The Anglo-Saxon poem *Beowulf* is also set in Denmark.

NORSE MAGIC
The Norse myths are full of magic. The great god Odin hung on a tree for nine days to learn the secrets of rune magic, while Freyja brought the gods the secrets of seidr.

Rune magic
The first Norse alphabet was made of runes, which were formed from straight lines that were easy to carve in stone. Vikings would use runestones to cast spells or curses, foretell the future, or protect people from misfortune.

Seidr
A type of magic that foretold the future, Seidr was brought to the gods of Asgard by Freyja (above). It was practiced in Norse society until the rise of Christianity.

PLACES OF WORSHIP

Viking worship of the gods quite often took place in areas of natural beauty, in sacred groves known as lundr. Norse people also built temples, which have become known as known as hofs.

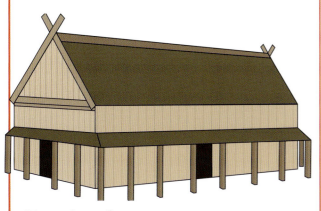

Norse temples
There is very little information about the hofs (sometimes known as heathen hofs) built by the Vikings. It's unknown whether these buildings were built to honor gods such as Odin, Frigg, and Frey and were only used as religious buildings or whether they were also places to host feasts or for people to live in.

Sacred sites
Important sites of worship, sacred groves known as lundr were believed to be inhabited by gods or spirits. They were often used to perform rituals, and it was believed that ceremonies held in these places would earn favor from the gods.

Breathtaking vistas
Scandinavia has many areas of dramatic natural beauty that would have made a fitting home for a god.

SUPERNATURAL CREATURES

The creatures of Norse myth are now familiar throughout the world. Tales of giants, dwarves, and dragons have become particularly popular over the past century.

Giants
Some of the first beings to come into existence were the frost giants, towering figures who lived in their icy home of Jotunheim.

Elves
Elves were split into light elves and dark elves. The dark elves lived underground while the light elves were "fairer than the sun."

Dwarves
Germanic dwarves were small but skilled craftspeople. They commonly lived inside mountains or at the bottom of mines.

Trolls
Fearsome giantlike creatures, trolls would often attack humans. They sometimes had magical powers. If exposed to sunlight they turned to stone.

NORSE WORSHIP

The gods of the Vikings were worshipped in a variety of ways. As in many cultures, believers offered sacrifices. Feasting was also a ritual for the Vikings, and feasts could last days. A more personal sign of worship was to wear jewelery depicting items sacred to the gods.

Feasts
Feasts, known as blots, were held to give thanks to the gods after good weather or great victories. These celebrations were an opportunity for the community to get together over hearty stews, roasted meat, ale, and mead.

Toasting the gods
At feasts, each guest would offer a toast to either the gods or an honored guest from a drinking horn.

Jewelery
Many Viking warriors wore pins or pendants in the shape of Thor's hammer. Jewelery in the form of an item associated with a god was worn for strength or for protection.

FREYA PENDANT

SACRIFICIAL SITE

Sacrifice
At feasts, animals such as horses would be sacrificed in a sacred place, and their meat would then be eaten at the feast.

Dragons
In north European stories, dragons were huge, fire-breathing reptiles that hoard gold. They were originally wingless, but in later tales they had wings like other European dragons.

europe o **NORSE CREATION STORIES**

On his death, the blood that flowed from **Ymir's body** drowned all the other **frost giants**, except for **Bergelmir** and his wife.

Norse creation stories

The spectacular landscape of northern Europe, such as the red-hot lava flowing from volcanoes and the ice sitting on mountaintops, inspired the Norse people's dramatic myths of creation.

In the beginning of time, a great void existed between the realms of ice and fire. From these powerful and opposing elements, the first being sprang forth. From his giant body, other giants emerged, born between the extremes of fire and ice, and they went on to create the first gods. These supreme deities brought order to the universe, using the elements they could find to forge the world, the sun, and the moon.

THE FIRST BEINGS

Ginnungagap was a void between the icy realm of Niflheim, and the fiery realm of Muspelheim. When the two worlds collided, the ice began to melt and filled Ginnungagap with water. From it, the first beings were created.

Ymir the giant

The first being was a giant whose name was Ymir. He was like an enormous ice sculpture, standing tall over the flaming and frozen lands. While he slept, the sweat from his body transformed into new creatures and crept away. They were an entirely new race of giants known as the frost giants.

FROM DARKNESS TO LIGHT

Odin, Vili, and Ve didn't stop at creating the world from Ymir's body. They brought light to the universe by throwing some of the sparks from Muspelheim into the sky, which became the sun and planets. Then the gods made the sun and the moon move across the heavens by putting them in separate chariots.

> "THE HORSE ON WHICH **DAY RIDES IS** CALLED SKINFAXE, AND WITH HIS MANE HE LIGHTS UP ALL THE SKY AND THE EARTH."
> Snorri Sturluson, *The Prose Edda*, c.1220CE

Always on the run

The god Mundilfari had two children whom he named after the sun and the moon. Odin put Sól ("sun") in charge of steering the sun's chariot, and Máni ("moon") as the moon's chariot driver. The two never rested because they were chased after by two hungry wolves. Sköll chased the sun, while Hati pursued the moon.

Ask and Embla

One day, Odin, Vili, and Ve found two trees while walking along the beach. They created the first man from the ash tree, and the first woman from the elm tree. Ask ("ash") and Embla ("elm") started the human race on Earth.

Shiny disk
The bronze disk was covered in a thin layer of gold on one side to represent the sun.

Drawn by horses
The dark goddess Nott ("night") and radiant god Dag ("day") were placed in the sky by Odin. They followed each other every 12 hours in their chariots.

Sun chariot
The Danish Trundholm sun chariot dates back to around 1400BCE. This ornament shows the ancient belief that celestial objects were drawn by chariots.

ASH ELM

Odin was by far the strongest of the **three sons of Bor**, with **supreme strength** on the battlefield.

4 The sky had **four corners**, and each one was assigned to **a dwarf**. They were known as **Austri** (East), **Vestri** (West), **Nordri** (North), and **Sudri** (South).

The sacred cow

As the ice continued to thaw, a colossal cow was revealed. Her name was Audhumla and she produced milk to feed Ymir and keep him strong and healthy. But soon the cow became thirsty herself, and started licking the surrounding ice. Her rough tongue scraped the ice to form the body of the first god—Buri.

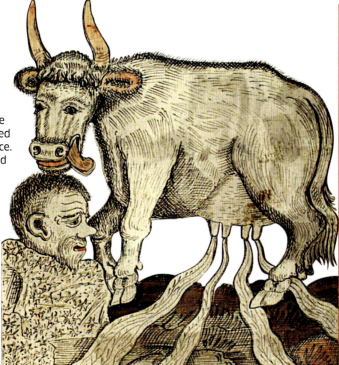

Sculpting the ice
Audhumla licked the ice for three days, forming the god Buri with her tongue.

Three brothers

Buri felt powerful as soon as he was born. He had a son named Bor who married the giantess Bestla. The couple had three sons: Odin, Vili, and Ve. They created a stable world from the chaos of ice and fire by killing Ymir. With his body parts they constructed the world—his head formed the sky and clouds, which they placed on the Earth.

THE FIRST WAR

The gods were once divided into two tribes: the Aesir, who were from Asgard, and the Vanir, who lived in Vanaheim. The Aesir were made up of warriors, led by Odin, while the Vanir were mostly magical peacekeepers. A conflict started between the two groups of gods, which went on for many years.

Execution of Freyja

The war began when the Vanir goddess of love, Freyja, went to Asgard and demonstrated her magic to the Aesir gods. When the Aesir began using her magic for their selfish gains, the Vanir gods were angered. Odin chose to punish Freyja for the tension between the gods, and gave the order for her execution by fire. Freyja used her magic to protect herself against the flames and survived all three attempts to burn her body. This made Odin even more angry, and the two groups went to all-out war.

Protected by cats
Freyja drove a chariot pulled by two cats. Feline creatures were sacred to the goddess and they protected her.

Exchanging hostages

After the long war, both sides called for peace. The Aesir and the Vanir gods agreed to exchange hostages. Hoenir and the wise god Mímir were given to the Vanir gods. But the gods angrily chopped off Mímir's head when they realized that Hoenir was a fool, and sent the head back to Odin. The Aesir god preserved the head, so it continued to give him advice.

Kvasir the wise

The gods did not restart the war. Instead, the two groups of gods united in peace. They took turns to spit into a cauldron, which created Kvasir, the wisest god in existence. His precious blood was later used to make the Mead of Poetry (see pages 50–51).

europe • THE WORLD TREE

Valhalla
The war god Odin was in charge of the hall of Valhalla in Asgard. Female warrior spirits known as Valkyries (see page 63) carried half of those slain in combat to Valhalla, while the other half were taken to the goddess Freyja's heavenly field of Fólkvangr. In Valhalla, the soldiers fought daily, their wounds healing after each battle. Viking warriors regarded Valhalla and Fólkvangr as ideal resting places in the afterlife.

A never-ending party
As well as eternal battles, Valhalla was a place of eternal feasting, with festivities overseen by Odin himself and his wife, the goddess Frigg.

The World Tree

With its mighty branches and twisting roots, the giant ash tree Yggdrasil connected the nine worlds of the Norse cosmos. Each world was primarily the home of either gods, giants, humans, elves, dwarves, or the spirits of the dead.

The nine worlds sat in the branches of the World Tree. Gigantic animals lived in its leaves and trunk. At its roots, the tree was nourished by three sacred wells.

Midgard was the world of humans. It was connected to Asgard, where the Aesir gods lived, by a rainbow bridge known as Bifrost. At the end of Bifrost, the god Heimdall kept watch and warned the gods of anything that might threaten their world.

The creatures that lived on Yggdrasil slowly devoured the tree over time. The serpent Nidhogg gnawed Yggdrasil's roots and the four stags, called Dvalinn, Duneyrr, Dáinn, and Durathrór, ate its leaves.

Ratatosk the squirrel scurried up and down the tree, sharing messages between Nidhogg and the eagle that lived in the canopy, who were sworn enemies.

At the tree's roots, Mímir's Well gave wisdom to anyone who drank from it, while the water of Hvergelmir was full of snakes and dragons. The Well of Urd was guarded by three all-knowing female spirits, the Norns, who took care of the tree. Without them, the tree would have died.

Alfheim
The magnificent home of the light elves was ruled by the Vanir god Freya.

Bearer of worlds
Yggdrasil was described in ancient Norse texts, but the exact position of the realms are unknown, so there are many versions of the tree.

Vanaheim
The Vanir gods of fertility, wisdom, and fortune-telling set up home in this realm.

Niflheim
Law-breaking and disloyal people spent the afterlife in this cold and cloudy realm.

The Norns
Three wise women, known as the Norns, cared for and watered Yggdrasil daily. They repaired the tree using mud mixed with water from the Well of Urd.

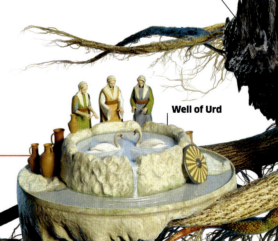

Well of Urd

52 europe • ODIN, THE ALLFATHER

Odin was married to **Frigg**, the goddess of marriage, motherhood, and the sky.

Odin is the father of all gods and men, and of all things that were made by him and by his might.

Snorri Sturluson,
Prose Edda, c.1220CE

One-eyed god
Odin traded his eye at a magical well for wisdom.

Eight-legged horse
Sleipnir, Odin's eight-legged gray horse, was swift, intelligent, and could fly.

Hungry wolf
Geri ("the greedy one") followed Odin into battle.

Odin's **mother** was a giant named **Bestla** and his **brothers** were **Vili** and **Ve** (see pages 48–49).

It is foretold that **Odin** will die in the Norse apocalypse of **Ragnarok** (see pages 56–57).

Feathered companion
Huginn, meaning "thought," was one of Odin's ravens. The other was Muninn, meaning "memory."

Magical weapon
Gungnir, Odin's spear, never missed a target, regardless of the attacker's skill.

A great sacrifice
At the roots of Yggdrasil was a magical well belonging to the wise god Mímir. The well's water gave secret knowledge to its drinker, and Odin was only allowed to drink from it once he had sacrificed something important to him, so he pulled out one of his eyes. Mímir accepted Odin's offering and gave him some water from the well. As he drank it, Odin gained not only wisdom, but the ability to see into the future.

The water from Mímir's Well
Mimir dipped his Gjallarhorn (drinking vessel) into the well and offered Odin the sacred water. The small amount he drank empowered him with wisdom.

Riding into battle
Together with his ravens Huginn and Muninn, his ferocious wolves Geri and Freki, and his eight-legged horse Sleipnir, Odin charged into battle as a fierce warrior god. The Vikings honored Odin as the highest of all the gods and called upon him to triumph over their enemies.

Protecting Odin
Freki ("the ravenous one") was one of Odin's loyal wolves.

Odin, the Allfather

King of Asgard and the Norse god of war and wisdom, Odin was all-knowing and all-powerful. As a bearer of secret knowledge and protector of the gods, Odin was given the name "Allfather." He was known for going to great lengths to gain insight into the future.

Odin was both a rugged warrior and a wise seer. His long beard and wide-brimmed hat gave him the appearance of an old wizard. Odin ruled from his throne Hlidskjálf, with his wife Frigg by his side, watching over the Aesir and the Vanir gods, his one eye shining bright like the sun.

As a warrior god, Odin fought with his loyal animals by his side. His wolves Geri and Freki feasted on the bodies after each battle.

As he tirelessly sought knowledge, Odin sent his two ravens, Huginn and Muninn, to fly over the worlds daily and report what they had seen every evening.

Odin once tore out his eye in exchange for wisdom (see above) and brought the gift of poetry to the Aesir gods and humans (see below).

To understand the runes, a set of magical symbols, Odin pierced himself with a spear and hung upside down from the world tree Yggdrasil's branches (see pages 50–51). After nine nights, the runes and their meaning appeared to him, carved clearly on Yggdrasil's trunk.

The Mead of Poetry
The Mead of Poetry was a drink created by the dwarves Fjalar and Galar. It turned anyone who drank it into a poet. The dwarves gave the mead to the giant Suttung, who hid it in a mountain and set his daughter Gunnlod to guard it. Odin tricked Gunnlod into giving him the mead. He drank it, turned himself into an eagle, and flew away. Suttung chased after Odin, also in the form of an eagle. As Odin flew over Asgard, he spat the mead into containers for the gods.

A gift worth stealing
As Odin approached Asgard in the form of an eagle, the gods placed containers in the courtyard so he could spit into them and share the potent drink that turned them all into great poets. Some of the mead accidentally trickled into Midgard, the world of humans.

europe • THOR AND LOKI

*Thor was the **eldest son** of **Odin** and the Earth goddess **Jord**.*

⊙ GOD OF THUNDER
Thor's immense size and considerable strength made him a fearsome opponent. Rumbles of thunder filled the air whenever he threw his magical hammer, which never missed its target.

Flame-haired fighter
The thunder god was built as strong as a rock, and armed with his trusted hammer and protective shield.

Powerful hammer
After being flung, Thor's hammer Mjolnir always returned to his hand.

Megingjord
The belt worn by Thor doubled his strength and endurance.

Thor and Loki

Two major figures in Norse mythology were the thunder god Thor and trickster god Loki. Although they were total opposites, their paths often crossed in stories, acting as either friends or foes.

Thor and Loki shared little in common. Thor never shied away from a fight and relied on his strength and weapon in battle. His name meant "thunder" because he was quick to deliver his blow. By comparison, Loki was a more complex character, using his wit to cause mischief, stirring up problems for the gods. He could transform into animals and different people to create havoc and make a quick getaway. But there were times when he stepped in to help the gods.

Fishing trip
One day Thor and the giant Hymir went out fishing together. Against Hymir's wishes, Thor took them into the waters of the terrifying serpent Jörmungandr. It wasn't long before the monster emerged from the deep. Hymir was frightened and let the serpent go. In a fit of rage, Thor pushed the giant overboard.

Catching a monster
When Thor ate all of Hymir's food, they went fishing, but Thor decided to hunt Jörmungandr instead.

Thor's sacred symbols

Mjolnir
The magical hammer Mjolnir was forged by the dwarf Sindri.

Megingjord
Thor's magic belt equipped him with extraordinary strength.

Jarngreipr
These gloves gave Thor a stronger grip when holding his hammer.

Thunder and lightning
Thor could send terrible thunderstorms down to Earth whenever he chose.

Oak tree
The oak was easily struck by lightning, and so it was sacred to Thor.

Goat
Thor's two goats were often eaten by the god and brought back to life.

Dangerous duel
When Thor and the mighty giant Hrungnir got into an argument, they agreed to a duel the next morning. The pair threw their weapons at the same time. As usual, Mjolnir was on target, killing the giant instantly. Too fast for Thor, Hrungnir's whetstone hit Thor in the face, shattering into a million shards. One of them remained stuck in his forehead for the rest of time.

3 Thor's three main possessions were his **hammer**, **gloves**, and **belt**.

Loki turned into a fly to annoy the dwarves as they worked on Thor's hammer, so **its handle** was sculpted too short.

55

THE TRICKSTER

Loki was originally a frost giant who came to live in Asgard. A mischief-making god, Loki could shape-shift at will, but most of the time he looked like an ordinary man. He was an unpredictable character, flitting between being good or evil on a whim to entertain himself.

Red alert
Loki's red hair stood up like flames, to show the chaos he caused.

Armed and dangerous
Loki killed his rivals and enemies with a dagger.

"LOKI IS PLEASING, EVEN **BEAUTIFUL** TO LOOK AT, BUT HIS NATURE IS EVIL ..."
Snorri Sturluson, *Prose Edda*, c.1220CE

A calculated character
Loki was tall, a trait he inherited from his family of giants. He had red hair, sharp features, and a mischievous smile.

UNLIKELY ALLIES

As youngsters, Thor and Loki built a solid friendship and when they grew up, they became allies. Thor acted as a protector to Loki, while Loki helped Thor fulfill his ambitions. However, their bond was often challenged by Loki's sly nature and infuriating practical jokes.

Thor's wedding

When a frost giant stole Mjolnir, the thunder god hatched a cunning plan with Loki. Thor promised the giant Freyja's hand in marriage and arranged a wedding. Thor disguised himself as the bride and ripped off the veil at the altar. He grabbed Mjolnir and killed the giant.

Disguised as a bride
The frost giant was so stunned to see Thor as his bride that he forgot to defend himself.

Sif's golden hair

Thor's wife Sif was renowned for her golden hair, which flowed down to the floor. While she slept, Loki cut it all off with his dagger. Sif was devastated by the loss of her hair, and told Thor. He knew it was one of Loki's tricks and confronted him. Loki realized he had gone too far and asked the dwarves to spin a mane of gold that was just like Sif's real hair.

Stolen jewels

One day, Loki decided to play a trick on the love goddess Freyja, and stole her beautiful necklace. Her husband, the war god Heimdall, spotted a seal in the sea sparkling with jewels, and knew Loki had shape-shifted again. Heimdall transformed into a seal himself and fought with the trickster god until he gave up the necklace.

Loki's children

Loki produced unusual offspring because his shape-shifting abilities meant he could give birth as a woman and incorporate traits of animals and monsters. Like their father, Loki's children were both good and bad, and couldn't be trusted.

Hel
The death goddess Hel ruled over the dead in the gloomy realm named after her.

Jörmungandr
This supersize serpent encircled the human world with its body.

Fenrir
The powerful wolf Fenrir was chained in the mountains by the gods.

Sleipnir
This speedy horse galloped on eight legs and was given to the god Odin as a gift.

Making Mjolnir

Loki challenged the blacksmith dwarves of Svartalfheim to make something better than Sif's hair. The dwarves worked hard in their forge, creating Thor's Mjolnir. When it was ready, the gods agreed it was their best creation.

Precious pendant
The Vikings wore pendants of Mjolnir because they believed it gave them strength and protection.

europe • TWILIGHT OF THE GODS

Ragnarök comes from an **ancient Norse** word meaning "twilight of the gods."

Twilight of the gods

According to prophecy, a catastrophic battle known as Ragnarök will see the Norse gods face off against giants and monsters. This event will bring horrifying scenes of chaos as the world is destroyed.

In the Norse world, nothing was permanent, and even the gods could not escape death. The end of the world was described in the terrifying tale of Ragnarök.

First, the sun will darken, resulting in three long years of winter (the "Fimbulwinter"). In the human world, there will be endless wars and violence. The wolf Sköll, who had been chasing the sun since the world was created, will finally achieve his aim of swallowing it, while the wolf Hati will do the same with the moon. The chains binding the trickster god Loki and his son, the wolf Fenrir, will shatter, setting them loose to unleash their revenge upon the gods. As the sky splits apart, the fire giants of Muspelheim will ride out bearing flaming swords.

Thrashing his way ashore, the World Serpent known as Jörmungandr will be killed by Thor, who soon after will collapse and die. In fact, many of the gods will die during Ragnarök, including Odin, the king of the gods, who will be devoured by the wolf Fenrir. Vidar, Odin's son, will avenge his father's death immediately and destroy Fenrir, grasping his jaws and tearing him apart. After a long period of fighting, almost every living being will be erased from the nine worlds.

But from the destruction and chaos, the world will rise again. This world will be a peaceful paradise in which a new generation of humans will emerge, in a reborn world lit by a new sun.

Death of Balder
Balder, the son of Odin and the goddess Frigg, was a beautiful god. When his death was foretold, Frigg asked all living things to promise not to harm him, but forgot to ask the mistletoe. Loki knew this, and had the god Hodur use mistletoe to kill Balder. His death reminded the gods that they too will one day die in the fated Ragnarök.

Mistletoe mistake
Loki tricked the blind god Hodur into shooting Balder with a piece of mistletoe.

Loki's punishment
The gods punished Loki for Balder's death by chaining him to a rock under a snake that dripped poison on his face. Loki writhed from the pain, causing earthquakes. At the time of Ragnarök, Loki will break free and seek revenge on the gods.

Giant wolf
Fenrir produces burning flames from his eyes and nostrils.

Vidar
Odin's son will wound Fenrir with his sword and tear him apart.

Among the Norse gods who **survive** Ragnarök are **Hoenir, Hodur, Magni, Modi, Njord, Vali,** and **Vidar.**

1220 The story of Ragnarök was written in the *Prose Edda* by Icelandic author **Snorri Sturluson** c. 1220 CE.

57

Deadly blow
With hammer in hand, Thor will kill Jörmungandr, and die from a poisonous bite.

An end foretold
In the aftermath of Ragnarök, a man named Lif, meaning "Life," and a woman named Lifthrasir, meaning "Longing for Life," will emerge from the branches of Yggdrasil (see pages 50–51). Together they will start a family and repopulate the world.

The end of the world
In one account of Ragnarök, darkness will engulf the world, and mountains will topple, trees will be uprooted, and terrible monsters will destroy the gods.

Spewing poison
Son of Loki, Jörmungandr hisses deadly poison.

Battle of the giants
Armies of giants that have crossed Bifrost, the rainbow bridge, will fight to the death against the gods.

Loki seeks revenge
Loki will go head-to-head with the war god Heimdall, but neither will survive the battle.

War god
Heimdall will play a key role in Ragnarök because he was tasked to announce the coming of danger to the gods.

The Kalevala

The Finnish national epic, the *Kalevala*, is based on traditional poems and tales collected by the poet Elias Lönnrot between 1828 and 1837. Its stories of the hero Väinämöinen became a source of national pride and helped form the modern Finnish language.

Lönnrot collected hundreds of tales while traveling through the Finnish countryside. He wove these stories together to create one continuous epic, which tells the adventures of Väinämöinen, a sorcerer and the first man, who travels around the countries of Kalevala (or "land of heroes," which is another name for Finland) and Pohjola, found in the far north. Other characters that alternately help or hinder Väinämöinen include the smith Ilmarinen and the warrior Lemminkäinen.

2 Lönnrot published **two versions**: the *Old Kalevala* in 1835, and the *New Kalevala* in 1849.

ADVENTURES OF THE HERO

In the beginning, there was nothing but the sky and an endless expanse of sea. Then Ilmatar, the air-daughter, came out of the sky, and the sea made her pregnant. She was now the water-mother.

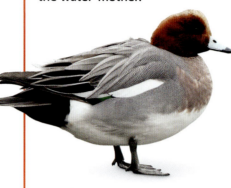

Cosmic duck
The duck could find nowhere else to settle, so she made a nest on Ilmatar's knees and laid her eggs there.

Väinämöinen's birth
A duck laid her eggs on the water-mother's knees, but they rolled off and smashed as they hit the water. Ilmatar formed the land out of the eggshells, creating mountains, valleys, plains, and coastlines from the fragments. Still pregnant, it took 700 years for her son, Väinämöinen, to be born. Already an old man, he floated in the ocean for nine years before he reached Kalevala.

COURTING THE MAID

When Väinämöinen met Louhi's daughter, the Maid of the North, she agreed to marry him without the sampo if he would carry out four seemingly impossible tasks.

Impossible tasks
The Maid told Väinämöinen he must tie a knot around an egg that she couldn't see, peel a stone, split a hair with a blunt knife, and build a boat from a weaving shuttle and move it to the sea without touching it. He succeeded in the first three, but spirits sent by Louhi distracted him while he constructed the boat, and he cut himself so badly he had to give up.

Knot an egg
Väinämöinen had to tie a knot around an egg, but it had to be invisible.

Peel a stone
The Maid gave the sorcerer a stone to peel.

Split a hair
Using a blunt knife, Väinämöinen had to split a horse hair.

Make a boat from a weaving shuttle
The hero was tasked with making a boat using fragments from a shuttle.

Ilmarinen and the sampo
Väinämöinen returned to Kalevala and told his brother Ilmarinen, a great blacksmith, to make the sampo for him. But as the maker of the sampo, Ilmarinen got to marry the Maid of the North. Their marriage ended tragically when, some years later, she was trampled to death by a herd of cows set loose by her servant Kullervo, whom she treated badly.

Forging the sampo
Out of Ilmarinen's forge came first a golden bow, then a golden boat, and finally a golden cow. Ilmarinen broke them all and, finally, out of the fires emerged the sampo.

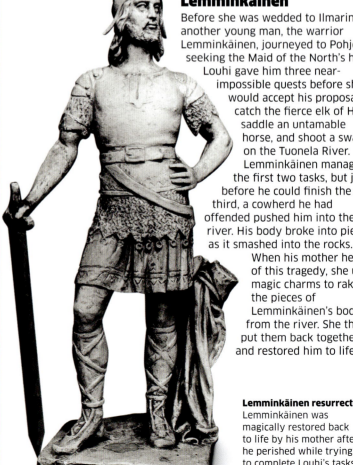

Lemminkäinen
Before she was wedded to Ilmarinen, another young man, the warrior Lemminkäinen, journeyed to Pohjola seeking the Maid of the North's hand. Louhi gave him three near-impossible quests before she would accept his proposal: catch the fierce elk of Hiisi, saddle an untamable horse, and shoot a swan on the Tuonela River. Lemminkäinen managed the first two tasks, but just before he could finish the third, a cowherd he had offended pushed him into the river. His body broke into pieces as it smashed into the rocks. When his mother heard of this tragedy, she used magic charms to rake the pieces of Lemminkäinen's body from the river. She then put them back together and restored him to life.

Lemminkäinen resurrected
Lemminkäinen was magically restored back to life by his mother after he perished while trying to complete Louhi's tasks.

22,795 The *Kalevala* is **22,795** lines long, divided into **50 cantos**, or sections.

The *Kalevala* is drawn from **Karelian myth** as well as Finnish.

Musical competition

Väinämöinen planted forests, sowed barley, and learned the secret of fire. But a young Sami magician, Joukahainen, grew jealous of Väinämöinen and challenged him to a singing contest. The magician lost but refused to give in, so Väinämöinen brought out his kantele, a magical musical instrument, and sang, causing Joukahainen to sink up to his shoulders in boggy ground. Only when he promised that Väinämöinen could marry his sister Aino was he set free.

The kantele
The power of Väinämöinen's kantele was so strong, its music caused Joukahainen to sink deep into a swamp.

Louhi

Aino threw herself into the sea to avoid marrying Väinämöinen. Her brother Joukahainen was furious at her death, and shot at Väinämöinen with a crossbow. Väinämöinen tumbled into the ocean, but an eagle saved him and flew him to the land of Pohjola. Its queen, Louhi, who could transform herself into a giant bird, promised him her daughter in marriage if Väinämöinen would make her a sampo, a magical mill that could make gold, flour, and salt.

LOUHI, QUEEN OF POHJOLA

JOURNEY TO POHJOLA

Some time after Ilmarinen's wife's death, Väinämöinen and Ilmarinen decided to sail to Pohjola and steal back the sampo. They met Lemminkäinen along the way, who agreed to join them. On the journey, they struck a large object, which turned out to be a mighty pike. Väinämöinen killed the pike, and created a magical musical harp, or kantele, from its bones. When he played the harp, it enchanted every living being.

Stealing the sampo

When the trio reached Pohjola, they confronted Louhi, asking for half of the sampo. She refused and sent her army against them. Väinämöinen used his kantele to lull the warriors to sleep, and while all of Pohjola slept, the three traveled to the hidden mountain where Louhi had embedded the sampo into the rock. Using the strength of a mighty ox, they freed the sampo, brought it to their warship, and made their escape.

Kantele
Väinämöinen's magical kantele was made from the bones of a giant pike.

The sampo breaks

Lemminkäinen was triumphant and sang a loud victory song, but this woke up Louhi, who set off in a warship to catch the thieves. During the fight, Väinämöinen's prized kantele and the sampo both fell into the sea. The sampo was smashed into pieces.

Louhi transformed
Louhi took on the form of a giant bird, and conjured up fog and a great storm during her battle against Väinämöinen.

Väinämöinen departs

Väinämöinen rescued as many pieces of the sampo as he could, and even these few fragments brought great prosperity to Kalevala. After a while, a mysterious child was born, who even at two weeks old could speak. The baby was then baptized as king of Kalevala. Väinämöinen could sense that with the coming of this child his magical powers were waning. So he summoned up a magic boat and sailed away to a land between earth and sky.

Louhi's curse

In revenge for the destruction of the sampo, Louhi cursed Kalevala's people with nine plagues. She sent a great bear to attack their cattle, but Väinämöinen killed it. She stole the sun and moon and hid them inside a mountain, and she took fire from the humans and concealed it inside a fish. Väinämöinen found the fish and released the fire, and Ilmarinen tried to make a new sun and moon in his forge, but they would not shine. However, Louhi became afraid the real sun and moon would burn her, so she let them go anyway.

Hiding the sun
Ilmarinen could not open the mountain where Louhi hid the sun and moon.

Leaving Kalevala
Väinämöinen left behind his kantele and his songs, as well as a prophecy that, one day, he would return to make a new sampo.

Tough skin
Grendel had tough skin that couldn't be pierced by a typical sword.

Great warrior
With great strength, Beowulf forced Grendel to the ground.

Fighting the beast
As Beowulf and Grendel came together in a fierce battle, benches crashed to the ground and Grendel's cries of pain rang out across the hall.

3,182 The original manuscript of *Beowulf* consisted of 3,182 lines.

Beowulf

Set in Scandinavia, the epic poem *Beowulf* describes the incredible feats of strength and courage by its hero of the same name. Beowulf defeated three terrifying monsters and was honored by royalty. First, he killed the savage Grendel, then the beast's mother, and finally, a fire-breathing dragon.

Mead hall
Heorot, which means "stag" in Old English, was built from wood.

King Hrothgar of Denmark held feasts in his great mead hall of Heorot, entertaining nobles and warriors. But every night for 12 years, a beast called Grendel crept out of his underwater cave, broke into the hall, and killed anyone who got in his way.

Beowulf, a warrior of the people known as the Geats, heard of King Hrothgar's troubles. He offered to slay the troublesome beast, and Hrothgar welcomed him into his palace. One night, when everyone was asleep, Beowulf stayed awake and listened for the monster. When Grendel arrived, Beowulf attacked him with his bare hands. Grendel tried to fight him off, breaking Heorot's benches and tables, but the mighty warrior tore out his arm. Crying in agony, Grendel stumbled back to his cave, where he bled to death.

The next day King Hrothgar held a great feast in his hall in Beowulf's honor. The Danes believed they were safe, but Grendel's mother soon came to avenge her son's murder. She was not as strong as her son, but she was driven by fury, and wanted to see his killer dead. After she caused devastation in King Hrothgar's mead hall, Beowulf followed her to her cave and killed her with a magical sword. The blade mysteriously melted leaving only the hilt after the deed was done. Finding Grendel's body in the cave, Beowulf sliced his head off, and took it, along with the hilt, as trophies.

Beowulf later became the king of the Geats, and ruled peacefully for 50 years until he was faced with another enemy. This time a dragon began attacking his realm and killing his people. By now, the hero was much older and not as strong as he used to be. After a long duel, Beowulf managed to defeat the beast, but died from his injuries.

> "I will not with my sword give him the sleep of death, although **I well could.**"
>
> *Beowulf*, translated in 2014

Grendel's mother

Grendel's monstrous mother wanted revenge for her son's death. She entered Hrothgar's mead hall and tore one of his men apart before returning to her lair beneath a lake. Beowulf followed her, but found his sword useless against her tough, scaly hide. Desperate, Beowulf seized another sword from the creature's treasure hoard, and this blade sliced her flesh and killed her.

The deadly dragon

Many years later, a fire-breathing dragon attacked the Geats. The aged Beowulf went out to face it. The valiant Wiglaf helped him and delivered the killing blow, but Beowulf was so badly wounded that he died.

Treasure hoarder
The dragon began terrorizing the Geats when someone stole an item from its treasure hoard.

europe ○ **SIGURD THE DRAGON SLAYER**

The name of the desirable ring **Andvaranaut** means "Andvari's gem."

Andvari's curse
The treasure originally belonged to the dwarf Andvari, who could transform into a fish. The god Loki came up with a plan to catch him and forced him to hand over his gold. Andvari, who was angry to see his riches go, cursed the gold before handing it over. Loki gave the gold to Hreidmar, Regin's father and king of the dwarves.

Rich haul
Andvari transformed into a pike to escape from Loki, but Loki cast a net and captured the fish.

Slaying the dragon
After slaying Fafnir, Sigurd accidentally licked some of the dragon's blood, which gave him the power to speak with birds. They revealed Regin's plans to steal the gold.

Dragon's flesh
Sigurd removed Fafnir's heart and cooked it for Regin. The blood gave Sigurd magical powers.

Son of a hero
Sigurd was the son of another hero, Sigmund, who was the son of a king.

Piles of treasure
The dragon hid the treasure in a cave nestled deep in a forest, where no one would think to approach him.

> "The dying creature thrashed about fiercely, thundering, **Who are you who dares to attack me?**"
>
> *Saga of the Völsungs*, 1260 CE

1260 — The *Saga of the Völsungs*, which features the hero Sigurd, was written in around 1260.

This story **inspired a love of dragons** in *The Hobbit* author **J. R. R. Tolkien** as a young boy.

The Valkyries
Brynhild belonged to a group of supernatural creatures known as the Valkyries. They took the souls of dead warriors to the gods to spend an eternity either in Valhalla or Fólkvangr (see pages 50–51).

Battle ready
Valkyries were portrayed as beautiful but fierce female warriors wearing armor.

Sigurd the dragon slayer

When the hero Sigurd heard of the treasure guarded by the dragon Fafnir, he went in search of it, and hoped to defeat the beast. Little did he know that he would spend the rest of his life being haunted by the treasure's curse.

The dwarf Regin raised the orphan Sigurd as his own child. One day, the dwarf told Sigurd about the treasure called Otter's Ransom, which the Aesir gods had given to Regin's father. The gold was cursed to destroy anyone who possessed it. Regin's brother Fafnir had murdered his father for it, ran away, and turned into a dragon to guard it.

When Sigurd heard about the gold, he went to find it and defeated the dragon, Sigurd soon found out that Regin plotted to kill him and seize the treasure for himself, so he beheaded the dwarf.

Sigurd went on to become a famous hero and fell in love with the Valkyrie Brynhild. He gave her a ring called Andvaranaut taken from the treasure hoard, which cursed her as well. The evil queen Grimhild wanted Sigurd's gold, so she gave him a potion that made him forget Brynhild and instead fall in love with her daughter, Gudrun. They were soon married.

Grimhild's son Gunnar wanted to marry Brynhild, but the Valkyrie declared she would only marry a man who could pass through fire. She knew that only Sigurd could perform this feat, so Sigurd helped Gunnar by walking through the fire in his place. Brynhild married Gunnar, but when she found out that she had been deceived, she had Sigurd killed. She soon regretted her actions and threw herself into the flames of Sigurd's funeral pyre.

Andvaranaut
When Loki captured Andvari, he told the dwarf to keep the ring, but Loki lied and took it anyway, so Andvari cursed the ring along with the treasure.

Greedy dwarf
As Sigurd took care of slaying the dragon, Regin stuffed his chest with the treasure.

EARLY CELTIC GODS

The early Celts did not leave written records, so we have little firsthand knowledge about their religion. Much of what we do know comes from the Romans, who left descriptions of Celtic deities and their rituals. Finds at archaeological sites have also shown that the Celts worshipped many different gods and goddesses.

Cernunnos
Also known as the horned god, Cernunnos had the horns of a stag. He was often shown surrounded by animals as "Lord of the Beasts." His horns suggest that he may have been a god of fertility.

Epona
A horse goddess, Epona was the only Celtic deity to be worshipped by the Romans, who made her the patron of cavalry. Rhiannon in the *Mabinogion* (see pages 74-75) may be a later version of Epona.

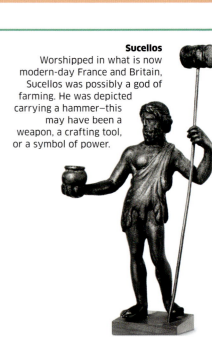

Sucellos
Worshipped in what is now modern-day France and Britain, Sucellos was possibly a god of farming. He was depicted carrying a hammer—this may have been a weapon, a crafting tool, or a symbol of power.

WESTERN EUROPE

The ancient Celts were people from a group of tribes that once lived in settlements across all of Europe. As the Roman Empire expanded, the Celts were pushed out to the edges of Europe, particularly to Ireland, Wales, Scotland, and parts of western France. The Celtic stories that we know and love today were first recorded in these regions, and many of the earlier myths have been lost to time.

THE CELTIC OTHERWORLD

In Celtic stories, heroes can visit a magical world where people do not age and live without a care. This Otherworld can sometimes be the realm of the gods or of the dead. It exists either parallel to our world, or far away over the ocean.

Tír na nÓg
Meaning "Land of the Young," Tír na nÓg is a name for either the Otherworld or a region within it. The hero Oisin went to Tír na nÓg and lived there happily for centuries. Eventually, he got homesick, returning to Ireland. When his feet touched the land he became old and died.

Otherworld gateways
The burial mounds that dot the Irish landscape were believed to be portals to the Otherworld. Some say that the Tuatha de Danaan (see pages 68-69) retreated to the Otherworld through these gateways after the first Celts arrived in Ireland.

NEWGRANGE BURIAL MOUND

CELTIC STORIES AND CHRISTIANITY

Many of the stories from Ireland and Wales were first written down by medieval Catholic monks. The godlike powers of some Celtic heroes suggests that they may once have been gods who were rewritten as human heroes by Christian storytellers.

St. Brigid
Before the arrival of Christianity, Brigid was a goddess of spring, but she was turned into a Christian saint. Her symbol, the St. Brigid's Cross, is the same as a symbol for the goddess Brigid, and the pair share a feast day on February 1st.

ST. BRIGID'S CROSS

Bag noz
Some Celtic stories of the Otherworld survive as folklore in parts of France. In Brittany, the people of the coast speak of a ship that takes the dead to their final resting place. The Bag noz ("boat of night") belongs to Ankou, the servant of death. He picks up the recently deceased souls of the dead and drops them off at the entrance to the afterlife.

Taranis
A major deity in Britain, Taranis was a sky god who controlled thunder and lightning. He was also described by the Romans as a god of war.

ARTHURIAN LEGEND

Early appearances of Arthur, the legendary British king, are in Welsh myths, with the first stories being written down in the 9th century. But the story of Arthur would not be fully developed in writing until the great Arthurian romances of French poet Chrétien de Troyes in the 12th century.

THE GREEN KNIGHT AND SIR GAWAIN

The Green Knight
Arthurian romance is full of smaller stories that highlight the ideals of knighthood. The tale of Gawain and the Green Knight is a story of Sir Gawain's courage in the face of impending death.

LANCELOT AND GUINEVERE

Love triangle
One of the greatest love stories is the triangle between Arthur, his wife Guinevere, and his knight Lancelot. Guinevere and Lancelot attempt to ignore their love for each other, but this eventually leads to disaster.

FESTIVALS

In Ireland, four major festivals divided up the Celtic year. Samhain was the origin of today's Halloween, when people dressed up in disguises and spirits could travel to the real world. Imbolc was a spring festival, while Beltane celebrated the start of summer. Lughnasadh marked the beginning of the harvest season.

Samhain
On October 31st, the boundaries broke down between the living world and the world of the spirits, allowing them to travel to our world using portals found in burial mounds.

Imbolc
On February 1st, Celts observed the feast day of Brigid, the spring goddess in charge of dairies. Both milk production and the birth of lambs were celebrated at this festival.

Beltane
On May 1st, the beginning of summer was marked by a ceremony in which cattle were driven between pairs of bonfires to purify them. This festival of fire gave thanks for the sun's return.

Lughnasadh
On August 1st, great gatherings took place on Lughnasadh, dedicated to the god Lugh. Events that might take place included athletic competitions, betrothals, and trades.

SUPERNATURAL CREATURES

There were many spirits in the Celtic world. Some had their origins in early Celtic mythology while others sprang from folklore or from the cultural traditions of a region.

Banshee
A "fairy woman," the banshee was an Irish female spirit that shrieked and screamed when a person's family member was about to die. Her screams were based on the tradition of "keening," a wailing song sung for the dead.

Aos Sí
Also known as the Sidhe, the *aos sí*, or "folk of the fairy mounds" were possibly descended of the Tuatha de Danaan. They may also have been spirits of nature, or gods themselves. They were believed to live in burial mounds, which were portals to the Otherworld.

Kelpie
This horselike creature inhabited bodies of water in Scotland. It was a shape-shifter, able to take human form. Kelpie preyed on people they encountered, dragging them into the depths to devour them, then leaving their remains on the shore.

Brownie
A household spirit of Scottish folklore, the brownie came out at night to perform chores around the home. It would only do this if it was left a bowl of milk or cream by the fire. Mischievous beings, brownies played tricks on those who insulted them.

A standing stone atop the Hill of Tara in County Meath is thought to be the legendary Lia Fáil.

The Island of Destiny

According to Irish Celtic mythology, in ancient times a supernatural race of people arrived in Ireland under the cover of magical dark clouds. These divine beings were known as the Tuatha Dé Danann.

The Tuatha Dé Danann were led by King Nuada, and their ranks included The Dagda, The Morrigan, and the sun god Lugh, among many others (see pages 68–69). Carrying four supernatural treasures brought from afar, they traveled through the heavens and landed in Connaught in western Ireland. One of the treasures they carried was the Lia Fáil (the Stone of Destiny), and so Ireland became known as Inis Fáil, or "the Island of Destiny."

Upon their arrival, the Tuatha Dé Danann confronted the Fir Bolg, who were at that time the rulers of the island. The newcomers defeated the Fir Bolg at the First Battle of Mag Tuired, and became Ireland's new overseers. However, Nuada lost an arm in the fighting, so he was replaced as king by Bres, a tyrant who was in part descended from the Fomorians, a race of creatures from underground or under the sea.

When Nuada received a new arm and took back the kingship of the Tuatha Dé Danann, Bres called on the Fomorians to fight them, leading to the Second Battle of Mag Tuired. The Fomorians were led by the giant Balor of the Evil Eye, who could kill anyone he looked upon. The sun god Lugh defeated Balor by shooting a stone into his eye. The stone pierced all the way through Balor's skull and killed him. Though the Tuatha were victorious once again, King Nuada had been killed by the Fomorian leader, and Lugh became the new king of Ireland.

The Tuatha Dé Danann were themselves later defeated by another race that came to Ireland. The Milesians were Gaelic-speaking people and the ancestors of the Irish Celts. They fought for control of the land, and when they were victorious, the Tuatha Dé Danann retreated into the Otherworld.

The Four Treasures
The Tuatha arrived in Ireland from four mystical cities called Falias, Findias, Gorias, and Murias. From each of the cities they brought a magical treasure to help them conquer the island: a stone from Falias, a sword from Findias, a spear from Gorias, and a cauldron from Murias.

Stone of Destiny
Known as Lia Fáil, the stone roared when the true king of Ireland put his foot against it.

Sword of Light
Wielded by King Nuada, this magical blade emitted a blinding light.

Spear of Lugh
Deadly accuracy was the special power of this spear carried by the god Lugh.

Cauldron of plenty
The Dagda's cauldron provided an unlimited source of food for any who ate from it.

Fighting the Fir Bolg
The Tuatha's first battle, against the ruling Fir Bolg, took place on a mythical plain known as Mag Tuired. The Tuatha won a particularly bloody encounter–in some versions of the story, 100,000 Fir Bolg were killed.

Direct hit
Lugh fired his slingshot as Balor's eye opened, striking the giant directly in his eye and killing him.

Hero's chariot
Lugh arrived at the battlefield riding a chariot and laid down a challenge to the monstrous Balor.

Lebor Gabála Érenn, which described the **origins of the Tuatha Dé Danann**, was written **around the 11th century**.

In some accounts of the myth, **Balor** was **Lugh's grandfather**.

Evil eye
Balor's giant single eye had deadly powers—anyone it gazed upon immediately died.

Team effort
It took many Fomorian attendants working together to open Balor's huge eyelid so that he could see his rival.

Lugh defeats Balor
Riding his chariot, Lugh approached the battle with the Fomorians. The giant Balor told his warriors to lift the lid of his massive eye so he might gaze upon Lugh. But as they did so, Lugh shot a stone with his slingshot that pierced the giant's eye, went through his brain, and shot out the back of his head. Balor's eye fell to the ground facing his own army, where its gaze desolated many of the Fomorian warriors.

> **In this wise they came, in dark clouds ... and they brought a darkness over the sun for three days and three nights.**
>
> *Lebor Gabála Érenn*, translated by R. A. S. Macalister, 1941

The Tuatha Dé Danann

At the heart of Irish Celtic mythology is a tribe of supernatural beings known as the Tuatha Dé Danann ("the folk of the goddess Danu"). These beings were immune to ageing and disease, and had the power to shape-shift and cast magic.

The Tuatha Dé Danann possessed supreme knowledge and magical powers. They became the rulers of Ireland soon after arriving on the island and defeating the Fir Bolg (see page 66). Their reign marked a new era of ambition and achievement as they shared their skills and knowledge with everyone.

LUGH

A key member of the tribe was the warrior god Lugh, whose skill with weapons was unmatched on the battlefield. He waged war against the terrifying demonic race of the Fomorians and won. His softer side included expert knowledge of arts and crafts, as well as healing and prophecy.

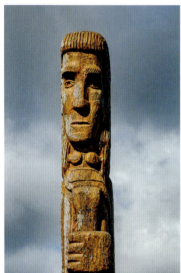

Wooden warrior
This giant wooden statue of Lugh in County Donegal is one of many across Ireland that pay homage to the mythical warrior.

ÉRIU

The name Ériu is the origin of the Irish name for Ireland: Éire. This celebrated goddess of the Tuatha Dé Danann requested for all the land to be blessed with her name, which is an ancient Irish word meaning "plentiful." Together with her two sisters, Ériu enriched the landscape and protected the people against invasion.

Sacred statue
An ornate statue of Ériu stands on the lofty hill of Uisneach, in the Irish county of Westmeath.

THE DAGDA

The lead warrior of the Tuatha Dé Danann was The Dagda (meaning "The Good God"). This brave hero carried a magical staff capable of killing with one end and giving life with the other. He was blessed with a magical cauldron that spilled over with food without ever going empty, keeping the land thriving.

In Celtic mythology, **Manannán mac Lir** was the first ruler of the **Isle of Man**, and this island in the Irish Sea is **named after him**.

Every February 1st **Brigid is celebrated in the festival of Imbolc**, to mark the start of spring.

69

THE MORRIGNA

Depending on the story, the Morrigna were sometimes depicted as one Celtic goddess with triple aspects, and sometimes as a trio of sisters. Their combined forces on the battlefield meant they could predict the winners of conflicts.

The Morrígan
With a name that means "great queen" or "phantom queen," The Morrígan was associated with the fury of battle. In some tellings she was married to The Dagda. Often appearing as a raven, The Morrígan would swoop down onto battlefields to peck at the flesh of the fallen.

The Badb
The arrival of this sister was a terrifying omen of death in battle. The Badb had the ability to shape-shift into a crow and give a bird-like battle cry, a sound that sealed the fate of any enemy warrior that she encountered.

Macha
Two very different personalities collided in Macha. On one hand, she was a mother goddess and guardian of fertility and childbirth. On the other, she was a horse goddess, fiercely riding into battle determined to defend her territory.

AENGUS

Accompanied by a flock of birds at all times, Aengus (meaning "one strength") had blue eyes and golden hair, and was forever young. In some myths, his father was The Dagda. Aengus was the god of love and poetry, and charmed whoever he met, making him adored by the rest of the Tuatha Dé Danann.

MANANNÁN MAC LIR

The sea god Manannán mac Lir ruled the waves in Irish myth, and was a protector of sailors. He had a special ship that traveled across the ocean without oars or sails.

Sea sculpture
A sculpture of Manannán on his boat overlooks the sea in County Londonderry.

Brave warrior
This statue in County Donegal shows Nuada armed with his sword and shield.

NUADA

The original king of the Tuatha Dé Danann was the warrior god Nuada. When his arm was severed in battle, he was removed from the throne because the ruler had to be without imperfection.

DIAN CÉCHT

The physician god Dian Cécht helped to heal the injured on the battlefield. When his brother Nuada lost an arm in conflict, Dian created a new arm from silver to replace it. However, Dian's son Miach exceeded him by making Nuada an authentic human arm. Dian didn't appreciate being outdone, and killed his son in a jealous rage.

BRIGID

The Dagda's daughter was Brigid, goddess of spring, who brought new life after long winters. As protector of cattle, she was always accompanied by her four trusty animals—two oxen, a boar, and a ram.

europe • THE HOUND OF CHULAINN

The Ulster Cycle is one of **four main cycles of Irish mythology**.

The Hound of Chulainn

The Ulster Cycle is a collection of tales about the rivalry between Connacht in the south of Ireland, and Ulster in the north. The longest story, *The Cattle Raid of Cooley*, centers on the young hero Cú Chulainn.

Originally named Sétanta, Cú Chulainn was the nephew of King Conchobar of Ulster. As a child, he visited the house of the blacksmith Chulainn, where he killed a ferocious guard dog that attacked him. To repay the blacksmith, Sétanta resolved to take the dog's place to protect the Kingdom of Ulster. From then on, he was known as "Cú Chulainn" ("Hound of Chulainn"), and he grew into a fearless warrior.

In Connacht, evil Queen Medb was jealous of her husband, King Ailill, who owned Finnbennach, a magical, white-horned bull. So Medb decided to invade Ulster and launch a cattle raid to steal Donn Cúailnge (or Cooley), the only other magical bull in the land, belonging to King Conchobar.

A curse had made all the Ulstermen sick, and so it fell to Cú Chulainn alone to hold Medb's army back. Transformed into a giant by the war goddess Morrígan, he slaughtered all of the Connacht troops. Medb then sent forward Ferdiad, a former friend of Cú Chulainn.

The pair fought for five days, until Ferdiad finally wounded Cú Chulainn. Fearing for his life, Cú Chulainn grabbed the Gáe Bolg, a magical spear, and killed Ferdiad with it. Upset at killing his friend, Cú Chulainn withdrew from the battle. The rest of the Ulster warriors woke from their curse and drove Medb back, but not before she managed to capture Donn Cúailnge anyway.

Medb was not willing to accept her army's defeat. Her men armed themselves with spears and attacked Cú Chulainn. Refusing to die lying down like an animal, the young hero tied himself to a standing stone and died upright. The goddess Morrígan appeared as a raven on his shoulder, symbolizing his death.

Learning the Salmon Leap
When he was young, Cú Chulainn was sent to the kingdom of Alba in Scotland to learn how to fight from Scáthach, a female warrior skilled in martial arts. She taught him the "salmon leap"—a way of jumping high and long to cross great chasms.

Finding a teacher
Cú Chulainn trapped the sleeping Scáthach inside a yew tree and made her promise to train him.

Watchful student
Cú Chulainn paid close attention as Scáthach performed the salmon leap.

The whole cycle was recited by **the ghost of Fergus MacRoich, former king of Ulster**, about five centuries after his death.

Scáthach's skill
Scáthach leaped from the ground, higher than Cú Chulainn's head.

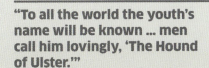

"To all the world the youth's name will be known … men call him lovingly, 'The Hound of Ulster.'"

Eleanor Hull, *The Boys' Cuchulain*, 1910

Gáe Bolg
Scáthach gave Cú Chulainn her spear, which inflicted terrible wounds when it was pulled out of a victim's flesh.

Donn Cúailnge
After Medb stole Donn Cúailnge, she set him against Ailill's white-horned bull. Donn Cúailnge killed his rival, but was mortally wounded in the fight. He managed to make his way back to Ulster, where he died.

STATUE OF DONN CÚAILNGE, IN COUNTY LOUTH

Queen Medb
Queen Medb hated King Conchobar of Ulster because he used to be her husband. He then married her sister, whom Medb ultimately murdered. In revenge, her nephew killed her with a piece of hard cheese fired from a sling.

QUEEN MEDB OF CONNACHT

europe ○ FIONN MAC CUMHAILL

40,000 The approximate number of **columns of basalt rock** that make up the Giant's Causeway

A bridge for giants
The giants Fionn and Benandonner provoked each other, until finally Benandonner challenged Fionn to a fight. The Irish giant Fionn threw enough rocks into the sea to build a pathway that would enable him to cross to Scotland. According to the myth, the largest rock Fionn threw into the Irish Sea became the Isle of Man.

Not so giant
Even though Fionn was a giant, he wasn't nearly as large as his rival Benandonner.

Giant rocks
Fionn threw large rocks into the Irish Sea so he could cross to Scotland and face off with Benandonner.

The Salmon of Knowledge
A young Fionn helped the poet Finnegas catch the Salmon of Knowledge, a mystical fish that held all the world's wisdom. Finnegas asked Fionn to cook the salmon but not eat it. But Fionn accidentally burned his thumb on the cooking salmon. He sucked his thumb, which gave him the salmon's knowledge.

The birth of Oisín
In one tale, Fionn found a deer, which transformed into a woman called Sadhbh. They married and Sadhbh became pregnant, but a druid changed her back into a deer. While searching for his wife, Fionn discovered another young deer, who was actually his son Oisín.

SADHBH AND OISÍN

The **Salmon of Knowledge** is believed to have been **caught in the Boyne River**.

Some stories say that Fionn is **not dead, but sleeps in a cave surrounded by the *Fianna*,** ready to once again become Ireland's greatest defender.

Scottish conqueror
The giant Benandonner wanted to conquer Ireland, but he had to defeat Fionn first.

Coastal views
On a clear day, the coast of Scotland can be seen from the Giant's Causeway in Ireland.

Diarmuid and Gráinne
Fionn was to marry the high king's daughter Gráinne, but she fell in love with a *Fianna* warrior called Diarmuid and ran away with him. Years later, when Fionn could have saved an injured Diarmuid with his healing hands, he instead allowed him to die.

The tragic lovers
A sculpture in Kilbaha, County Clare, depicts Gráinne and Diarmuid. Diarmuid was mortally injured by a boar while protecting his lover.

Fionn mac Cumhaill

The heroic figure Fionn mac Cumhaill is at the heart of many colorful Irish myths. Often portrayed as a giant, Fionn fiercely defends Ireland and protects its people. He leads a brave band of fighters known as the *Fianna*.

Central to various legendary tales, Fionn mac Cumhaill, also known as Finn MacCool, is considered one of the great heroes of Irish mythology and folklore. He was the hero of a collection of myths known as the Fenian Cycle, and has been associated in folk tales with the creation of various features of the landscape of Ireland.

In one such legend, Fionn is responsible for the creation of the Giant's Causeway, a formation of hexagonal stone pillars on the north coast of Ireland. According to this tale, the giant Fionn lived in Ireland while the giant Benandonner lived across the Irish Sea in Scotland. Benandonner decided he was going to conquer Ireland, so Fionn angrily began digging up rocks and throwing them into the sea, creating a causeway, or land bridge, that would enable Fionn to cross the sea and confront the Scottish giant. However, when Fionn approached Benandonner, he realized that his opponent was much bigger than himself. Fionn quickly retreated back to his home.

Benandonner followed him, but Fionn's wife, Oonagh, came up with a clever ruse. She disguised Fionn as a baby, and upon arriving at their home in Ireland, Benandonner saw Oonagh with her giant "baby." He assumed that the baby's father, Fionn, had to be colossal. In fear, Benandonner fled back to Scotland, tearing up the causeway as he went so that Fionn could not follow him.

Annwn is the name for the Otherworld in Welsh mythology.

Brân was a giant who could wade across to Ireland without the need of a ship.

The Mabinogi

Four stories from Welsh mythology are recorded in the *Mabinogi*, which is part of a wider collection of Welsh myth and legends known as the *Mabinogion*.

The four branches (parts) of the *Mabinogi* are a rich treasury of stories about early Celtic deities and heroes in Wales. They were first written down by Christian monks in the 12th century. The first branch of the *Mabinogi* deals with the adventures of Pwyll, Prince of Dyfed, especially his visit to the Otherworld. The next two branches relate stories of the children of Llŷr– Bran, Branwen, and Manawydan. The last branch follows events surrounding Math, king of Gwynedd.

PWYLL, PRINCE OF DYFED

One day, Pwyll was out hunting, and claimed a freshly killed deer slain by the hunting dogs of Arawn, lord of the otherworldly realm of Annwn. To appease a furious Arawn, Pwyll agreed to change appearance with Arawn and take his place.

King for a Year
Pwyll ran Arawn's kingdom for a year, and at the end of that time he killed Arawn's rival Hafgan in single combat. Arawn was pleased with Pwyll, and the two became lasting friends.

BRANWEN, DAUGHTER OF LLŶR

The Irish king Matholwch came to Britain to ask for the hand in marriage of Branwen, sister of the king of Britain, Brân the Blessed. Brân agreed to the marriage, but during the ceremony Branwen's half-brother Efnisien wounded Matholwch's horses, angry that he had not been consulted about the marriage.

The magic cauldron
In compensation, Brân offered Matholwch a magic cauldron, which could bring the dead back to life. Pleased with the gift, Matholwch returned to Ireland with Branwen.

The dead return to life
This mythological scene embossed into a Celtic cauldron shows warriors lining up to be returned to life by a figure placing them in a cauldron.

MANAWYDAN, SON OF LLŶR

A direct sequel to the story of Brân and Branwen, this branch follows their brother Manawydan and his friend Pryderi, Pwyll's son from the first branch. After burying Brân's head, Manawydan traveled to Dyfed with Pryderi.

A cursed land
On arriving in Dyfed, Pryderi was reunited with his wife Cigfa, and Manawydan married Pryderi's widowed mother, Rhiannon. A magical mist then covered the whole of Dyfed, leaving it empty of all humans except for Manawydan, Pryderi, Cigfa, and Rhiannon.

Pryderi vanishes
While hunting, Manawydan and Pryderi came across a white boar and followed it to a fort. Manawydan would not go inside, but Pryderi entered the fort and found a beautiful golden bowl. On touching the bowl his hands were stuck to it. Rhiannon entered the fort to look for Pryderi and also got stuck on the bowl. The fort then disappeared in a blanket of mist.

Manawydan lifts the curse
Determined to lift the curse from Dyfed, Manawydan sowed three fields of wheat. Manawydan caught a mouse destroying the fields. He was asked to spare its life by the enchanter Llwyd, because the mouse was his wife in disguise. Llwyd lifted the curse from Dyfed, which he had placed upon the land in revenge for the treatment of his friend Gwawl.

Manawydan son of Llŷr is a Welsh version of the Celtic sea god **Manannán mac Lir**.

Blodeuwedd ("flower faced") was turned into an owl, a bird whose face was thought to **resemble a flower**.

Marriage to Rhiannon
Pwyll fell in love with Rhiannon. She returned his love, but was engaged to a man named Gwawl. Pwyll arrived at their wedding dressed as a beggar asking for food. The bag he held could never be filled no matter how much was put into it. Gwawl was tricked into stepping into the bag, and Pwyll beat him until he agreed to allow Rhiannon to marry Pwyll.

Horse goddess
Rhiannon was associated with horses, and may have been a version of the early Celtic horse goddess Epona.

The birth of Pryderi
Pwyll and Rhiannon had a son, but he disappeared from his cot one night. Rhiannon was falsely accused of murdering her son. Meanwhile, Teyrnon, the lord of Gwent, was dealing with a monster that was stealing foals from his stable. He cut off the beast's hand, and at that moment heard a baby crying. He found a young boy in the stable, and raised him as his own. Realizing later that the boy was Pwyll's son, Teyrnon returned him to Dyfed to reunite him with his parents. Rhiannon named him Pryderi, which means "care."

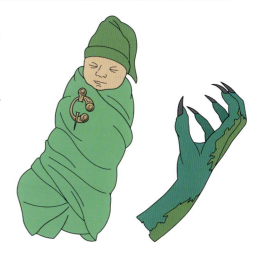

Branwen's woes
When the people of Ireland heard what happened at the wedding, they turned Matholwch against Branwen. He treated her cruelly and made her work in the kitchens. Branwen tamed a starling, and sent it to her brother with a note telling of her woes. Brân gathered an army to invade Ireland and to bring his sister home.

A STARLING

Brân in Ireland
The war in Ireland did not start out well for the British invaders, because Matholwch used the cauldron to bring his dead warriors back to life. Efnisien jumped into the pot and broke it from the inside, dying in the process. Britain eventually won the battle.

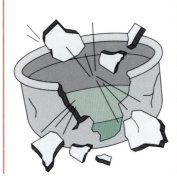

Brân's head
Brân was fatally wounded in the battle, so he asked his men to chop off his head and bury it in Britain, where it would protect the land from further invasions. Brân's head constantly talked to them until they made it back home.

Head of the feast
Brân's men stopped many times on the way home to feast and tell stories with their king.

MATH, SON OF MATHONWY
The king of Gwynedd, Math son of Mathonwy, had to rest his feet in the lap of a young woman when he was not at war. In need of a new foot holder, he tested his niece Arianrhod for purity. She failed the test, and immediately gave birth to two sons. She abandoned the children in shame.

The creation of Blodeuwedd
Furious at being tricked, Arianrhod lay another curse on Lleu Llaw Gyffes, this time declaring that he would have no human woman for his wife. So Math and Gwydion made a woman for him to marry out of oak blossom, broom flowers, and meadowsweet. Her name was Blodeuwedd ("flower faced").

OAK BLOSSOM   **BROOM FLOWERS**   **MEADOWSWEET**

Lleu Llaw Gyffes
Arianrhod's first son left to become a sailor, but her second son was raised by his uncle, the magician Gwydion. Arianrhod cursed the boy to have no name except one given by her. Gwydion tricked her into naming the boy Lleu Llaw Gyffes ("the fair one of the skillful hand") by disguising him as a cobbler come to fix her shoes.

Blodeuwedd's treachery
Blodeuwedd was not a faithful wife, and fell in love with a nobleman, Gronw Pebr. She knew that her husband could only be killed a certain way, so asked him to demonstrate. Gronw was waiting, and threw a spear at Lleu. Rather than dying, Lleu turned into an eagle.

BLODEUWEDD AND GRONW

Revenge of Lleu
Gwydion rescued Lleu and turned him into a man again. He found Blodeuwedd, and turned her into an owl. Gronw begged Lleu for his life, but he would accept nothing except the opportunity to throw a spear at him. Gronw stepped behind a rock now known as Llech Gronw, but Lleu's spear smashed a hole right through it and killed him.

OWL

THE SLATE OF GRONW

europe • THE LEGEND OF KING ARTHUR

1485 The year *Le Morte d'Arthur* by **Sir Thomas Malory**— the **most famous account of Arthur**—was published.

The legend of King Arthur

King Arthur is one of Britain's most celebrated legendary figures. It is unknown whether he was based on a real person, but some writers have portrayed him as a brave king with mystical powers.

Arthur was the son of the British king Uther Pendragon and Queen Igraine of Cornwall. As a baby he was taken by the wizard Merlin to be raised in secret. When Arthur grew up, he had to prove he was the rightful heir to the throne. Before his death, King Uther devised a challenge—whoever could pull a sword named Excalibur out of a stone would become the next king. Many valiant knights tried and failed to perform the feat before a young Arthur stepped forth and easily removed the sword from the stone.

Later, King Arthur broke the sword in a duel and his advisor, Merlin, took him to the magical land of Avalon to replace it. The new sword, also called Excalibur, was raised from a lake by a hand, and Arthur had to sail through its misty waters to take it.

The center of Arthur's realm was Camelot, where he assembled a group of trusted soldiers known as The Knights of the Round Table. They set off on journeys in search of the Holy Grail—a sacred cup that Jesus drank from—which was discovered by the knight Sir Galahad. When his father, Sir Lancelot du Lac, fell in love with Arthur's wife, Guinevere, the king declared war on Lancelot and left Camelot to fight him in France.

While Arthur was away, his power-hungry son, Mordred, took over as Britain's ruler. In the Battle of Camlann, Arthur fought with Mordred to take back his throne with the help of his knights. Arthur killed his son, but was badly wounded himself. As the heroic king lay dying, he ordered one of his knights to throw Excalibur into the lake, and the arm rose up to take it.

Finding Excalibur
An ethereal being known as the Lady of the Lake took care of the sword. She told Arthur to sail to the center of the lake, where an arm held up the sword in its scabbard (sheath).

Magical scabbard
The scabbard had healing powers— Arthur could not be wounded when he had the scabbard with him.

Mythical king
Arthur sailed alone to get the sword while Merlin waited for him at the edge of the lake.

Although considered a **force of good**, Merlin's **magical powers** came from a **demon** who was also his father.

Some people believe that the **Holy Grail** was used by Jesus Christ at the ceremony called the **Last Supper**.

The magic of Merlin
Legends describe Merlin as a great sorcerer and prophet who served as a guide to Arthur throughout his life. As a seer, he could see into the past and future.

Mysterious Merlin
Not much is known about Merlin. In some stories, he was thought to be the son of a demon.

Valiant knights
There were often thought to be 12 Knights of the Round Table, but some versions of the story reported that the table could seat more than 250 people. The knights were equal to one another and they were in charge of maintaining peace in Arthur's kingdom.

KNIGHTS OF THE ROUND TABLE

Quest for the Holy Grail
Sir Galahad went in search of the Holy Grail after receiving a divine vision at the Round Table. Enlisting the help of Sir Bors de Ganis and Sir Percival, Sir Galahad went on an epic journey to find it. Galahad drank from the cup when he found it, an act which killed him instantly and sent him to heaven.

> "Whoso pulleth out this sword of this stone and anvil, is rightwise king born of all England"
>
> Sir Thomas Malory, *Le Morte d'Arthur*, 1485

Lady of the Lake
Also known as Viviane or Nimue, the Lady of the Lake was a water fairy who lived beneath the lake.

Sword bearer
A slender arm dressed in white satin rose out of the water, holding the mighty sword.

77

FOLK TALES

Most early myths of Eastern Europe have become lost over time because they were passed on by word-of-mouth, without being written down. The Slavic lands are known for their folklore and fairy stories—tales of the fantastical and the unexplained, often sprinkled with elements of magic.

Sadko
Set on the shores of Lake Ilmen, one tale tells of a poor man named Sadko. He played such a beautiful tune on his lyre that the Sea King helped him win a wager with the local merchants. The king filled the lake with golden fish, and for every merchant that wouldn't believe it was true, Sadko won the bet and became rich.

Winning the bet
Sadko was given fine goods by the merchants who had bet against him.

The wood dove
A woodcutter was once poisoned by his wife so she could marry a younger man. After some time, an oak tree took root over the woodcutter's grave. Each time the woman passed, a wood dove perched in the tree would coo at her. Thinking it was the voice of her murdered husband, the woman threw herself in the river, tormented with guilt.

WOOD DOVE, OR COMMON PIGEON

Vasilisa the Wise
A character that appeared in multiple Slavic tales, Vasilisa the Wise was also known as Vasilisa the Beautiful (see pages 82–83). She was often depicted in the role of a beautiful maiden who was rescued from danger by a handsome prince.

Sea princess
In one story, Vasilisa is the daughter of the Sea King. After marrying a foreign prince, the pair are pursued by the king after they escape from his underwater kingdom.

EASTERN EUROPE

From a region of rich history and varied traditions, Eastern European folklore brings together the beauty of the natural world with elements of the supernatural. Slavic mythology strikes a bewitching balance between light and darkness, framing powerful monsters and spirits against a backdrop of ancient forests, deep lakes, and rushing rivers.

SPIRITS OF NATURE

A landscape of dense forests and deep, misty lakes, the Slavic lands were home to a treasure trove of nature spirits. Some were kindly and harmless, but others were a danger to unwitting travelers who could easily wander down the wrong path, and become forever lost.

Mavka
Sometimes called Nyavka, Mavka was the spirit of a playful young girl trapped between the worlds of the living and the dead because she had died young.

SUPERNATURAL CREATURES

The folklore of Eastern Europe often referred to abnormal beings and strange events. Tales of the supernatural could include deadly and dangerous foes, as well as bizarre but friendly creatures, all set against the real-world landscape or even the family home.

Vampir
A creature from Serbian folklore, vampirs lived on a diet of human flesh and blood. It was believed they could shape-shift into moths, drawn to gather around moonlight.

Werewolf
European legends tell of humans who could shape-shift into bloodthirsty wolves when the moon was full. It was believed that plants and natural herbs such as wolfsbane could protect against one of these creatures.

Domovoy
The domovoy were house spirits known across all Slavic countries. Living close to the hearth or up in the attic, it was a guardian of the household and its inhabitants. This creature was often depicted as a tiny, middle-aged man, or sometimes similar to a bundle of hay.

Kikimora
Kikimora was believed to be married to the domovoy. But in contrast to the helpful domovoy, this female house spirit would scare naughty children and disrupt the household with noise.

CHRISTIANITY ARRIVES

The Christian faith arrived in the Slavic world in the 9th and 10th centuries, bringing with it beliefs that challenged the folklore of the region. Today, many Eastern Europeans follow the teachings of Orthodox Christianity, but the traditional stories still have their place.

Monster evolution
Christians regarded the creatures and monsters of folklore as enemies of the faith. Missionaries discarded the spirits and ancient deities in favor of Christianity, but many Slavic people continued to believe in both.

Weapons of faith
Stories evolved to tell of vampirs being banished by the crucifix and holy water.

Traditional customs
Today, decorating eggs is a traditional custom in Czechia to celebrate the religious holiday of Easter. The eggs now symbolize the Resurrection, but this practice actually has much earlier roots in Eastern Europe as a symbol of rebirth and renewal.

Painted eggs
Chicken eggs are hollowed out and painted with bright colors and patterns.

Nix
Nixes were kindly water spirits that lived in lakes. One legend tells of a nix that granted a mortal three wishes after striking up a friendship.

Rusalka
Rusalkas were beautiful water nymphs associated with fertility. Mortals could be enchanted by their bewitching songs and end up drowning.

Vodyanoi
A well-known water spirit, the Vodyanoi was a dangerous creature that would lure travelers into its lair in order to drown them.

Vila
Depicted as a beautiful, young girl, the Vila was believed to be born from dew drops. She lived far from humans, close to rivers, or even in the clouds.

Early Slavic gods

The Slavs once worshipped a variety of powerful deities who influenced their daily lives and the wider world. Little is known about these gods, because most writings about them come from inaccurate accounts by later Christian writers.

Before the spread of Christianity, the Slavs believed that their gods controlled every aspect of the cosmos. Perun unleashed thunder and lightning, Mati Syra Zemlya watched over crops, and Veles ruled over the dead. To repay the gods, the Slavic people gave offerings to appease them and held festivals in their honor.

VELES

A malicious trickster, Veles was god of the underworld. This chaotic shape-shifter earned a bad reputation for stealing cattle, kidnapping people, and issuing harsh punishments on a whim. Perun was his enemy, and the pair regularly waged war against each other to settle disputes.

Horned god
Veles is shown with a horned head to reflect his position as god of cattle and his links to the animal kingdom.

PERUN

The greatest of the Slavic gods, Perun was the god of lightning and his voice was the sound of thunder. His main role was to protect the Slavs. A generous god, he brought rain in times of drought and rewarded honorable warriors with victory on the battlefield.

Storm breaker
The circular spiral symbol held by this idol of Perun is the thunderbolt he used to break apart the clouds so the sun would shine again.

SVAROG

The mighty fire god Svarog created the world from an egg, using its shell to make the land and sea. With his fire and the remains of the egg, he forged humans, the sun, and the moon. When his work was done, he retired, allowing his sons and daughters to take charge of ruling the universe.

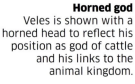

Divine tool
As the celestial blacksmith, Svarog used a hammer and other tools to help shape elements of the world from his divine forge.

Perun was thought to create order, while Veles brought destruction.

745 A beautiful temple dedicated to Ziva in the middle of Lake Bled, Slovenia, was destroyed in 745.

JARILO

The god of spring and fertility, Jarilo was kidnapped as a baby by the death god Veles. He spent his childhood years in the underworld, where it was always spring. When Jarilo finally escaped, he brought springtime with him to the land. Although he was mainly a fertility god, Jarilo was also a violent god of war.

Trickster god
Since Jarilo grew up in the underworld, he adopted the trickster traits of its ruler Veles.

DAZHBOG

The sun god Dazhbog brought light and warmth to the world. His golden palace was situated in a land of eternal summer. In the morning, he traveled across the sky in a chariot pulled by fire-breathing horses, while at night, he crossed an ocean on a boat pulled by geese, ducks, and swans. His daughter was Zorya.

MATI SYRA ZEMLYA

The earth goddess Mati Syra Zemlya is one of the oldest gods in Slavic mythology. Her body was the earth and soil that ensured the growth of crops. The Slavs made holes in the ground and filled them with offerings of bread and wine to show Mati their appreciation.

Spirit of the earth
The spirit of Mati Syra Zemlya could be found in the land, from ears of wheat to moist, dark soil.

SVETOVID

The four-headed war god Svetovid had the ability to see from multiple viewpoints at the same time, making him wise and powerful. His white horse could predict the outcome of every conflict and remained his faithful companion on and off the battlefield.

> "EVERY YEAR, EVERY MAN AND WOMAN **PAID A COIN** AS A DONATION FOR THE WORSHIP OF SVETOVID'S IDOL."
>
> Saxo Grammaticus, *Gesta Danorum*, 13th century CE

Equipped for battle
Svetovid was often depicted with four heads, allowing him to see in all directions (north, south, east, and west), and he carried a drinking horn, a silver sword, and a bow.

ZIVA

A giver of life, the fertility goddess Ziva made all plants, flowers, and fruit flourish with her magical touch. As well as enabling growth, she had the ability to heal wounds. She was also a mother-like figure who protected all life, nurturing children in particular.

Feathered friend
Ziva was associated with the cuckoo, which represented the flow of life and healing. The goddess was often depicted holding this bird.

ZORYA

The goddess of the dawn was Dazhbog's three-headed daughter Zorya. Each of her heads represented a stage in a woman's life: a young girl, an adult woman, and an old lady. It was Zorya's daily duty to open and close the palace gates for Dazhbog when he left for his travels each morning.

82　europe　○　BÁBA YAGÁ

Spooky hut
The witch's home was an old hut made out of wood and bones.

Riding on chicken legs
The wooden hut where Bába Yagá lived was tucked away in the forest, propped up by chicken legs that could sprint after fleeing children. It was furnished with moss and twigs, as well as bones and skulls left over from the witch's dinner.

Made for running
Bába Yagá commanded her hut to chase after her next meal using its chicken legs.

1755 The year tales of Bába Yagá were first published in a book.

Some legends claim that Bába Yagá could grant wishes if she were offered roses.

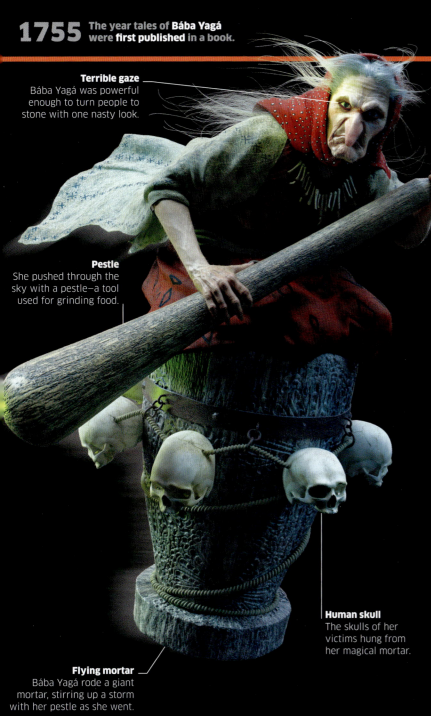

Terrible gaze
Bába Yagá was powerful enough to turn people to stone with one nasty look.

Pestle
She pushed through the sky with a pestle—a tool used for grinding food.

Human skull
The skulls of her victims hung from her magical mortar.

Flying mortar
Bába Yagá rode a giant mortar, stirring up a storm with her pestle as she went.

Bába Yagá

The mysterious witch Bába Yagá is a figure who appears many times in tales from Slavic folklore. In some of her appearances she took on the role of the villain, but sometimes she was a wise woman who helped the main character.

The word "baba" means "grandmother" in many Slavic languages, but Bába Yagá was not always as innocent as her name implies. In many tales she was depicted as an evil sorceress with a ravenous appetite for children. Stories described her as having bony legs, iron teeth, and a nose long enough to stick to the ceiling. According to some tales, Bába Yagá was not a single being, but a trio of identical beings who shared the same name. Often two of these beings were helpful, while the third was dangerous.

When Bába Yagá captured her victims, she turned them into stone, and then turned them back into flesh at her home, where she cooked and devoured them. Bába Yagá lived in a chicken-legged hut deep in the woods of a mysterious realm separated from the ordinary world by dense forests, deep gorges, and other natural barriers. A visitor could greet the hut and ask it to turn around and face the front if they wished to enter. The fence of the hut was decorated with human skulls, which lit up like lanterns at night. Inside, Bába Yagá sat at her stove or slept, her long body stretched from one corner of the hut to the other.

Children captured by Bába Yagá often used her own magic against her to flee, such as in the tales of Vassilisa and Mariassa (below). The boy Ivan in the story *The Maiden Tsar* visited three Bába Yagás. The first two warned him about the third, and Ivan took their advice when this last Bába Yagá tried to harm him. He sounded Bába Yagá's three magical horns, summoning a firebird that carried him away from Bába Yagá, leaving her with a fistful of feathers.

> I saw Bába Yagá, **galloping in a mortar** that she urged on like a horse, with an **iron pestle.**
>
> Vasilii Levshin, *Russian Fairy Tales*, 1780

Vassilisa and the skull
When Vassilisa's mother died, her father remarried. Her stepmother and stepsisters treated her badly by giving her lots of chores to do. One day, Vassilisa's stepmother sent her to get some tapers (wicks covered in wax used to carry flame) from Bába Yagá to light the lamps at home. Instead of giving her some, Bába Yagá set her a series of impossible tasks. Vassilisa was able to complete them, but the witch kept giving her more to do. At night while Bába Yagá slept, Vassilisa crept out of the hut, and took a glowing skull from the witch's fence to guide her home.

Eerie glow
Vassilisa made her way through the forest using a magical skull.

Mariassa's lucky escape
Mariassa's stepmother didn't like her and sent her to borrow a needle and thread from Bába Yagá. Before going, the girl's aunt told her how to talk to the witch's cat. Bába Yagá tried to imprison Mariassa, but the cat told her to run away with a towel and a comb. Hearing the witch approaching as she ran, Mariassa threw the towel down, which turned into a river, and the comb, which grew into a forest, trapping Bába Yagá behind her.

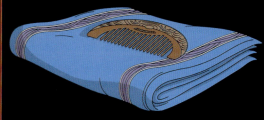

84 europe · KOSCHEI THE DEATHLESS

Koschei could take on multiple forms, including a **man**, a **monster**, a **snake**, and a **tornado**.

IVAN AND MARYA
The story begins with Prince Ivan, who fell in love with the warrior queen Marya Morevna. They had many encounters with the evil Koschei before finally defeating him.

Three sisters
Ivan had three sisters, who all married shape-shifting beings. Each husband could transform into a bird—a raven, an eagle, and a falcon. When the sisters went away to settle down with their husbands, Ivan missed their company and set out on his horse to find them.

RAVEN   EAGLE   FALCON

Passing the battlefield
While traveling through the countryside, Ivan discovered hundreds of dead and wounded soldiers in a field. They were warriors fighting for Koschei, who had been defeated by an army led by Marya Morevna. The warrior queen had taken Koschei captive.

Two lovers
Ivan met Marya on the battlefield. They fell in love and were soon married. Marya told Ivan that she must soon leave to fight in another war. Before Marya left their palace, she warned him that no matter what, he must not open the door of her wooden closet.

Wandering prince
On his travels, Ivan (sometimes referred to by his full name of Ivan Tsarevich) especially yearned for the company of his sisters because their parents had recently died.

Love at first sight
Ivan met Marya in a field where she had set up camp with her fighters.

THE EVIL KOSCHEI
Koschei managed to escape from Marya's palace and then kidnapped her as she was on her way to war. Koschei used his power to throw obstacles in Ivan's way to prevent him from reuniting with his wife.

Koschei's escape
Ivan couldn't keep himself from opening the closet. Inside, he found a feeble old man tied up in chains, who asked Ivan to show him mercy and give him some water. Ivan, not suspecting it was Koschei, did so. The old man quickly regained his strength and broke free, telling the prince he was going after Marya.

The man in the closet
In one version of the story, it was only after Ivan gave Koschei a third bucket of water that Koschei returned to his normal self and escaped.

Hard to kill
Koschei was known as the Deathless because he couldn't be killed easily. It was said that he hid his soul in the eye of a needle that was inside an egg that had been placed first in a duck and then a rabbit. The rabbit was locked inside a chest that had been buried under an oak tree on an island.

Koschei the Deathless

Also known as *Marya Morevna*, this Slavic folk tale follows the hero Ivan, who goes on a quest to defeat an almost invincible force of evil.

In Eastern European legend, Koschei the Deathless was a monstrous figure who prolonged his life by keeping his soul well hidden. In this tale, Koschei kidnaps the female warrior Marya Morevna, and it is up to her husband, the brave Prince Ivan, to rescue her. But first, Ivan must find a way to accomplish the almost impossible—killing the evil Koschei.

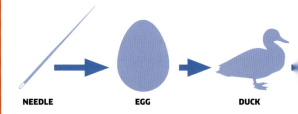

NEEDLE   EGG   DUCK

In this story, **Baba Yaga** rode a **magical horse** across the **whole world** every day.

The name **Koschei** comes from **the Slavic word** for **bone**, which describes the **villain's slender appearance**.

The search for Marya
Over many days, Ivan searched far and wide for Marya. On his travels, he met his brothers-in-law, the raven, eagle, and falcon. They consoled him and wherever each bird parted with Ivan, they placed a silver item on the ground: a spoon, a fork, and a snuffbox.

Capturing the queen
While Ivan searched for her, Koschei brought Marya back to his kingdom.

Death and rebirth
Prince Ivan eventually reached Koschei's palace, where he found Marya alone. They fled, but were pursued and caught. Koschei released Ivan, but carried Marya back home with him. This happened two more times, and on the third occasion Koschei chopped Ivan up and placed the pieces of his body in a barrel that was thrown into the sea. Fortunately, the three brothers-in-law were able to find the barrel and put Ivan back together.

Tarnished silver
Ivan's brothers-in-law knew that something had happened to him when the three silver items on the ground turned black.

> "THANK YOU, IVAN THE PRINCE!" SAID KOSCHEI THE DEATHLESS. "NOW YOU WILL NEVER AGAIN SEE MARYA MOREVNA, JUST AS YOU'LL NEVER SEE YOUR OWN EARS!"
>
> Nicholas Kotar, *In a Certain Kingdom*, 2021

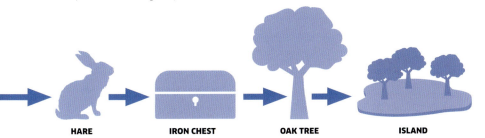

HARE → IRON CHEST → OAK TREE → ISLAND

DEFEATING THE DEATHLESS
Every time Ivan tried to take Marya away from Koschei, the evil kidnapper would catch up with them on his speedy horse and grab her back. Ivan needed a horse that could outrun Koschei's, and for that, he asked for help from the witch Baba Yaga (see pages 82–83).

Seeking help
Baba Yaga lived in a land beyond a river of fire, and she had many magical horses. To get across the fiery river, Ivan waved a magical handkerchief over it three times and a bridge appeared. He found the witch in her chicken-legged hut and asked her for her best horse. The witch gave him a simple foal that became a speedy horse as he rode on it, enabling him to return to Marya.

An encounter with the witch
Ivan found Baba Yaga in her hut. Before helping him, the witch set the prince a series of tasks to complete.

The final chase
When Ivan reached Koschei's kingdom, he grabbed Marya and set off back to their palace. It didn't take long for Koschei to catch up with them. When Koschei's horse stumbled, he fell to the ground and Ivan killed him with a sword, then burned his body so he never returned. Prince Ivan and Marya lived together in peace thereafter.

europe • THE FIREBIRD

1910 The year **the ballet** *The Firebird* was first **performed** by Russian composer **Igor Stravinsky**.

Fire in the sky
The firebird was described as being like a living bonfire, lighting up the night sky as it flew. Each night it visited the czar's orchard and pecked at his golden apples.

Fiery plumage
The firebird has long feathers in fiery colors of red, yellow, and orange.

Magical apple
The golden apples were said to give strength and youth to those who ate them.

The firebird

Eastern European folktales are bursting with magic, wonder, and unexpected twists. A famous story featuring the strikingly beautiful firebird and the boy Ivan is one such example. Its message is one of determination and loyalty in the face of adversity.

Ivan the stable boy worked for the czar (king), who had a magnificent orchard of golden apples. One day, when the king noticed that some of his apples were missing, he asked Ivan to find the thief. That night, Ivan stayed up in the orchard and waited. In the middle of the night he saw a small light growing brighter and brighter, until the entire orchard lit up. It was the firebird! Ivan tried to catch it, but it flew away, leaving him with a feather in his hand.

In the morning, Ivan took the feather to the czar, who ordered him to capture the bird. After a day of searching for the firebird, Ivan came across a wolf. It advised Ivan to give the firebird food that had been dipped in beer, which would slow the creature down, making it easier to catch. Following the wolf's advice, Ivan caught the firebird and took it to the czar. He locked it up in a cage and ordered Ivan to find his love, a princess called Yelena. Yet when Ivan located her, he fell in love with her.

To trick the czar, the wolf turned into a beautiful princess, with whom the czar fell in love and married. Just before their first kiss, the wolf returned to its animal form and the czar died of shock. Ivan then took the throne and married Yelena. He set the firebird free because it had changed his life.

The majestic firebird is found in many other tales from the region, such as *The Little Humpbacked Horse* and *The Firebird and Princess Vasilisa* (see right).

The firebird was believed to **come from the heavens** or an unknown **distant land**.

Ivan is the **main character** in most of the **firebird folktales**.

Precious fruit
The czar was furious to find his golden apples missing because only he was allowed to pick them.

Bright feather
The power of the firebird is such that even a single feather can bring good or bad fortune to the person who finds it.

Slavic hero
In another version of the story, Ivan is called Ivan Czarevitch—literally the czar's (king's) son.

The humpbacked horse

In this story, the boy Ivan found a white mare with a golden mane. This horse gave him three other horses, one being tiny and magical with humps on its back. On his way to sell the horses to the czar, Ivan discovered a feather belonging to the firebird. The czar set Ivan a few tasks, including finding the firebird. Thanks to the little humpbacked horse, Ivan was able to catch the firebird, finish his tasks, fall in love, and marry a princess.

Classic folktale
The tale of the little humpbacked horse has been depicted in art, film, animation, and even in a ballet.

The Firebird and Princess Vasilisa

One day, a huntsman captured the firebird and brought it to the czar, who decided to present it to Princess Vasilisa. The huntsman was sent to find the princess, who was rowing on a lake. When brought before the czar, he asked her to marry him, but she refused unless the czar asked the huntsman to bathe in boiling water. The huntsman's magical horse charmed him so that he emerged from the boiling water unharmed and handsome. The czar then decided to enter the water, but without magical help he died. The huntsman then married the princess.

AFRICA

The deities of ancient Egypt are no longer worshipped, but they once influenced all aspects of Egyptian life. South of the Sahara Desert, sacred stories and folktales featuring gods, tricksters, and heroes are still at the heart of many cultures.

ANCIENT EGYPT

Dating back to 3500 BCE, ancient Egypt was one of the world's earliest civilizations, forming around the fertile Nile River. It developed a complex culture, with more than ten thousand gods and goddesses overseeing all aspects of life, from childbirth to mummification.

SOURCES OF THE MYTHS

The oldest myths of the ancient Egyptians have survived today because they took great care in recording them. Hieroglyphics were used to provide guidance and describe important events.

HIEROGLYPHICS

Pyramid texts
Religious inscriptions were carved on the walls of the pyramids, where pharaohs were buried. These writings acted as a guide for the dead, containing useful spells for them to use on their hazardous journey in the afterlife.

THE WEIGHING OF THE HEART CEREMONY

Book of the Dead
Written on papyrus, the Book of the Dead was a religious text and a magical book of spells illustrated to show what took place in the afterlife. This included the weighing of the heart ceremony performed by the jackal-headed god Anubis.

GODDESS IMENTET AND SUN GOD RA

Tomb painting
Ancient Egyptian wall paintings were typically found in the tombs of wealthy people. These paintings were important, not only because they expressed the spiritual beliefs of the dead person, but because they conveyed high status in society. Colors were used symbolically—for example, red represented the sun and power.

ANIMAL-HEADED GODS

The ancient Egyptian gods were often depicted with the head of an animal attached to a human body. The gods were thought to have the strengths of the animals they were associated with. Many of them had the ability to shape-shift and combine with other gods to become a "composite" deity.

Sekhmet
With the head of a lioness, Sekhmet was a fierce warrior goddess who also took care of the sick.

Hathor
This goddess was a protector of women and oversaw love, beauty, music, dancing, and fertility.

Bastet
A cat-headed deity, Bastet was a goddess of protection and motherhood who brought good health.

Taweret
This protector of children had the head of a crocodile, the body of a hippo, and the legs of a lion.

ROLES OF THE PHARAOHS

Pharaohs had great power over the land. They were the heads of state and religious figures that people worshipped as earthly representations of the gods. When pharaohs died, they became divine and joined the god Osiris in the underworld. On Earth, their power transferred to their heir.

RAMSES II SITTING WITH GOD AMON AND GODDESS MUT

Pharaohs as gods
The ancient Egyptians believed that pharaohs were chosen by the gods to rule the land. They acted as messengers of the divine. During the coronation, the pharaoh was thought to become an earthly version of the god Horus.

GREAT PYRAMID OF GIZA

Pathway to heaven
Constructed of giant stone blocks, the staircases of the pyramids were thought to be pathways to the sky. They were aligned with stars of religious importance, so that when the pharaoh died, they could walk up to heaven.

PREPARING FOR THE AFTERLIFE

When a rich person died, an elaborate process known as mummification was performed on them to ensure that their soul made it safely into the afterlife.

Mummification
The complex ritual of mummification involved removing the organs, washing, and wrapping up the body. The only organ that remained inside the body was the heart.

Personal items
During mummification, protective amulets were tucked inside the bandages.

Organ removal
Firstly, the organs were taken out, including the brain, which was removed through the nose.

Applying salt
A special salt called natron was used to coat the body to prevent it from rotting.

Wrapping up
The body was then rubbed with oil to preserve it and wrapped in linen bandages.

Final ceremony
A ceremony was performed to bring back the mummified person's senses in the underworld.

Inside the coffin
The mummy was placed inside the coffin, which was decorated with spells and prayers.

Protective eye
Amulets were usually decorated with the Eye of Horus to protect the dead from evil forces.

Keeping the organs
Canopic jars stored important organs, including the lungs, liver, intestines, and stomach. The jars were usually carved with heads of deities and placed in the tomb.

CANOPIC JARS

Important goods
Because the afterlife was thought to be a continuation of a person's life on Earth, people were often buried with items they would need. This included items such as food and household goods.

Model boat
Carved model boats were believed to help the deceased on their journey to the underworld.

Food for the soul
Models of scenes depicting baking were thought to teach people how to cook in the afterlife.

PLACES OF WORSHIP

Temples were sacred places considered to be the home of the gods. Rituals were performed daily, often by pharaohs, and festivals were held at special times of the year.

Temple sacrifice
As offerings to the gods, the Egyptians sacrificed animals and mummified them. These offerings were made to temples by visitors to appease the gods and gain their favor. Crocodiles were sacrificed to the god Sobek, who took the form of the animal and represented royalty.

Opet Festival
During the Nile flood season, the Opet festival was held in honor of the god Amun, his wife the goddess Mut, and their son Khonsu. Priests carried statues of the gods through the streets of ancient Thebes, and made their way onto river barges. They would end up at the temple of Luxor, where the statues were kept for 24 days.

Karnak Temple Complex
Dedicated to the god Amun, the temple complex of Karnak was an impressive religious site, containing temples, shrines, columns, and gateways. It dates from around 2055 BCE.

The Egyptian story of creation

Time began when the god Ra (often known as Atum in his role of creator), emerged from an endless ocean known as Nun. From his body he made the deities Tefnut and Shu who, along with their children Geb and Nut, took on the task of creating the universe.

Ra rose alone out of the waters of Nun. Realizing his solitude, he sneezed, and Shu, the god of dry air, was born. Then Ra spat, and Tefnut, the goddess of moist air, was created. They left Ra and set off on a journey far away.

To make the universe work in harmony, Ra created the goddess of order–Maat. Next, he drew up an island, known as the Benben stone, to stand on, and imagined everything he wanted to create. Then he conjured up all the plants and animals of the Earth by speaking their names. He ordered his eye, known as the Eye of Ra, to find Shu and Tefnut, and when his eye returned with them after two days, it saw that Ra had replaced it with another eye. The Eye of Ra was distraught and wept, its tears transforming into the first humans.

Shu and Tefnut had two children: Geb and Nut. They fell in love, but their parents were jealous of their relationship. Shu kept the two apart and they were forbidden from having children on any day of the year. But the god Thoth pitied Geb and Nut, and asked for five extra days as his prize for winning a game. Nut gave birth to five Egyptian gods on each of these days.

The divine family

Ra was the first of many deities in the Egyptian pantheon. His grandchildren Nut and Geb were parents to five Egyptian gods, one of which was Horus the elder. When Horus died, he was born again as the child of Isis and Osiris (see pages 96–97).

Arched over — Nut's body was the sky that held all the stars, and every night she swallowed the sun.

Waters of Nun — The universe and the gods arose from the bubbling, chaotic ocean of Nun.

2,000 The ancient Egyptians worshipped more than 2,000 deities.

God of air
As the god of dry air, Shu was in charge of the clouds, which were thought to be his bones.

Staring at the sky
Geb was the Earth, and from his body, all the plants and trees grew.

Winning the days
Thoth played the game Senet with the moon god Khonsu in the hopes of winning some extra days for Nut to have her children. If Khonsu won, he wanted Thoth to tell him all the secrets of the universe. The gods played for hours until Thoth finally won.

An ancient game
In the popular ancient Egyptian game of Senet, players competed to be first to move their pieces to the other side of the board.

Held apart
In Egyptian art, Geb was green to represent the Earth's plants and trees, while Nut was as blue as the sky and shimmered with stars. They were pushed apart by Shu, their father.

Ptah the creator
In an alternative story of Egyptian creation, the sculptor god Ptah made the universe with his bare hands. He crafted the gods out of stone and metal using his forge and chisel, then brought them to life.

An artistic god
The ancient Egyptians worshipped Ptah as a god of crafts and skilled laborers.

africa • JOURNEY OF THE SUN

Hawk-headed god
By day, Ra had the head of a hawk on a human body, and held a scepter.

Divine headdress
Ra's headdress was the shining Sun that he wore and guided across the sky.

> **Hail to thee, Ra,** at thy rising; the night and the darkness are past.
>
> Ancient Egyptian prayer

In the Duat
The world was in darkness every night when Ra visited the underworld. He journeyed through the Duat's realms for 12 hours in the *Mesektet*. Each hour was crucial as he battled evil forces to make it out in time to bring light into the world again.

The first hour
Ra passed through the gates leading to the Duat. Awaiting his arrival were the gods of the night and baboons in celebration. Ra's hawk head changed into a ram's. A nearby boat carried the divine scarab beetle Khepri.

The second hour
In this hour, Ra's nightly journey officially began as he entered the Duat and set sail aboard the *Mesektet* with a fleet of four other boats. They crossed the dark Waters of Nun that coursed through a fertile land known as Wernes. The goddess Maat, who was one of the gods present to protect Ra, was often depicted as a feather in the barque.

The third hour
The Waters of Nun slowly became the Waters of Osiris, a gloomy place of stagnant ponds and muddy marshes. Osiris appeared and sailed with Ra at this time. The Duat got steadily darker the deeper they sailed. In the darkness, Ra's light grew dim and he could barely see anything. He hardly spoke or moved.

The fourth hour
The *Mesektet* passed through Imhet, a desert wasteland ruled by Sokar – a hawk-headed god who was one of Osiris's many forms. In this pitch-black, snake-riddled realm, the *Mesektet* had to be towed across the sand, and it turned into a serpent whose fiery breath cut the darkness.

The fifth hour
The land of Sokar was so vast that the serpent barque continued to be towed here, this time with the additional help of Khepri. Ra passed through a narrow cave, which led to a pyramid. Below the cave was the burial mound of Osiris situated on a Lake of Fire. It was a place that blessed good souls with cold water, but bad souls suffered a scorching punishment.

3 Ra took on the form of **a scarab beetle at dawn**, a hawk-headed man during the day, and **an old man in the evening**.

Ra had a **secret name** that could be used to **control him**, but only he and the goddess Isis knew it.

95

Journey of the sun

The sun god Ra was the king of the ancient Egyptian gods. He controlled the sun's movements and could even turn into the sun itself. Every morning Ra rose up and sailed across the heavens aboard his barque (boat) and descended into the underworld, known as the Duat, in the evening.

Solar sailor
Every day Ra journeyed across the sky in *Mandjet*, also known as the "Boat of a Million Years." As it approached noon, Ra was at his strongest, and the sun he wore as a headdress shone brighter than at any other time.

Transporting souls
The barque ferried souls and the prayers of the living to the underworld.

Ra was among the first and most important gods in ancient Egypt. According to some, he created himself and the universe. His worshippers prayed to him to bring light and life into the world.

Whether in the sky or in the Duat, Ra was constantly on the move. At the break of dawn, he set sail aboard his barque *Mandjet*, and changed form throughout the day. People watched him on his route across the sky as the sun traveled from east to west. At sunset, his barque crossed the horizon and made its way down into the Duat.

There Ra boarded his other ship *Mesektet*, and throughout his underworld journey, he was joined by many deities, such as the goddess of order and justice, Maat, and the ruler of the Duat, Osiris. The divine serpent Mehen formed a protective canopy over him on his dangerous journey.

The serpent Apophis tried to attack Ra each night, but the gods defended him and killed the serpent, so Ra could emerge victorious in the morning. The ancient Egyptians gave thanks for each new day when they saw Ra rising in the sky.

Creature of the night
In the Duat, Ra transformed into the ram-headed god Iuf as he merged with the soul of Osiris. His evening barque was called the *Mesektet*. It was also known as "the Boat of Millions of Souls" because it took the souls of the newly dead to the Duat. During his nighttime sailing, the scepter in Iuf's hand and his barque turned into snakes.

RAM-HEADED RA AT NIGHT

The sixth hour
At this critical point in the journey, Ra's soul combined with the body of Osiris to give him the power he needed to regenerate his light. The serpent Mehen, a symbol of eternity, arched over Ra's barque, which was now back on the Waters of Nun. The serpent protected Ra as he approached his most dangerous hour.

The seventh hour
Ra's enemy was the serpent Apophis, who wanted to end all life on Earth by preventing the sun from rising. The goddess Isis cast spells on him, while the goddess Selkis bound him. At the end of this battle, Apophis was destroyed.

APOPHIS THE SERPENT

The eighth hour
Having avoided the threats of Apophis and with his power renewed, Ra faced five doors, called knives. He used a magical spell to open them and sailed through. The souls of the dead celebrated as Ra passed them, and an eerie cry like that of a tomcat pierced the air.

The ninth hour
Ra headed toward the land of the living in the east, assisted by 12 strong oarsmen who helped Ra get there on time. Next to them in the barque were three baskets filled with grain to feed the dead in the underworld.

The tenth hour
The journey was nearly over, and Ra was protected by the 12 oarsmen, who were now armed with weapons to prevent enemy attacks. The goddess Sekhmet appeared and cured Ra's eyes so he could see better. Osiris kept watch nearby in the form of a snake with a falcon's head.

The 11th hour
A bright red sun disk, circled by a serpent, appeared on the prow of the barque to indicate that the end was in sight. Joining Ra in front of the barque were 12 deities, each carrying a serpent. The snakes were not to touch the ground until the final hour.

The 12th hour
After 12 long hours in the Duat, Ra's journey was finally over. Many gods joined him in a celebratory parade as he made his way through the final gates. Ra was reborn as the scarab beetle Khepri, and emerged from the horizon to begin his voyage across the sky all over again.

Osiris and the underworld

An epic battle between good and evil raged when the god Set plotted to take the throne from his brother Osiris. Set thought he had succeeded, but Osiris became the ruler of the dead, while his son Horus took back Egypt's throne.

Osiris ruled Egypt with his wife and sister Isis. He was a kind-hearted king, who taught his people how to live and farm. After he was killed by Set, he became the ruler of the Duat (the underworld). The story of Osiris's revival after death gave hope to the Egyptians. Years after his death, Horus, the son of Osiris, struggled against the ruthless Set, and in the end, good triumphed over evil.

KING OF MORTALS
Together with his wife Isis, Osiris ruled Egypt during a period of peace and happiness. The royal couple were fair and generous, and in return, their people adored them. Unfortunately, the reign of Osiris did not last forever.

The eternally good
At first, Osiris taught his people how to cultivate wheat and use tools, while Isis showed them how to weave. Then Osiris traveled the world to share his skills with all humans. This act of goodness earned him the name Wennefer, which means "the eternally good." His brother Set was so jealous of his success that he devised a clever plan to overthrow him.

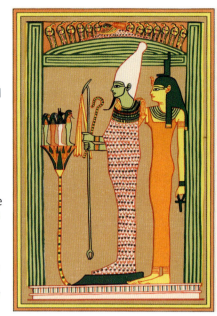

DEATH OF OSIRIS
Osiris passed away inside the casket. Isis mourned the loss of her husband dearly and ensured that his body was treasured. With the help of the gods Anubis and Thoth, Osiris's body was preserved through mummification.

The grief of a queen
Isis scoured the Nile River looking for the lost casket, but it had been swept out to sea. When she finally found it, she was heartbroken to find her husband dead, and brought the casket home with her. Exhausted from crying, Isis fell asleep. Set appeared, broke open the casket, and tore Osiris's body apart, scattering the remains. Isis, with the help of her sister Nephthys, searched for his body parts and collected them together.

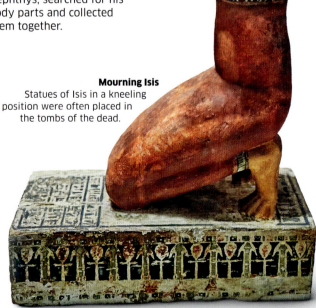

Mourning Isis
Statues of Isis in a kneeling position were often placed in the tombs of the dead.

Descent into the Duat
The sun god Ra (see pages 94–95) ordered the underworld gods Anubis and Thoth to help Isis in her time of need. They carefully put Osiris's body back together as it once was. Then Anubis mummified the body by applying special creams and lotions before covering it in linen bandages to prevent decay. Isis sang a spell to resurrect the body of Osiris and the pair were reunited one last time before Osiris descended into the underworld of the Duat to become its ruler.

Anubis mummifies Osiris
The jackal-headed god Anubis invented the process of mummification and was highly respected in ancient Egypt.

9 The Ennead consisted of nine deities.

At one point during their feud, **Set tore out Horus's eye**, which was the moon.

Set's banquet
When he returned to Egypt, Osiris received a hero's welcome. His brother Set hosted a banquet for the king, and during the celebration, he brought out a casket. Set told the guests that whoever fitted perfectly inside the casket could keep it. The guests tried to squeeze themselves in, but it was a trick because Set had made sure that only Osiris could fit into it. Once Osiris was inside, he was trapped. Set shut the lid, secured the casket, and pushed it into the Nile River.

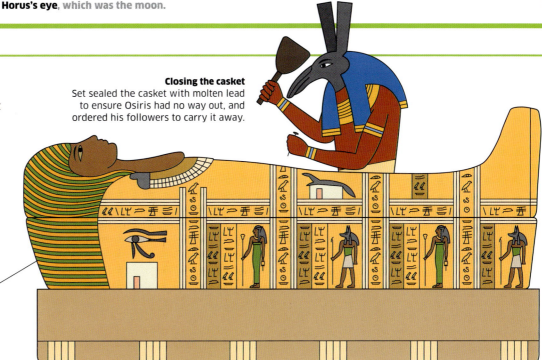

Closing the casket
Set sealed the casket with molten lead to ensure Osiris had no way out, and ordered his followers to carry it away.

Alive inside
At first, Osiris banged on the casket and shouted for help, but Set ignored him.

ROYAL CONTESTS
After Osiris's death, Isis gave birth to their son Horus. When he grew up, Horus sought to take the throne from his uncle. Horus and Set went before the Ennead, the council of gods, to decide who was entitled to the throne. Fearing they would vote against him, Set arranged his own contest instead.

Symbol of evil
Male hippopotamuses were often associated with evil and Set, the god of chaos and destruction.

Underwater challenge
Set challenged Horus to see who could stay underwater the longest. They both turned themselves into hippopotamuses and dived to the bottom of the Nile River. The contest was well underway when suddenly Horus was hit by a harpoon. Isis had attempted to attack Set for killing Osiris, and accidentally targeted her son. Horus was so enraged, he leapt out of the water and chopped her head off (it was later restored by magic). The contest was canceled with no clear winner.

The rightful king
Thanks to his father Osiris, falcon-headed Horus ruled over Egypt for thousands of years as a sky god.

Egypt's new ruler
With no decision made over the rightful king of Egypt, the gods of the Ennead wrote to Osiris in the Duat and asked him to decide. Osiris vouched for his son Horus to inherit the throne and become the new king of Egypt. The gods of the Ennead accepted his decision, and Horus was crowned king. As Set was burning with rage, the sun god Ra took him into the sky and transformed him into thunder.

The boat race
The contest between Horus and Set continued. This time a boat race was arranged, but first the pair had to make their own vessels out of stone. Horus cheated by making his boat out of wood, and had it plastered to look like stone. Set's was made out of mountain stone. Out on the Nile River, Set's boat sank. Furious at this outcome, Set transformed into a hippopotamus and capsized Horus's boat.

Deities of the dead

The ancient Egyptians worshipped certain gods and goddesses to ensure their soul's safe journey through the Duat and to be granted an eternity in the Field of Reeds. In the Duat, a god could appear in the form of an animal. For example, the goddess Isis could turn into a scorpion. Some gods assisted the souls on their journey, while others judged a specific aspect of the soul.

Osiris
Ruler of the Duat, Osiris made the final decision on the fate of a soul.

Isis
Protector of the dead, the goddess Isis stood by the side of Osiris.

Tefnut
Goddess of moisture, Tefnut was one of the judges of the dead.

Horus
The son of Osiris and Isis, Horus led souls to their judgment before Osiris.

Nephthys
The sister of Osiris and Isis, Nephthys helped with funeral rituals.

Hathor
A sky deity, Hathor guided souls on their way into the Duat.

The Hall of Two Truths

The ancient Egyptians believed that when they died, they went to an afterlife known as the Duat. The soul journeyed through the Duat to reach the Hall of Two Truths. Here, the gods weighed the hearts of the dead, and decided whether a person deserved to be punished, or to spend eternity in a blissful place.

Before the souls could be judged in the Hall of Two Truths, they had to pass through seven gates, each of which led to a dangerous land. Here they might encounter venomous snakes and hungry crocodiles. A dog-headed beast dwelled by a Lake of Fire, ready to pounce, tear out hearts, and swallow shadows. The deceased were often buried with a copy of the *Book of the Dead* that was full of magical spells and practical advice to help them navigate this terrifying obstacle course.

Once through the gates, the jackal-headed god Anubis led the souls into the Hall of Two Truths, where each heart was weighed on a balance against a feather from the wings of Maat, the goddess of truth and justice. The god Thoth stood nearby to record the result.

If the heart was heavier than the feather, it meant that the person was wicked and had to suffer a second death. Ammit the devourer of the dead awaited this result— she was always hungry and could not wait to feast on the bad heart. The divine baboon Babi also hungered for the souls of the dead.

If the heart was lighter than the feather, the god Horus led the soul to Osiris, god of the underworld, and the judges who assisted him. They decided whether the soul was to serve Osiris, join Ra in his great barque (see pages 94–95), or spend a happy life with their loved ones in the Field of Reeds.

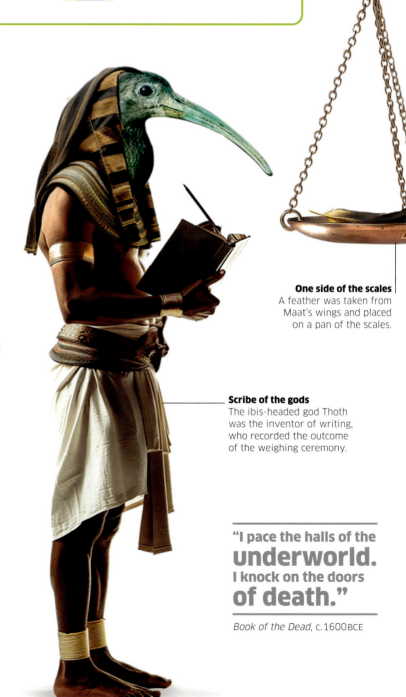

One side of the scales
A feather was taken from Maat's wings and placed on a pan of the scales.

Scribe of the gods
The ibis-headed god Thoth was the inventor of writing, who recorded the outcome of the weighing ceremony.

> "I pace the halls of the **underworld. I knock on the doors of death.**"
>
> *Book of the Dead*, c. 1600 BCE

75 The process of mummification involved seventy-five rituals.

42 There were forty-two **judges in the Hall of Two Truths**, along with **Osiris**, who **decided on the fate** of the soul.

The **Field of Reeds** was thought to be a **perfect version** of Egypt.

99

Monkey deity
Babi was the bloodthirsty, soul-eating chief of monkeys, who looked down at the ceremony from the top of the scales.

Winged goddess
The goddess Maat kept the universe in order. She was usually depicted sitting down with her wings spread out.

Heart of the dead
The heart of the deceased was placed on a pan to be judged on its weight.

A final check
Anubis checked the level on the scales before each weighing to ensure that the result was always fair.

Ammit
This beast had the head of a crocodile, the upper body of a lion, and the rear of a hippopotamus.

Weighing of the heart
In the Hall of Two Truths, a person's heart was weighed against a divine feather. If the heart did not outweigh the feather, the soul of the person was considered to be good.

Judged soul
The soul awaited their judgment in the hall, hoping its heart was lighter than the feather.

SUPREME DEITIES

Most cultures believe in an all-powerful creator, who usually lives in the sky. This being is capable of bringing order to the universe and creating humans. They tend to distance themselves from the world, instead communicating with humans through lesser gods, such as nature spirits.

Mbombo
The creator god of the Kuba people from the Congo Basin was a giant called Mbombo. Feeling a pain in his stomach, he vomited the sun, the moon, and the stars. Once the Earth was created he threw up nine animals, one of which was the iguana, and then he created the first men.

IGUANA

Enkai
In the tales of the Maasai people from East Africa, Enkai is the sky god (see pages 108–109). He once told people to leave their enclosures open at night, but not everyone obeyed him. Those who did were given cows, sheep, and goats. They became the Maasai. The ones who didn't remained hunters and became the Dorobo.

Unkulunkulu
When the god Unkulunkulu of the Zulu people created humans, he sent Unwaba the chameleon to tell people that they would live forever. Unwaba was slow. In the meantime, the god changed his mind and sent the gecko Intulo to tell humans that they were mortal. He was faster and when he delivered the message, it became law.

Chameleon
Known as Unwaba, the chameleon basked in the sun for too long.

Gecko
The lizard Intulo took his job seriously and delivered the message.

SOUTH OF THE SAHARA

Myths from south of the Sahara began to be recorded in the 19th century, although they have existed for thousands of years. Due to the migrations of people that took place over time, new beliefs have spread from group to group, leading to a rise of new stories. There are many cultural groups, so there isn't one common element in their tales. But tricksters, heroes, and animal spirits make a regular appearance.

ANIMAL SPIRITS

Certain animals are considered to be helpers and guardians. These animals are not allowed to be killed. For example, the lion is a totem for the Bataung people of South Africa and lions cannot be harmed or eaten. Some groups believe that spirits can appear in the form of animals to guide humans.

Following the python
A mythical python plays a central role in a tale explaining how the Kom people found their current settlement in Laikom, Cameroon. While the leader of the Kom lay dying, he told his people to watch for a snake. After his death, a python appeared and led the people from Babessi to Laikom.

CULTURE HEROES

There are a number of inspiring figures from south of the Sahara. They are often people born with outstanding abilities and weapons ready in hand. A popular hero from the Congo Basin is Mwindo (see pages 110–111), whose powers and magical fly swatter could defeat even the gods.

Moshanyana
Chief of the Basuto people of Southern Africa, Moshanyana was born fully armed and wearing a necklace of bones that could be used to cast spells. As a young boy, he killed a monster and cut open its belly, releasing all the people it had eaten.

Woot
The Kuba, who are often known as the "children of Woot," believe that Woot was the first human. He named all the animals and taught people languages. As a hunter, Woot's ability and strength were unmatched.

Kuba mask
Masks representing Woot are worn in dances during festivals.

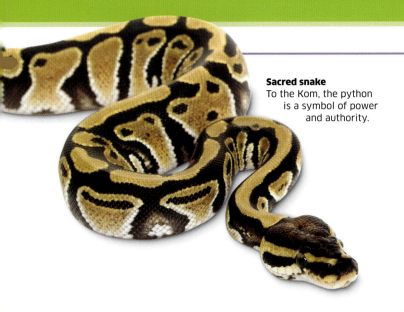

Sacred snake
To the Kom, the python is a symbol of power and authority.

Tumbuka tales
In the mythology of the Tumbuka, a people of Malawi, stories are told accompanied by drumming and song to teach and entertain children. Popular characters include Kalulu the trickster hare, Fulu the wise tortoise, and Chimbwi the evil hyena.

Kalulu
This clever hare could outwit anyone to get out of a tricky situation.

Fulu
The wise tortoise taught the value of patience and intellect.

Chimbwi
The hyena's selfishness and greed always led to his downfall.

Lonkundo
The founder of the Mongo people of the Congo Basin was Lonkundo. The first people didn't have any survival skills, so Lonkundo taught them how to hunt. He set a trap using a long, flexible twig where animals were known to pass by.

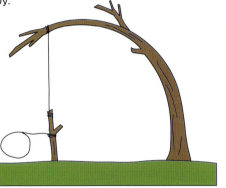

TRICKSTERS
The most well-known trickster in Africa is Ananse, whose stories have spread from West Africa as far as the Caribbean and the US (see pages 106–107). There are many other tricksters from Africa who are able to triumph over others by using creativity and wit.

Ture
In the tales of the Zande people, Ture liked to steal things, including fire for humans and a special shield that made the sound of a drum.

Hlakanyana
Stories from the Xhosa and Zulu peoples describe Hlakanyana as someone who enjoyed tricking people out of food.

Shamba Bolongongo
Based on a real king from the Congo Basin who ruled in the first half of the 17th century, Shamba taught his people many skills, such as making clothes from raffia fibers, cooking cassava root, and extracting oil from palm seeds. He disliked violence and only used his dagger when it was absolutely necessary.

Wooden figure
Shamba was often depicted sitting cross-legged, holding a ceremonial knife.

THE AFRICAN DIASPORA
The communities around the world descended from African people are together known as the African diaspora. Africans carried their languages and traditions with them across the Atlantic during the slave trade, and their sacred stories blended with local beliefs in the Americas and the Caribbean.

Br'er Rabbit
Tales of the trickster Ananse traveled with the Ashanti people of Ghana to the United States and the Caribbean. Ananse's exploits were adapted in the stories of Br'er Rabbit who, like Ananse, used clever strategies to outsmart his foes.

Smart rabbit
Br'er rabbit featured in short stories, in which he outsmarted his enemies Br'er Fox and Br'er Bear.

Haitian loa
The traditions of the Yoruba and the Fon formed the "voodoo" religions as a result of the slave trade. Haitian Vodou developed in Haiti and spread to the United States. In Vodou, the spirits known as loas get their name from African deities.

Papa Legba
Holding a cane, Papa Legba stands at the gates of the spirit world.

Baron Samedi
This loa of healing and death wears a top hat, glasses, and a tail coat.

Maman Brigitte
Associated with the black rooster, this loa blesses gravestones.

africa ○ YORUBA SACRED STORIES

Olorun is a **Yoruba word** meaning **"Lord of Heaven."**

⊙ THE ORISHA
The natural world is a source of inspiration for the Yoruba and they show their love for Olorun by caring for all the creatures of the world. Most of the spirits known as the orisha are spirits of nature, representing its many aspects, while some are also the spirits of ancestors and even saints.

Nature spirits
Worshippers connect with the orisha because they provide strength and help as the earthly representatives of the Yoruba's powerful god, Olorun. In order to gain an orisha's favor, people make offerings to them, which might include their favorite food and gifts. There are hundreds of orishas. Below are a selection of the main ones.

Eshu
Also known as Elegua, Eshu opens doors and clears obstacles.

Yemaya
This spirit protects women and is known as the Queen of the Ocean.

Oshun
River spirit Oshun brings good fortune in the form of love and wealth.

Chango
With a hammer in hand, Chango brings violent thunderstorms.

Obatala
The benevolent creator Obatala is symbolized by a white dove.

Oya
By unleashing powerful storms and winds, Oya brings change.

Orunmila
A spirit of prophecy, Orunmila shares the wisdom of Olorun.

Ogun
This spirit is a master metalworker who makes weapons of war.

Yoruba sacred stories

The Yoruba people of West Africa have a rich heritage of stories evolved from a mix of different communities. Their myths, which have been passed down through many generations, reflect this diversity.

The supreme god of the Yoruba is Olorun, who created the universe, day and night, and the seasons, and who decided the fate of every living being. Since Olorun has no gender and is considered to be everywhere, there are no depictions of them. The Yoruba do not contact their supreme god directly, but through their worship of the orishas—spirits that represent the positive and negative sides of nature.

Passing messages
The orisha Eshu served as a messenger between the heavens and Earth. It was also his job to protect the other orishas so they didn't come to any harm. As an unpredictable figure, he caused mischief as a way of getting the attention of his followers.

Eshu's instrument
This ornate wooden figurine of Eshu carved by the Yoruba people in Nigeria shows the orisha playing the flute.

Young and old
Eshu could be depicted as a young boy or as an old man, as shown here, because he symbolized the beginning and end of life.

Hat trick
In one story, two women were happily working in the fields when Eshu walked past them wearing a hat that was white on one side and red on the other. When he was gone, the first woman remarked how nice his red hat looked. This angered the second woman who argued that his hat was white. They fought, and only found peace by offering a sacrifice to Eshu.

1,400 Some **West African myths** claim there are more than **1,400** orishas.

The **clever trickster tortoise** named **Ajapa** is a **popular character** in West African folklore.

CREATION OF THE WORLD
In the Yoruba creation myth, there was nothing but sky and sea in the beginning. Obatala, the son of Olorun, wanted to make dry land for creatures to thrive, so he visited Orunmila for advice. With her help, Obatala created the new and vast land he named Ife, meaning "sacred place."

> "TO EACH GOD OBATALA SAID, I PLAN TO CREATE SOLID LAND WHERE NOW THERE IS NOTHING BUT WATER."
> Yoruba creation myth

A destructive flood
The water deity Olokun was unhappy with Olorun's creation, as Olorun had taken over her oceans without permission. She sent terrible floods, which almost completely submerged Ife, but Orunmila cast spells to calm them, and Ife returned to normal.

Ingredients for creation
Orunmila told Obatala to take a hen, a cat, a palm nut, and a sand-filled snail shell to Earth. On arrival, Obatala emptied the shell and freed the hen, which scattered the sand to form hills. The palm nut grew immediately, filling the landscape with trees. Ife was beautiful, and the cat kept Obatala company, but he eventually became lonely. So after drinking some palm wine, he dug into the sand and found clay from which he drunkenly created humans.

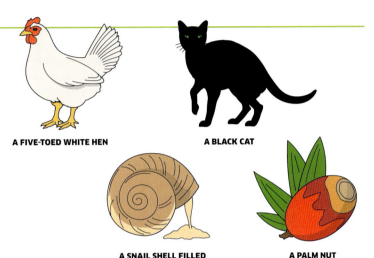

A FIVE-TOED WHITE HEN

A BLACK CAT

A SNAIL SHELL FILLED WITH SAND

A PALM NUT

WEST AFRICAN FOLKTALES
The Yoruba stories told to children are bursting with humor. Some tales seek to warn them of the dangers in the world, while others aim to explain how something came to be.

Tortoise and Lion
Lion was always showing off his strength and speed, so Tortoise challenged him to a race. As Lion sped off, Tortoise asked some birds to carry him over the finish line. Lion was so stunned when he saw that Tortoise had beaten him that he learned not to underestimate others again.

Leopard's spots
One day, a young boy was on his way home from playing in the forest when he remembered that he had left behind his yam. He returned to find it, but saw that the scary Leopard was stalking him. The boy poked at Leopard with a stick dipped in dye, which covered him with spots. And this is how the leopard became dotted all over!

Tortoise and Baboon
Baboon once tricked Tortoise by inviting him to dinner, but kept the cooking pot in a tree, far from his guest's reach. Tortoise took revenge by asking Baboon over for dinner the next day and telling him the food would only be served once his hands were clean. Because Baboon used his hands to walk, they always got more mud from the floor on them after washing, so they were never clean.

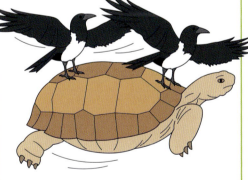

> "MY LITTLE YAM— MY LITTLE YAM O I LEFT YOU BEHIND IN THE BUSH MY MOTHER WARNED ME NOT TO LEAVE YOU ABOUT."
> Ayodele Ogundipe, *Esu Elegbara*, 2018

A LEOPARD MASK FROM BENIN

Crocodile's knobbly skin
Long ago, Crocodile had skin as smooth as silk. He would bask under the light of the full Moon each month to receive praise from the other animals. He sought their compliments more frequently, so he started sunbathing every day. His skin soon burned and became rough under the heat and the animals began laughing at him instead. Crocodile was embarrassed and disappeared underwater. He rarely emerges to this day.

A CHACMA BABOON

A WEST AFRICAN CROCODILE

104 africa ○ MAWU-LISA

Among **Mawu-Lisa's** children were **Da Zodji**, god of the Earth; **So**, god of thunder; and **Agbé**, god of the sea.

Four days of creation
Mawu-Lisa's first children were the gods and goddesses of the Fon. After they were born, humans were created. Mawu made the Earth and, together with Lisa, taught people how to survive. All this took place in just four days.

Day one
Mawu-Lisa gave birth to seven major deities and made humans out of clay.

Day two
Aido-Hwedo and Mawu made the Earth, a place fit for humans to live.

Day three
Humans received the gifts of sight and speech.

Day four
Mawu-Lisa taught humans the skills of farming and metalworking.

Mawu-Lisa and the cosmic serpent
Mawu was the goddess of the Earth and the moon, while Lisa was the god of the sky and the sun. Aido-Hwedo was a blue and red serpent, although some myths claim that he was a dragon.

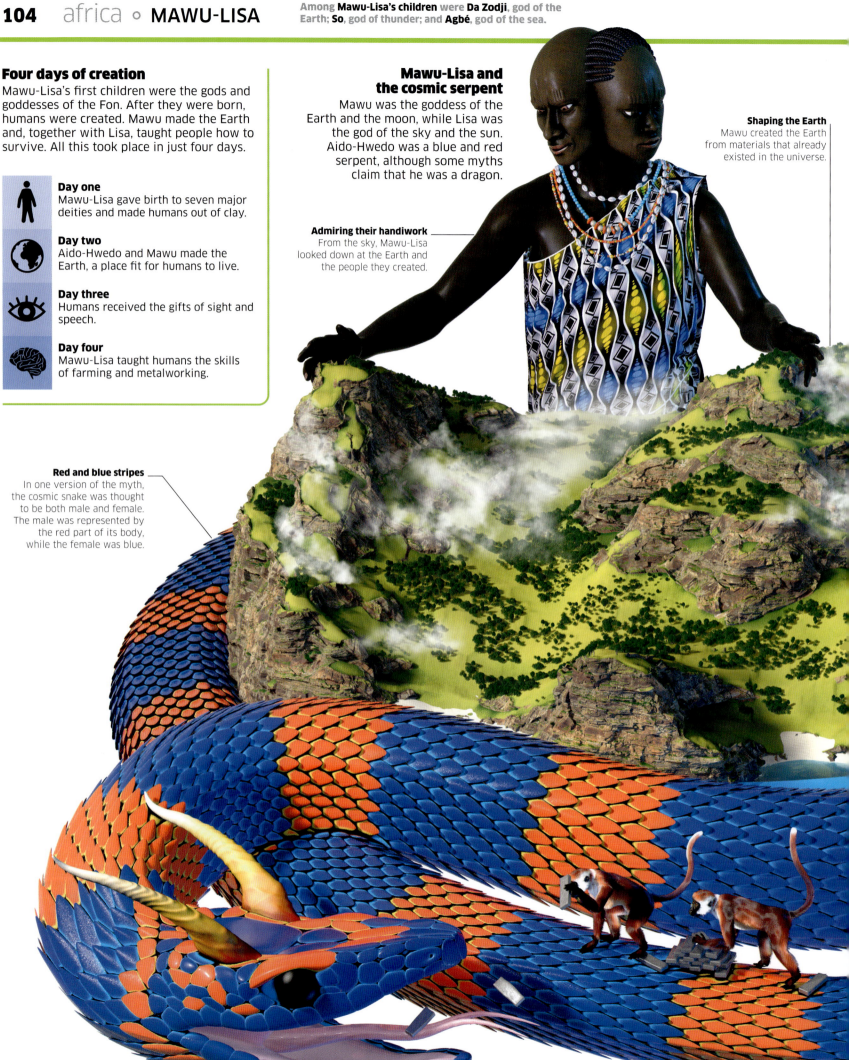

Admiring their handiwork
From the sky, Mawu-Lisa looked down at the Earth and the people they created.

Shaping the Earth
Mawu created the Earth from materials that already existed in the universe.

Red and blue stripes
In one version of the myth, the cosmic snake was thought to be both male and female. The male was represented by the red part of its body, while the female was blue.

In one version of the myth, the cosmic serpent arched across the sky from **edge to edge** and **curved around** the world.

2,000,000 More than **2,000,000** people from the countries of **Benin**, **Nigeria**, and **Togo** speak the **Fon language**.

Aido-Hwedo
Also known as the rainbow serpent, Aido-Hwedo was a powerful deity to the Fon. He was created before Mawu-Lisa and became a faithful servant to the god. A generous spirit, the cosmic snake provided good health and love to his worshippers.

Swallowing his tail
This circular sculpture of Aido-Hwedo is located at a shrine in Ouidah, Benin.

Mawu-Lisa

The Fon people of modern-day Benin in West Africa believe in a powerful twin deity called Mawu-Lisa, who often share the same body. Mawu, the female twin, created the world with the help of the sacred serpent Aido-Hwedo.

At the beginning of time, there was Mawu, the goddess whose eyes were the moon. Lisa was a god whose eyes were the sun. The two deities often united as Mawu-Lisa and sometimes they were two separate deities. From their union, the other gods and goddesses were born.

Mawu moulded the first humans from clay. Deciding that they needed a place to live, she called on the divine serpent Aido-Hwedo. Mawu took her seat in the serpent's mouth and rode through the universe. Together, they made the Earth, carving its slopes and valleys with the sinuous coils of Aido-Hwedo as he moved. Wherever they stayed the night, the serpent's manure would harden into towering mountains enriched with gold, iron, and other minerals. When their job was done, the pair stopped to rest and admire their handiwork. It looked as though the weight of the hills, rivers, and trees would cause the Earth to collapse. So Mawu asked Aido-Hwedo to place himself underneath the Earth to support it. The serpent coiled around the world, which kept it from falling apart—but his movements caused earthquakes.

To keep Aido-Hwedo cool, Mawu created the sea. To feed the snake, monkeys who lived under the sea forged iron bars and threw them into his mouth. These monkeys worked tirelessly to keep the serpent alive. At the end of time, it is believed that these bars will run out and a starving Aido-Hwedo will chew his own tail. This will cause him to lose balance, and the Earth and everything on it will slide into the sea.

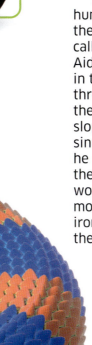

Red helpers
A troop of red monkeys were in charge of feeding the giant snake.

Mawu and Monkey
Once Mawu had created people, she started making animals out of clay. She told Monkey that, since he had fingers, she would make him equal to humans, but first he must help her make more animals. Instead of following this task, Monkey boasted that he was better than the other animals. Hearing this, Mawu cursed Monkey from ever walking upright.

Monkey's mischief
Monkey was caught singing "Tomorrow I will be a man! Tomorrow I will be a man!" so Mawu punished him.

Tales of Ananse

The trickster god Ananse has weaved his way into the legends of West Africa for centuries. These tales have come to be known as the spider stories.

Ananse (also spelled Anansi) first appeared in the stories told by the Ashanti people of Ghana. They described a cunning trickster who could outsmart anyone. Sometimes he played pranks to get out of danger, or simply to prove that wit was superior to strength. At the beginning of time, he was a messenger of the sky god Nyame. As more people talked about this sneaky spider, word of Ananse spread across the African continent, and eventually, the world.

WORKING FOR NYAME

The sky god Nyame created humans, but he was never directly involved with them. Ananse lived on Earth and heard people complaining about having no time to rest after work. The spider god asked Nyame for help and he created night as a time for sleeping, and made the moon so people wouldn't be afraid of the dark. When people shivered from the cold, Ananse told the sky god, who created the sun.

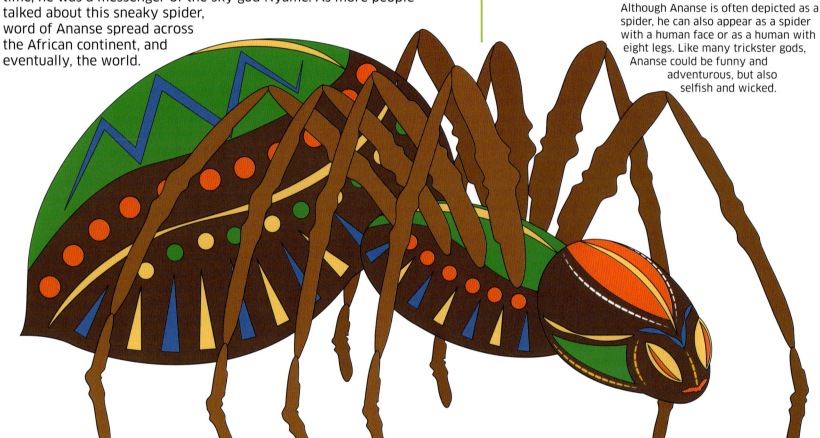

The spider god
Although Ananse is often depicted as a spider, he can also appear as a spider with a human face or as a human with eight legs. Like many trickster gods, Ananse could be funny and adventurous, but also selfish and wicked.

THE OWNER OF STORIES
Ananse had an endless thirst for knowledge. He wanted to buy all the stories in existence from Nyame, but he had to bring the sky god some animals as a form of payment.

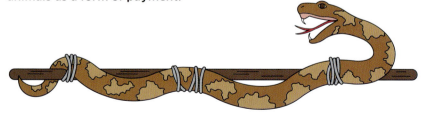

Snake snare
Ananse tricked the python by asking him whether he was longer than his staff. When the python lay next to it to check, Ananse quickly tied him to it.

Completing tasks
Nyame ordered Ananse to bring him a collection of creatures, including a python, a leopard, and some hornets. Ananse told the hornets to take shelter from the rain in a calabash gourd and sealed it shut, and tied the python to a branch. He then dug a hole and covered it with branches, which the leopard fell into. When he gave them to the sky god, he received all the stories.

Calabash containers
In West Africa, gourds are made from the dried-out shells of the calabash fruit, and they are used as containers for carrying liquids such as water.

Gourd full of wisdom
Once Ananse had all the stories, he needed to keep them safe. He stored them in the gourd of a calabash fruit and carried it to the top of a tree where no one could reach it. He tried tying the gourd to a branch, but it fell and shattered. The rain washed away the contents of the gourd and the wisdom and stories spread all over the world.

Ananse had **six children**. They were named **See All**, **Roadbuilder**, **Riverdrinker**, **Fishcutter**, **Spellcaster**, and **Cushion**.

The **Ashanti of West Africa** believe that Ananse taught people the skills of **writing**, **agriculture**, and **hunting**.

STORIES OF ANANSE AND TIGER

Ananse couldn't resist playing tricks on other animals, especially Tiger. Tales featuring Ananse and Tiger are told in the Caribbean, where many people of West African descent now live. Tiger stands for any big cat, and represents strength.

Tiger in the pit
One day, Ananse heard a distressed roar. He saw Tiger trapped in a deep, dark pit. As he was struggling to claw his way out, Ananse teased Tiger for his own amusement. When Tiger was almost at the top, Ananse told him to pray for more strength. Tiger foolishly put his paws together to pray and fell all the way back down again.

Tasty treat
Peanuts are grown across West Africa, Haiti, Dominican Republic, and Jamaica and are used in dishes such as soups.

Ananse and the tar-stump
Tiger set a trap to catch the thief who kept stealing his delicious peanuts. He covered a tree stump in sticky tar and waited. It wasn't long before Ananse came to steal some peanuts and got stuck. Tiger told Ananse he would burn him as punishment, and set up a fire. Ananse thought quickly, telling Tiger it was good luck to jump near the fire. When Tiger jumped, Ananse pushed him into the flames.

Test of strength
Another time, Ananse and Tiger clashed over who was the strongest. Ananse whacked Tiger over the head with a hammer that was hidden up his sleeve. Tiger was shocked at Ananse's strength, and warned him he would get him back next time. Later that day, Ananse asked Deer to his house and let him answer the door to Tiger. Assuming it was Ananse, Tiger hit Deer so hard it killed him. Having escaped another blow, the trickster ate Deer for dinner.

Escape plan
Tiger once became so hungry that he tried to eat Ananse and Goat. They ran away and came to a river, but Goat couldn't swim so Ananse turned Goat into a pebble and leapt to the other side of the river. When Tiger arrived at the water's edge, Ananse taunted him, so Tiger threw the pebble at him and when it landed on the other side, it turned back into Goat. Ananse and Goat escaped safe and sound.

GREEDY ANANSE

In some stories, Ananse is a selfish spider with a big appetite. He was too lazy to find food himself, so he let others do the hard work and used trickery for his own gain. In the end, he learned that he had to suffer the consequences for acting selfishly.

Grandma's pot of beans
Ananse paid a visit to his Grandma, but she wasn't home. In her kitchen, she left a note warning him not to eat her bean stew in the pot as it was too hot. But he couldn't help himself and lifted the lid. After taking in a whiff, he spooned the stew into his hat and began eating. Soon he heard his Grandma approaching the house. In a panic, Ananse put his hat back on and the hot beans cooked the hair off his head!

Hot cooking pot
Traditional cooking pots are used across West Africa to heat food over open fires and make tasty stews.

> "ANANSE IS A SPIDER WHO LOVES TO BREAK THE RULES, HE'S REALLY RATHER CLEVER 'THOUGH HE'S NEVER BEEN TO SCHOOL."
>
> "Ananse the Spider," Ghanaian song

Ananse and Vulture
After stealing Rabbit's fruit and vegetables, Ananse took them to the market and sold them all. He put the money in a basket and bought some corn for his dinner. On the way home, he left the basket on the side of the road to shelter from the rain. He thought the corn would hide the money, but Vulture spotted the basket and spread out his wings to protect it. When Ananse emerged to thank him, Vulture claimed it was his basket. The village chief settled the debate by giving the basket to Vulture. Ananse burst into tears.

108 africa • THE BLACK AND RED GODS

Mount Meru in **Tanzania** is thought to be En-kai's **home**.

Red eye
The red god is sometimes depicted with fiery red eyes to symbolize the scorching sun.

Dark as the rainclouds
The color of the black god's skin symbolizes the dark clouds that deliver rain.

Nomadic farmers
Rain is crucial for the survival of the Maasai, which is why the two gods are central to their beliefs.

1 The Maasai people are **monotheistic**, which means they believe in **one god**—En-kai.

En-kai is **worshipped by the Maasai** through rituals and ceremonies, as a way of **showing their devotion** to the god.

109

Fighting in the sky
According to Maasai beliefs, the red god always wants to bring about chaos and destruction on Earth but the black god, who stands in his way, protects humanity.

Maasai dress
The gods are often shown to be wearing traditional Maasai clothing, although En-kai is believed to be formless.

The black and red gods

The forces of good and evil clash in this sacred story from east Africa. The nomadic tribe known as the Maasai believe in a black god, called En-kai Narok, who is at odds with a vengeful red god, En-kai Na-nyokie.

The Maasai people from Kenya and northern Tanzania rely heavily on rain to water their crops and feed their cattle. So they have a deep connection with the sky, which is closely linked to their spiritual beliefs. The powerful god En-kai can appear as two opposing gods: En-kai Narok ("black god") and En-kai Na-nyokie ("red god"). The gods' colors indicated En-kai's moods. Both gods are worshipped to bring rain.

As the black god, En-kai was kind, considerate, and embodied thunder. When En-kai was red, he was feared by his people because he was quick to anger and brought droughts. He existed in the form of lightning. The two gods lived in the sky, where the black god was closer to Earth and the red god lived above him.

One day, when a terrible famine spread across the land, the black god asked the red god to release rain for the starving people and animals. At first En-kai Na-nyokie hesitated, but later gave in and made it rain.

After some time, the red god complained that enough rain had fallen, but the black god begged him to continue releasing water from the sky because the ground was still dry. Again, the red god agreed, although he wasn't happy about it. A few days passed by and the red god decided that enough rain had fallen so he made it stop. The black god was displeased and the two gods argued and then fought.

The Maasai people believe that when there is thunder and lightning, it is the red god En-kai Na-nyokie fighting to get past the black god En-kai Narok. The red god seeks to punish people because he believes they are spoiled.

The first cattle
Cattle are central to the Maasai's way of life because they rely on them for food, clothing, and shelter. The first cattle are believed to have descended from the sky. The first Maasai man, Maasinta, had built an enclosure for the animals and in the night En-kai sent them down from a rope that hung from a thundercloud.

Respect for animals
The Maasai see it as their duty to respect and protect all living creatures created by En-kai, not just the cattle in their farms. Wild animals are rarely killed, even in times of drought or famine.

Birds
Birds are used to make elaborate headdresses but are never eaten.

Snake
Dead spirits are thought to inhabit the bodies of snakes.

Lion
Lions are symbols of courage and strength.

Aardvark spirit
Also believed to be a god, Ntumba ruled over his kingdom of Munundu in the underworld.

Ready for combat
Mwindo held an ax in one hand and his conga-scepter in the other, both of which he used as weapons.

Sharp weapon
Mwindo carried an adze-ax with him—a cutting tool he was born holding, along with his magical conga-scepter.

Fleeing father
Shemwindo hid behind the friendly aardvark spirit Ntumba who ended up being punished by Mwindo.

> "I am Mwindo,
> the one born walking,
> the one born talking."
>
> Aaron Shepard,
> *The Magic Flyswatter*, 2008

The jungle underground
The lush jungle of the underworld was full of obstacles and spirits. Blocking Mwindo's way out of the underworld was Ntumba, the generous aardvark spirit, who was cursed with a disease by the boy hero for protecting his father Shemwindo.

Hidden beauty
The underworld is depicted as an underground jungle rich in all kinds of animal, plant, and spirit life.

The adventures of Mwindo

Folktales from the Nyanga people of the Congo Basin describe the outrageous feats of the boy hero Mwindo. He could travel anywhere, including the sky, the sea, and the underworld. He used his magical conga-scepter (flyswatter) to attack anything that threatened him.

The evil chief Shemwindo ruled over the village of Tubondo and ordered his wives to give birth only to girls. When his son Mwindo was born, Shemwindo tried to kill him many times. Since Mwindo survived every time, the chief locked him in a drum and threw him into a river.

Farther downstream, Mwindo's aunt Iyangura found the drum and released him. The next day, Mwindo set out for Tubondo with an army of warriors, which included his uncles. At the start of the conflict, Mwindo stayed behind and let his forces attack the village. But just as Shemwindo was about to claim victory, the boy hero stepped in and burned the village to ashes. Seeing the destruction, Shemwindo ran away to the underworld. Mwindo followed him closely.

When Mwindo arrived in the underworld, its ruler Muisa gave him a set of tasks to complete before he would give up Shemwindo.

However, once Mwindo had successfully performed the tasks, Muisa confessed that Shemwindo had already left. In frustration, Mwindo beat up the underworld god and went to find his father.

Mwindo confronted Shemwindo on his way out of the underworld and was ready to strike him with his conga-scepter. But Shemwindo hid behind the giant aardvark spirit Ntumba, so Mwindo slapped the aardvark out of the way with his flyswatter, and chased his father to the sky. There, Mwindo was set more tasks by Sheburungu, the sky god. After Mwindo had completed them, the sky god released Shemwindo, who apologized for trying to kill Mwindo. Back on Earth, the boy hero rebuilt Tubondo and became its powerful ruler.

The trials of Mwindo
Muisa asked Mwindo to complete a "little task" for him in the underworld. It was, in fact, very difficult and so Mwindo resorted to using his powers to help him. When Muisa found out, he tried to strangle Mwindo with a magical belt, but he failed, so he gave Mwindo another task.

Growing bananas
Mwindo was given a day to harvest a banana crop. He cheated by using his powers to complete the task. A servant of the underworld god caught Mwindo and told his master.

Collecting honey
Mwindo had to collect a bucket of honey from a tree. He succeeded after smoking out the killer bees and asking Nkuba, the god of lightning, to blow up the tree with a thunderbolt.

112 · africa · STORIES OF THE SAN

100,000 The **oldest relatives** of the San people first inhabited Africa about **100,000 years ago**.

ACTS OF CREATION

The San stories of creation describe how !Kaggen emerged, and took part in creating the world. In these stories !Kaggen, also known as Mantis, is wise and generous.

White flower
The flower was waiting for the morning to arrive in order to open fully.

The first human
In the beginning, a bee carried Mantis over the dark waters of a river. The bee was exhausted and spotted a half-open white flower floating on the water. The bee dropped Mantis on the flower, placing the seed of the first human inside Mantis, and died. When the flower bloomed, Mantis woke up and the seed from inside him grew into the first human being.

!Kaggen's world
At first, humans and animals lived together in harmony and set up home underground. !Kaggen wanted everyone to live above ground, so he made a special tree, known as the "World Tree," to attract them. When the creatures relocated, !Kaggen warned them against using fire because it was destructive. One day, the people disobeyed him and lit a fire for warmth. The animals fled in panic, and from that day on, animals and people ceased to live peacefully together.

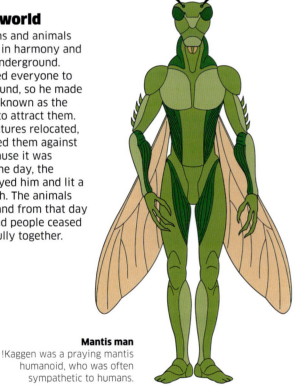

Mantis man
!Kaggen was a praying mantis humanoid, who was often sympathetic to humans.

Stories of the San

The grassy tropical plains known as savanna are central to the stories of the San people, a culture of hunter-gatherers who live in southern Africa. Their stories often feature the animals found around them.

Having roamed the regions of Botswana, Namibia, and South Africa for thousands of years, the San people have a vast knowledge of the animals and plants around them, particularly the bee, the praying mantis, and the eland (a type of antelope). The San people tell their stories in groups through elaborate performances and rituals, which often feature !Kaggen—a humanoid mantis and a trickster god.

Eland art
The eland is depicted in many cave paintings in southern Africa as a symbol of strength.

The sacred eland
!Kaggen made the first eland—a very large variety of African antelope. He soaked a shoe in water and fed it lots of honey, nurturing it into the eland. When the eland was grown, !Kaggen left it alone while he went to find food. The god Kwammang-a, who had been watching !Kaggen in secret, shot the animal dead. !Kaggen was devastated when he found it. He pierced its gall bladder, which released a dark fluid that covered the world. To give light, !Kaggen threw the gall bladder into the sky, where it turned into the moon.

Changing forms
Shape-shifting is common in San stories, with !Kaggen himself having the ability to take on many forms. Although the god was usually half-man, half-praying mantis, he could transform into other animals for many reasons, one of which was to trick people.

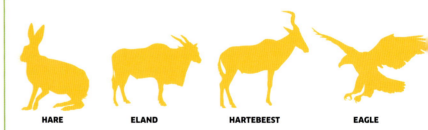

HARE   **ELAND**   **HARTEBEEST**   **EAGLE**

Story of the sun
The sun was once a man who lived in a hut and created enough light to brighten his home. One day, a group of children were told to go and visit the man when he was asleep and throw him up into the sky. When they tossed him into the air, the man remained in the sky, shining as the sun forever.

ADVENTURES OF THE MANTIS
As well as being an important god of creation, Mantis was thought to have humanlike characteristics and was not prayed to. Some stories describe him as being a playful figure who went on many adventures.

How Ostrich lost his fire
Before people had fire, they ate raw meat and spent the night in darkness. This changed when Mantis saw Ostrich sneakily dipping food in flames hidden beneath its wing before eating it. Mantis hatched a cunning plan and asked Ostrich to pick some ripe plums from the treetops. As Ostrich spread its wings out to reach the plums, the flames fanned out and Mantis grabbed the fire. He shared it with everyone and their lives were changed from that day on.

Embarrassed Ostrich
When Mantis stole fire from Ostrich, the bird was so ashamed, it never flew again.

The trickster hartebeest
One day, Mantis heard the noise of children approaching. He quickly transformed into a hartebeest and laid down in the grass, pretending to be dead. The children couldn't believe their luck and started cutting up the hartebeest for dinner, until the flesh began to move around and the head started talking to them. The children screamed and ran away. Mantis reattached his body and chased them.

Blessed hartebeest
The San people believe that the hartebeest has supernatural powers, so their bones are used to make special hunting tools.

TALES IN THE WILD
San stories are full of amazing adventures and humorous characters inspired by the southern African landscape and the animals that live there. These tales are sometimes told to teach morals—what's right and wrong.

Monkey's fiddle
Monkey had a bow and arrow, and a fiddle—a musical instrument—that could make anyone dance. When Wolf stole Monkey's bow and arrow, the pair fought over it. The animals sentenced Monkey to death, believing that the weapon belonged to Wolf. At this point, Monkey began playing his fiddle, forcing everyone in an endless dance. They begged Monkey to stop. He agreed, but only if Wolf gave up the weapon. Exhausted from dancing, Wolf returned the bow and arrow, and Monkey was freed.

"T-SIE, T-SIE, T-SIE, I AM THE HIGHEST, I AM KING," **TINK-TINKJE MOCKED.** THERE HE WAS AGAIN, HAVING CREPT OUT FROM UNDER THE WING OF VULTURE.
Tink-tinkje, South African story

Elephant and Tortoise
During a drought, Elephant found a waterhole and ordered Tortoise to guard it. While Elephant was away, some animals asked Tortoise for a drink but they were turned away. Lion, who wouldn't take no for an answer, drank all the water. When Elephant came back, he was furious and swallowed Tortoise. Inside his body, Tortoise tore Elephant's organs, killing him. Tortoise walked out of his body triumphantly.

Elephant paintings
The San were the first people to depict elephants in southern Africa, which are seen as symbols of power.

The Tink-tinkje bird
All the birds in the animal kingdom gathered to choose their king. One by one, each species was ruled out for a different reason. They agreed the best way to decide was to see which bird could fly the highest. Vulture looked like the winner as he flew to the sun, but then the tiny Tink-tinkje bird chirped above him, having latched on to his wing, so instead, the Tink-tinkje became king.

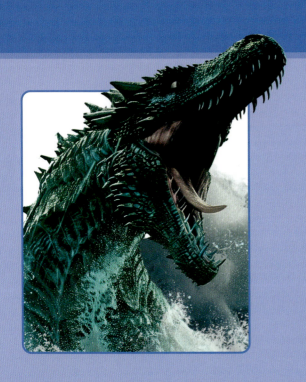

ASIA

The mythologies of Mesopotamia and other parts of West Asia contain some of the oldest known stories in the world. Farther east, sacred tales from India, China, and Japan form the basis for religions that are widely practiced today.

WEST ASIA

The site of some of the world's first cities, West Asia produced flourishing cultures that recorded many myths. Some of the world's first stories came from Mesopotamia, the land between the Tigris and Euphrates rivers in what is now Iraq. Cities such as Ur, Uruk, Babylon, and Ashur developed a highly organized religion that was based around enormous mud-brick temples known as ziggurats.

SOURCES

Much of what we know about Mesopotamian myths and the gods and creatures that appear in them was recorded in clay or stone. This has allowed these stories and images to survive until the modern day.

TABLET WITH PART OF THE EPIC OF GILGAMESH

Clay tablets
Mesopotamian priests inscribed religious stories on clay tablets. These tablets survived with their inscriptions still intact and legible despite centuries of exposure to the elements.

WINGED GENIE CARVING FROM ASSYRIA

Stone reliefs
The palaces and temples of Mesopotamian cities were decorated with stone reliefs (carvings on a flat surface). Many of these reliefs showed mythical creatures that were regarded as guardian figures who watched over the building and its inhabitants, protecting them from evil.

ASSYRIAN CYLINDER SEAL AND ITS IMPRESSION, SHOWING ISHTAR (RIGHT)

Cylinder seals
These engraved cylinders were used to mark ownership or identification. The cylinder was rolled over a block of clay to create an image. Many cylinders were engraved with mythological scenes that cannot be found elsewhere.

HOMES OF THE GODS

Each Mesopotamian city was the home of a deity, and its central ziggurat served to house the god. A statue of the god was placed inside the ziggurat, and a ceremony known as "mouth washing" was performed. This allowed the god to eat and drink. Once this ritual was complete, the god was believed to be present in the city.

Ziggurats
Mesopotamian ziggurats were large buildings with external stairs that were believed to allow the gods to climb up to and descend from the heavens. The steps led to high platforms on which the priests performed rituals in honor of the city deity.

Great Ziggurat at Ur
Built in the 21st century BCE to honor the god Nanna, the ziggurat at Ur has been partially restored.

City Patrons
The gods that looked after each city were believed to want to expand and evolve that city's civilization. These gods owned the city temples and the lands surrounding them, and were believed to control the city itself.

Ashur
The city of Ashur (or Assur) was named after its patron god. When the city-state expanded into an empire, it became known as the Assyrian Empire.

KINGS AND PRIESTS

Though each Mesopotamian city had a patron deity who looked after the city's spiritual needs, they also had a king who governed over more day-to-day affairs. The worship of the gods was very important, so priests also had a great deal of political power.

Divine kings
The kings of each city were believed to have been appointed by heaven, an idea that created a relationship between the king and the gods. The first king to declare his divine status was Naram-Sin of Akkad in the 23rd century BCE.

Receiving the law
This stele (an upright, inscribed column of stone) lays out the law code of King Hammurabi, who is shown at the top receiving the laws from the god Shamash.

A SUCCESSION OF CULTURES

The first Mesopotamian cities were independent city-states, with myths centered around the patron god of the city. Some cities, such as Babylon and later Ashur, expanded in power to create great empires, and their stories then spread across a wider region.

Same gods, different names
The various Mesopotamian empires shared similar myths but with variations in language. Gods and goddesses had different names in different parts of the region. For example, Inanna from Sumer became known in Babylon as Ishtar, while Utu became Shamash.

The Babylonian Empire
Babylon was the most powerful city of the Babylonian Empire. Its temples to Marduk, and the city gate dedicated to the goddess Ishtar, were impressive structures, and showed the power of the city's religion.

Marduk's dragon
The walls of Babylon were decorated with images of animals, including the mushkhushshu, sacred beast of Marduk.

Sumerian name	Babylonian name	Role
Abzu	Apsu	Fresh water, the void before creation
An	Anu	The sky, father of the gods
Dumuzi	Tammuz	God of grain, beer, the seasons
Enki	Ea	Controller of fresh water, god of wisdom
Gugalanna	Nergal	Husband of Ereshkigal, goddess of death
Inanna	Ishtar	Goddess of love, fertility, and war
Nammu	Tiamat	Saltwater oceans
Nanna	Sin	The moon
Utu	Shamash	The sun, law-giver

The role of priests
Each city was looked after by a patron god, and priests interpreted the god's will. Mesopotamian priests could also read and write, so they were the ones who recorded laws, contracts, and stories of the gods.

Stamp seal
The image on this stamp seal may show a priest kneeling in front of a representative of the god Marduk.

BEYOND MESOPOTAMIA
There were other centers of early civilization and myth in West Asia outside of Mesopotamia. Stories have been preserved from the city of Ugarit in Canaan, the Hittite Empire in Anatolia, and the Zoroastrian religion in Persia, which still has worshippers to this day.

Ugarit
The city of Ugarit in Canaan (in modern-day Syria) flourished around 1500–1200BCE. Its myths were lost until the 20th century, when they were discovered on a collection of clay tablets.

Baal
The main character of many surviving Ugarit myths, Baal was a weather deity and king of the gods.

The Hittites
Based in Anatolia, in modern-day Türkiye, the Hittites founded a powerful empire in around 1450BCE. Their myths included many weather deities, because the Hittites adopted the gods of the people that they conquered.

Teshub
Combining the roles of a war and weather god, Teshub kept the people fed and protected them from enemies.

AHURA MAZDA

Zoroastrianism
This religion originated in Persia (modern-day Iran). At its heart lies the struggle between good, represented by the god Ahura Mazda, and evil, represented by Ahriman. The religion still has followers in Iran and among the Parsi community in India.

Marduk and Tiamat

The story of Marduk and Tiamat and their fierce battle was told as a part of an ancient Mesopotamian poem called the *Enuma Elish*, found carved into clay tablets in the ruined Library at Nineveh in modern-day Iraq.

At the beginning of time there were two seas, named Apsu and Tiamat. Apsu, the male deity, was made up of sweet, fresh water, while Tiamat, the female deity, was formed of salty sea water. Together, Apsu and Tiamat gave birth to new deities, including Anu, god of the sky, and Ea, leader of the younger gods.

The noise of their children angered Apsu, so he decided to kill them. Before Apsu could carry out his plans, however, Ea cast a spell that put Apsu to sleep and then killed him. He then built a temple over Apsu, which Ea made his home and which became the birthplace of his son Marduk.

Tiamat was angry with her children for killing Apsu, so she gathered together a group of monsters, led by one of her sons, Kingu, to destroy them. The gods were unable to defeat Tiamat, so they asked Marduk to fight her in single combat. He accepted on the condition that he be named ruler of the land. The gods agreed, and Marduk went into battle against Tiamat.

Using the power of the four winds, created by Anu and given to Marduk to use against Tiamat, Marduk managed to overcome her, trapping her in a net and killing her with an arrow. Marduk then divided Tiamat's body in two and created the heavens from one half and Earth from the other. He also destroyed Kingu, and used Kingu's blood to create the first humans.

3,300 The *Enuma Elish* was possibly written more than 3,300 years ago.

Patron of Babylon
After defeating Tiamat, Marduk built Babylon as the gateway to the gods, and became its patron. Babylon, in modern-day Iraq, became the most powerful city in Mesopotamia. Symbols representing Marduk, such as dragons, were found throughout Babylon, including on the Ishtar Gate, the eighth gate to the inner city of Babylon.

Replica of the Ishtar Gate
This replica of the Ishtar Gate replaced the original, which was built in the 6th century BCE.

Sea dragon
Tiamat was depicted as a fearsome, dragonlike creature.

1851 The Library at Nineveh was **first excavated** by Austen Henry Layard in 1851.

30,000 More than **30,000 clay tablets** were uncovered in the ruins of the **Library at Nineveh**.

119

Deadly weapon
Marduk killed Tiamat with an arrow that "pierced her heart."

Trapped in a net
Marduk's net trapped Tiamat and her army of monsters.

Four winds
Marduk used the violent four winds to weaken Tiamat during their battle.

Pulling the chariot
The horses pulling Marduk's chariot were described as "ferocious," "destructive," and "swift of pace."

Marduk's victory
Riding into battle on his chariot, pulled by his mighty, ferocious horses, Marduk cast his net and trapped Tiamat. Enraged, she opened her mouth to its fullest extent to devour him, but he drove the four winds down her throat. With his arrow, he delivered the final blow, piercing her heart and killing her.

asia • INANNA, QUEEN OF HEAVEN

Inanna's twin brother Utu was god of the sun and truth.

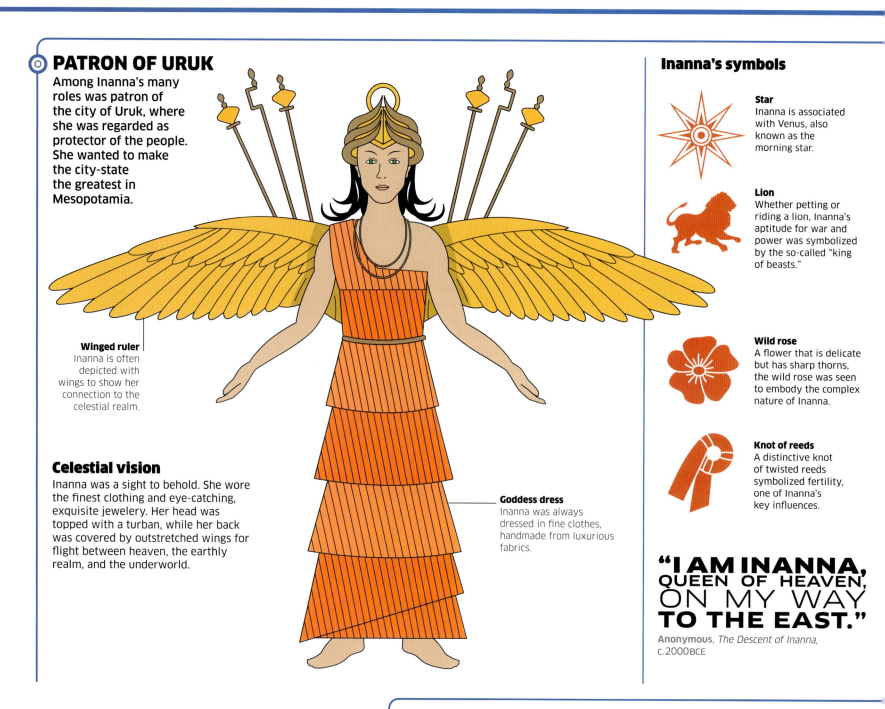

PATRON OF URUK
Among Inanna's many roles was patron of the city of Uruk, where she was regarded as protector of the people. She wanted to make the city-state the greatest in Mesopotamia.

Winged ruler
Inanna is often depicted with wings to show her connection to the celestial realm.

Celestial vision
Inanna was a sight to behold. She wore the finest clothing and eye-catching, exquisite jewelery. Her head was topped with a turban, while her back was covered by outstretched wings for flight between heaven, the earthly realm, and the underworld.

Goddess dress
Inanna was always dressed in fine clothes, handmade from luxurious fabrics.

Inanna's symbols

Star
Inanna is associated with Venus, also known as the morning star.

Lion
Whether petting or riding a lion, Inanna's aptitude for war and power was symbolized by the so-called "king of beasts."

Wild rose
A flower that is delicate but has sharp thorns, the wild rose was seen to embody the complex nature of Inanna.

Knot of reeds
A distinctive knot of twisted reeds symbolized fertility, one of Inanna's key influences.

> "I AM INANNA, QUEEN OF HEAVEN, ON MY WAY TO THE EAST."
> Anonymous, *The Descent of Inanna*, c. 2000 BCE

Inanna, Queen of Heaven

Inanna was the Sumerian goddess of love and fertility on Earth, but risked her life to visit her sister, the queen of the underworld.

For the people of ancient Mesopotamia, Inanna ranked among their most beloved deities because she played an important role in so many aspects of their lives, from love to war. Her influence over fertility was crucial for all life on Earth, and the story of her dangerous descent into the underworld explains the origins of the changing seasons.

THE SACRED LAWS
Ambitious and driven, Inanna worked hard to make Uruk the thriving center of Sumerian civilization, introducing sacred laws for her people to follow. One story tells how Inanna gained such knowledge.

Inanna visits Enki
Inanna asked for advice from the water god Enki, who was known as the "fountain of knowledge." In some stories, Enki and Inanna were father and daughter—there are many images of them talking, feasting, and drinking together. Enki would later become the only god who helped Inanna when she was held prisoner in the underworld.

Water god
Enki is usually shown with water flowing from his shoulders, in which fish can be seen swimming.

4,000 *The Descent of Inanna dates back more than* **4,000 years**, *making it* **one of the oldest surviving epic poems** *in existence.*

Originally a minor goddess, Inanna became more important as her worship **spread through Mesopotamia**.

Later incarnations
Inanna became known by different names as her worship spread throughout Mesopotamia. She was named Ishtar in the city-states of Babylon and Assyria. She was also called Astarte by the ancient Phoenicians, who inhabited coastal areas of the Mediterranean.

Alabaster Astarte
This alabaster figurine of Astarte was created by the Phoenicians during the 7th century BCE. Her hairstyle, costume, and the presence of two sphinxes either side suggest the influence of ancient Egyptian artwork.

Theft of knowledge
Inanna gave Enki lots of beer to take advantage of his wisdom. Drunk, he handed over all of his divine decrees regarding religion, faith, music, and rituals. When he woke the next morning, Enki had no memory of this because of all the alcohol he'd drunk. When he realized the decrees were missing, Inanna had already taken them to enforce the new laws in Uruk.

Sumerian beer
On feast days, Sumerians drank beer from communal pots using long straws.

THE MARRIAGE OF INANNA
As goddess of love and fertility, it was important for Inanna to marry a suitable god. This particular marriage would ultimately end up mirroring the repeated natural cycle of life, death, and rebirth.

A husband for Inanna
Many of the gods were attracted to Inanna, but in the end she had to choose between two. Both worked the land, one as a farmer and the other as a shepherd.

The farmer
God of agriculture, Enkimdu harvested bountiful produce in the form of grain, loaves, and beer.

The shepherd
God of fertility, Dumuzi was a shepherd who provided milk, wool, and cheese.

INANNA IN THE UNDERWORLD
Inanna's sister Ereshkigal was the queen of the dead in the Sumerian underworld of Kur. Inanna wanted to extend her own power over this realm, so she decided to visit the underworld under the pretence of missing her sister. Knowing the danger of the journey ahead, Inanna wisely told her maid Ninshubur to raise the alarm if she did not return within three days.

Descent into Kur
While Inanna was in the underworld, nothing grew in the world above. Kur was a gloomy and foreboding place, where demons roamed the darkness. The meeting between the sisters did not go well. Ereshkigal saw through Inanna's false intentions and made her remove her beautiful clothes and accessories, leaving her with nothing. Inanna was sentenced to death, because nobody could leave the underworld alive.

Sumerian jewelery
Inanna would have had to remove lavish jewelery similar to this necklace.

Happy union
Many stone carvings show Inanna and Dumuzi as a happily married couple holding hands.

Inanna chooses Dumuzi
For some time, Inanna deliberated over the choice of farmer or shepherd. Her brother finally persuaded Inanna to marry the shepherd, because he provided more for the people. The couple were both associated with fertility, and its connection with the rebirth and renewal of the land.

Escaping the underworld
When Inanna didn't return from Kur, her maid sought help from the gods. To rescue her, Enki created two creatures who were not truly alive, because it was difficult for any living thing to safely return from the underworld. But in return for her release, Inanna had to promise Ereshkigal another soul as her replacement. Her husband Dumuzi was sent to Kur for half of each year, and his sister would take his place for the other half. This led to the changing seasons, because Dumuzi's six months on Earth influenced the spring and harvest, before he spent the long winter in the underworld.

Clawed goddess
Ereshkigal was sometimes depicted with sharp, birdlike talons for feet.

The Epic of Gilgamesh

The earliest known written story is that of a Mesopotamian king called Gilgamesh, recorded on a series of ancient stone tablets. The epic poem tells of Gilgamesh's friendship with the wild man Enkidu, and his search for immortality.

> "Gilgamesh, like an expert butcher, **boldly and surely** approached the Bull of Heaven."
>
> *The Epic of Gilgamesh*, c. 21st century BCE

Gilgamesh was the king of Uruk, and a wise but selfish leader. He treated his people cruelly if it served his own desires. The people called on Anu, god of the sky, to restrain Gilgamesh. Anu created a wild man called Enkidu to tame Gilgamesh. When Gilgamesh met Enkidu, they faced off in a trial of strength. After hours of battle without a winner, Gilgamesh seemed to have finally met his match.

But the pair surprised the gods by becoming friends, and between them they made life even worse for the people of Uruk. To prove his own strength, Gilgamesh wanted to fight a great beast. So he took Enkidu with him to seek out a savage creature named Humbaba, the demonic ruler of a sacred forest. Together, the pair brought an end to Humbaba.

Impressed by Gilgamesh, the goddess of love Inanna approached him with an offer of marriage, but he turned her down. Angered, she sent the Bull of Heaven, the strongest of all creatures, to kill him. But Gilgamesh and Enkidu once again vanquished the beast together.

Slaying the bull came with a price. Enkidu had a dream in which he saw the gods Ea, Anu, and Shamash decide that his punishment would be death. Enkidu soon became gravely ill and died. After losing his friend, Gilgamesh was devastated, but was also determined to find a way to avoid the same fate.

Seeking eternal life, Gilgamesh sought out Utnapishtim, a man who had been granted immortality. Utnapishtim told him of a plant with the ability to renew youth. Gilgamesh found the plant, but before he could eat it, a serpent took it instead.

Finally accepting his mortality, Gilgamesh went back to Uruk, where he lived the rest of his days as a more gentle king.

Team effort
Enkidu pulled the tail of the bull to enable Gilgamesh to get closer to the animal.

Animal elements
As a wild man of the forest, Enkidu was sometimes portrayed with hooves and horns.

The demon Humbaba
Also known in some sources as Huwawa, Humbaba was the divine protector of cedar forests. He was often portrayed as a fire-breathing beast. The ancient tablets do not explain in detail what happened in Humbaba's meeting with Gilgamesh and Enkidu, but it is generally believed that the story tells of the forest guardian's death.

Mask of evil
This clay mask dating from 1800–1600 BCE depicts the demonic face of Humbaba.

12 The number of **stone tablets** telling the tale that were discovered in the **ancient Assyrian city of Nineveh**.

1872 The epic was only translated **into a modern language** for the first time in 1872.

The gift of immortality
Utnapishtim had survived the Great Flood of Babylonia by building a boat, onto which he packed many animals. He and his wife were the only humans to survive. For saving the lives of many animals with their boat, Enlil, the god of earth, wind, and air, granted them immortality. When Gilgamesh heard of this, he set out to learn Utnapishtim's secret to eternal life.

UTNAPISHTIM AND HIS WIFE

The Great Flood
The Great Flood of Babylonia is similar to destructive floods that can be found in a variety of mythologies and religions from around the world. These events are often brought about by the gods to cleanse the Earth and start humanity anew.

Flood warning
Utnapishtim was warned of the flood by the god Enlil, and built a boat to survive.

Thick hide
The bull's hide was meant to be impossible to penetrate.

Fatal blow
Gilgamesh used a dagger to deliver the blow that killed the sacred bull.

Bull's eye
The gigantic bull was sometimes said to have glowing red eyes.

Slaying the bull
After Gilgamesh and Enkidu slayed the Bull of Heaven, they removed the beast's heart and offered it to Shamash, god of the sun and justice.

asia • BAAL AND ANAT

*These stories of Baal, told on **six tablets** found at the **ruins of Ugarit**, are known as **the Baal Cycle**.*

BAAL, RIDER OF THE CLOUDS
A warrior god, Baal lived high up among the clouds on Mount Zaphon, to the north of Ugarit. He was the head of the council of the gods that ruled over the Earth, and he defended order against the forces of chaos. His main enemy was his brother Yamm, the god of the deep ocean.

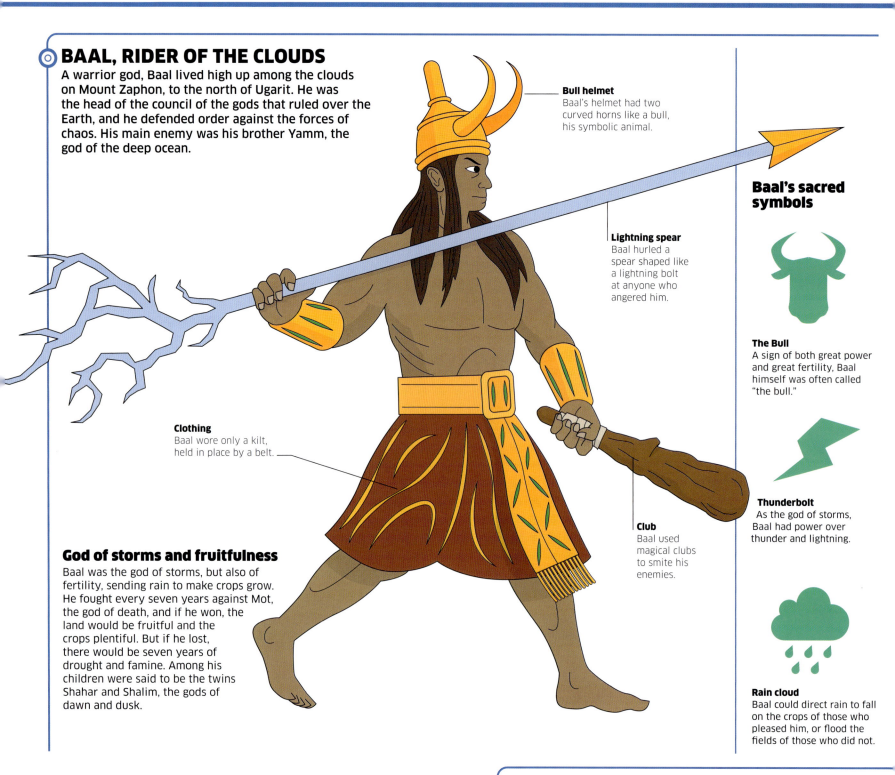

Bull helmet
Baal's helmet had two curved horns like a bull, his symbolic animal.

Lightning spear
Baal hurled a spear shaped like a lightning bolt at anyone who angered him.

Clothing
Baal wore only a kilt, held in place by a belt.

Club
Baal used magical clubs to smite his enemies.

Baal's sacred symbols

The Bull
A sign of both great power and great fertility, Baal himself was often called "the bull."

Thunderbolt
As the god of storms, Baal had power over thunder and lightning.

Rain cloud
Baal could direct rain to fall on the crops of those who pleased him, or flood the fields of those who did not.

God of storms and fruitfulness
Baal was the god of storms, but also of fertility, sending rain to make crops grow. He fought every seven years against Mot, the god of death, and if he won, the land would be fruitful and the crops plentiful. But if he lost, there would be seven years of drought and famine. Among his children were said to be the twins Shahar and Shalim, the gods of dawn and dusk.

Baal and Anat

Ugarit was a major city in an area once known as Canaan, along the west coast of the Mediterranean. The people of Ugarit worshipped a supreme god, El, as well as the storm god Baal and his sister, the violent Anat.

The city of Ugarit was destroyed by invaders at some point before 1200 BCE, but in the 1920s, thousands of clay tablets were found at the ancient site. These tablets described the gods and goddesses of the city's inhabitants, including Baal and Anat, and told their myths. The tale of Baal's struggle against his brother Yamm is the central story of Canaanite mythology.

BAAL'S STRUGGLE WITH YAMM
Yamm and Baal were both sons of El. Yamm, the god of the sea, was the favorite son of El, and thought he should become the next ruler of the gods when El stepped down.

Yamm's jealousy
As El grew older, Baal grew more powerful, and Yamm became jealous. He sent a messenger to the council of the gods demanding that Baal be handed over to him.

God of the ocean
Yamm symbolized chaos and was present in the crashing waves of the sea.

7 The number of days it took to build **Baal's palace**.

7 The number of years before **Mot** was **reborn to challenge** Baal again.

125

BAAL'S PALACE
After defeating Yamm, Baal wanted a magnificent palace of his own, one fit for a powerful god. His sister Anat went to El to persuade him to allow the construction of the palace, but it first needed to be agreed by Ashirat, El's wife.

A mother's favor
Ashirat was Baal's mother, but she preferred her other sons, Mot and Yamm. So Baal asked the craftsman god Kothar to make beautiful furniture and ornaments. He then persuaded his mother that these precious objects needed a home, and she agreed that the palace should be built.

Ugarit gold cup
Like the craft workers of Ugarit, Kothar may have made ornaments of gold to impress Ashirat.

A palace of his own
Kothar now built Baal's palace on top of Mount Zaphon. He made it with one single window on the palace roof. When it was completed, Baal invited all the other gods to a feast and opened the window, out of which came thunder and lightning, symbols of his power.

THE PEAK OF MOUNT ZAPHON

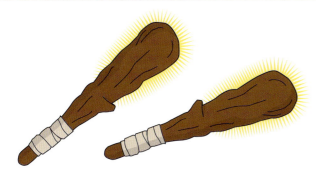

Magical weapons
Baal decided to fight Yamm, and the craftsman god Kothar wa-Khasis made him two magical clubs. When Baal hit Yamm once, the sea god was unhurt. But Baal struck him with the second club and Yamm fell. Baal became the ruler of the gods.

FEARSOME ANAT
Anat was the strongest of the goddesses of Canaan, and equal in power to Baal. She worked with him to overcome his enemies, but she had a dark side too. She was prone to bouts of extreme violence, and killed young men she lured into her temple.

Blood spatter
Anat was often shown covered in the blood of her enemies.

Goddess of fertility and war
Anat was both a goddess of fertility, giving life to the crops, and of war, bringing death on the battlefield. She was also a hunter goddess, performing a role traditionally carried out by men.

Anat's sacred symbols

Lion
The strongest and fiercest of the animals, the lion represented the power of Anat and her control of violence.

Serpent
Anat was sometimes shown wearing a serpent crown, a symbol of strength, fertility, and the right to rule over others.

Lily
A symbol of fertility and love, and also seen as a sign of purity, the lily was associated with Anat.

THE RESCUE OF BAAL
Baal invited Mot, the death god, to his feast, but insulted him by offering him bread to eat and wine to drink, rather than the flesh and blood Mot desired. So Mot swallowed Baal, sucking him into the underworld.

Furious Anat
Anat was angry at Mot and demanded Baal's return. She went to the underworld and searched for him, but without success. So she seized Mot, killed him, and ground up his body as though it were a grain. Eventually, both Mot and Baal were reborn and began to fight again, but the sun goddess Shapash made peace between them.

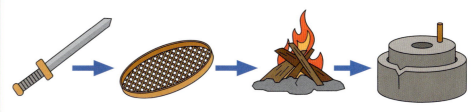

Sword
Anat used a blade to slice into Mot, cutting him into chunks.

Winnowing fan
She then strained him through her fan to make even tinier pieces.

Fire
Anat burned what was left of Mot's body, leaving it charred.

Millstone
Finally, she ground any pieces of Mot that were left into powder.

The struggle of good and evil

Twin brothers representing the forces of good and evil clash in a never-ending conflict in this ancient Persian tale. According to the myth, people on Earth have a choice—to follow the path of light or the path of darkness.

Zoroastrianism is a religion that was founded in Persia (present-day Iran) around the 6th century BCE. Its most fundamental principle is the eternal struggle between the opposing forces of good and evil. As recorded in the *Avesta*, the main Zoroastrian religious text, Zurvan, the ancient deity of time, wanted to create a son. To make this possible, the god of time gave up 1,000 years. However, toward the end of that time, he began to doubt his sacrifice. Because of this, instead of giving birth to one son, he gave birth to twins—Ahura Mazda, who represented his optimism, and Ahriman (sometimes known as Angra Mainyu), who represented his doubt and uncertainty.

Ahura Mazda embodied all things good, and he created the sun, moon, stars, and all life on Earth. In contrast, his brother Ahriman represented all things that were evil, such as death and disease. Ahriman attacked his brother with demons, but Ahura Mazda remained strong and exiled Ahriman into the darkness.

Ahura Mazda created the first human, Gayomart, but this angered Ahriman, so he broke free of the darkness where he had been trapped and brought evil to Earth in the form of pain, disease, and death. Ahriman fatally poisoned Gayomart, but Ahura Mazda took Gayomart's essence and used it to create Mashya and Mashyoi, the first mortal man and woman. The pair were born good, but they were given free will so they could choose between the paths of good and evil.

Meanwhile, the warring gods Ahura Mazda and Ahriman were unable to defeat each other, so Ahura Mazda put a limit on all of time, which trapped Ahriman in creation. The gods will continue to battle each other until the end of time, when a savior called Saoshyant will arrive to help Ahura Mazda defeat Ahriman. The dead will then be raised and purified, evil will be defeated, and the world will start anew, free from darkness.

Ultimate ruler
Chosen to be the creator and ruler of the world by Zurvan, the bearded Ahura Mazda is often portrayed wearing a crown and robes.

The Amesha Spentas

Ahura Mazda had six children known as the Amesha Spentas, who helped him by protecting and overseeing different aspects of the natural world. In Zoroastrianism, each of the three male and three female entities has their own festival and month of worship.

Asha
He stands for truth and justice, and protects fire.

Armaiti
She represents faith and devotion, and is a symbol of fertility.

Khshathra Vairya
A protector, he uses his weapons to keep the peace.

Haurvatat
Symbolizing perfection, she also safeguards water.

Ameretat
She is responsible for plants, and embodies eternal life.

Vohu Manah
Translated as "good mind," he oversees animal life on Earth.

10 Mashya and Mashyoi **gave birth to 10 different races** on Earth.   Zurvan was **androgynous** – neither male nor female.   **127**

> "They established Life and the Denial of Life; And so shall it be **till the world will last.**"
> The *Avesta*, c.6th century CE

Ring of kingship
Ahura Mazda is sometimes shown holding a ring of kingship or leadership.

The battle to rule
Ahura Mazda (translated as "wise lord") was often depicted holding the ring of kingship, which was passed down to each ancient Persian emperor and represented the divine right to rule. Ahriman ("destructive spirit") was locked in constant battle with Ahura Mazda as he attempted to overcome Ahura Mazda and become the ultimate ruler of the world.

Bird's feet
Ahriman is sometimes portrayed with the talons of an eagle.

Ahriman
In some depictions the wicked Ahriman is a griffin-type creature with the head of a lion.

Zurvan, god of time
At the beginning of time there was only the god Zurvan, the infinite god of time and space. He longed to create a son but doubted his own abilities, which led to the creation of the contrasting twins Ahura Mazda and Ahriman. Zurvan was often depicted as a winged, lion-headed deity with a snake encircling him.

The first humans
After forming the universe, Ahura Mazda created the original perfect human, Gayomart. When he was killed by Ahriman, Ahura Mazda wanted humankind to continue, so he formed Mashya and Mashyoi from the seed of Gayomart and gave them the ability to have children. All humans are descended from this couple.

GAYOMART

SOUTH ASIA

The mythology of South Asia has been dominated by Hinduism, a religion that has evolved over thousands of years. With a profusion of gods and goddesses, Hinduism has one of the largest collections of mythical and sacred stories in the world. Stories from Buddhism are also important in the region, and both religions play a vital role in traditions found throughout neighboring Southeast Asia.

VEDIC STORIES
The earliest known texts about Hindu gods and goddesses are known as the Vedas. These texts still attract readers, both for their poetry and for what they say about the beliefs of early people in South Asia.

The Vedas
The stories in the four books of the Vedas probably date to the 2nd millennium BCE, though they were written down much later. The oldest book, the *Rig Veda*, contains just over 1,000 hymns, each addressed to a deity.

The Vedic Deities
Many of the early gods and goddesses that appear in the Vedas relate to specific aspects of the universe. Among the most prominent are Indra, Surya, Vayu, Varuna, and Agni.

Surya
The sun god Surya, known as the Giver of Life, was a creator god in the Vedas, and brought light and knowledge to the world.

Indra
The god of thunder and lightning, Indra was the chief of the Vedic gods, and known for his strength.

Vayu
The god of the winds, Vayu was sometimes stormy, but at other times he was gentle.

Agni
Representing fire in all its aspects, Agni had three heads, each of which was aflame.

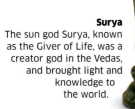

Varuna
God of the sky Varuna rode a *makara*, which was part crocodile and part fish.

HINDU WORSHIP
Many Hindus worship at shrines in their homes. They also make visits to Hindu temples, which are known as mandir. Many mandir will have statues of many different gods in the main shrine.

Hindu temples
Large mandir such as the Meenakshi Temple in Madurai, India, are often decorated with elaborate carvings that depict episodes in the lives of the gods.

Worship at shrines
Hindus place fruits, flowers, and other small items at shrines. They might also light lamps or ring a bell.

LATER DEITIES
In the centuries after the Vedas, another group of deities came to prominence. These included the Trimurti (see pages 130–133) and aspects of the Great Goddess (see pages 134–135). Around these figures clustered dozens of other popular gods.

Ganesha
Known as the breaker of obstacles, Ganesha was a god of good fortune and the son of Shiva and Parvati. One day, he stood guard for his mother while she was bathing. Shiva tried to approach her, but Ganesha stopped him. Furious, Shiva cut off his head. Regretting his actions, Shiva took an elephant's head and put it on Ganesha's body.

Hanuman
The monkey god Hanuman appeared in the story of the *Ramayana*, in which he accompanied Rama on his search for Sita (see pages 138–139). He represented the ideas of bravery and helping others.

Ganga
The Ganges River was worshipped as the goddess Ganga. She was the daughter of Himavat, who represented the Himalayas. Her waters once flowed through heaven, and they have the ability to wash away people's sins.

BUDDHISM

The religion of Buddhism also had its origins in South Asia, and its sacred stories quickly spread throughout the region.

Buddha and Mara
The demon Mara symbolized the senses and worldly pleasures. He tried to stop Buddha from achieving enlightenment by tempting him on various occasions.

Festivals
Hinduism has many religious festivals. Diwali, the annual festival of light, celebrates the return of Rama to his kingdom (see pages 138–139). During Kumbh Mela, which happens in full every 12 years, pilgrims travel to one of the sacred rivers to bathe and wash away their sins.

Siddhartha Gautama
According to Buddhist tradition, the prince Siddhartha Gautama wanted to free himself from suffering. Giving away his possessions, he began a life as a poor wanderer. He became the Buddha after achieving enlightenment.

Reaching enlightenment
The Buddha found enlightenment sitting underneath a banyan tree.

The forces of Mara
All beings associated with darkness and death, including demons and other evil beings, joined the forces of Mara.

SOUTHEAST ASIA

As Hinduism, and later Buddhism, spread into Southeast Asia, they had a major impact on the region's civilizations and their cultures.

Popular stories
The beliefs of Hinduism were absorbed by the peoples of Southeast Asia quite easily, and in some places Hinduism became the state religion. Epic poems such as the *Ramayana* were popular.

Parallel traditions
Buddhism spread throughout Southeast Asia from both India and China over several hundred years. Buddhism was often heavily promoted alongside Hinduism by many states in Southeast Asia.

Trading stories
Southeast Asia lay on major trading routes between India and China, and traders brought their own religions to the region. Hinduism arrived from India and its neighbors, while Buddhism spread from contact with both India and China. Over the centuries, each religion was absorbed to become a part of the many cultures of Southeast Asia.

Angkor Wat
The famous temple of Angkor Wat was built in Angkor, the capital of the Khmer Empire (in present-day Cambodia). It was originally a Hindu place of worship, but was converted to a Buddhist temple at the end of the 12th century.

Hanuman shadow puppet
Wayang kulit is a traditional form of shadow puppetry found in Java and Bali in Indonesia. Performances are usually based on Hindu epics such as the *Ramayana*.

Buddhist statues
Representations of the Buddha and other Buddhist figures in Southeast Asian art are distinct from those found in India or China.

asia • THE TRIMURTI

10 The number of **divine beings** made by Brahma to begin **populating the world**.

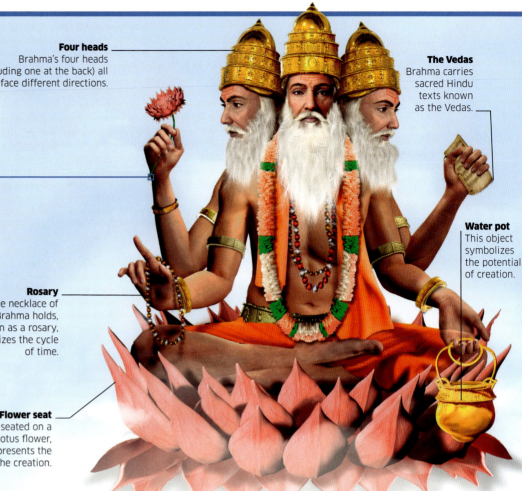

Four heads — Brahma's four heads (including one at the back) all face different directions.

The Vedas — Brahma carries sacred Hindu texts known as the Vedas.

Rosary — The necklace of beads Brahma holds, known as a rosary, symbolizes the cycle of time.

Water pot — This object symbolizes the potential of creation.

Flower seat — Brahma is seated on a huge lotus flower, which represents the purity of the creation.

Valmiki
The gifted author and poet named Valmiki was an avatar of Brahma—an aspect of the god in mortal form. Brahma gave Valmiki the inspiration to write the *Ramayana*, the first epic poem in Hinduism. This poem of more than 20,000 verses details the life of Rama, the seventh incarnation of the god Vishnu (see pages 138–139).

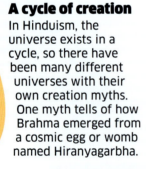

A cycle of creation
In Hinduism, the universe exists in a cycle, so there have been many different universes with their own creation myths. One myth tells of how Brahma emerged from a cosmic egg or womb named Hiranyagarbha.

Brahman
The collective of the Trimurti come together as Brahman, considered to be the ultimate reality of the universe. This principle has no physical form and is infinite. It does not change, but is the cause of all changes.

Hindu Om
The sacred symbol of Om consists of the letters A, U, and M. This special sound is considered eternal—it is the sound that emanates from the entire Universe. It is used by Hindus and followers of other faiths during mantras, meditations, and prayers.

The Trimurti

Brahma, Vishnu, and Shiva, known as the Trimurti, are worshipped as the supreme gods by followers of the Hindu faith. This trio look after the universe together, each representing a different aspect of it.

Trimurti means "three forms"—as the three supreme gods represent different parts of the ultimate reality of the universe. The three gods are Brahma the creator, Vishnu the preserver, and Shiva the destroyer.

In one creation myth, Brahma emerged fully formed from a lotus flower. Seeing the emptiness around him, he imagined the universe, and it began to take shape. He made the divine beings that gave birth to the many deva (gods) and asura (demons). The sun, moon, and stars appeared. Brahma also made the first woman, Shatarupa, from his own body. She tried to escape from him by turning into different animals, but he turned into the male form of each animal. In this way, the pair created all the animals of the world.

When Brahma had finished creation, Vishnu the preserver was tasked with maintaining harmony and keeping order. Shiva the destroyer would eventually undo all of creation by ending the universe.

Although this may sound like a negative outcome, in Hindu belief, destruction is the road to rebirth and renewal. Each time Shiva destroys the universe, it is born again. Hindus celebrate this repeated cycle of birth, preservation, destruction, and rebirth through the three gods of the Trimurti.

Shatarupa later took the form of the goddess **Saraswati**, who became **Brahma's wife**.

131

Creator, preserver, and destroyer

In Hinduism, a *murti* is a devotional icon (a representation of a deity). These three *murtis* of Brahma the creator (left), Vishnu the preserver (right), and Shiva the destroyer (below) are typical representations of the three deities and their sacred symbols.

Spinning discus
Vishnu holds a gold discus, known as the Sudarshana Chakra, to symbolize protection.

Lotus flower
This represents Vishnu's serenity and purity.

Blue skin
The distinctive blue skin of Vishnu reflects his role as preserver of the great oceans and skies.

Gada and conch shell
These are symbols of strength and power.

Giant serpent
Vishnu is seated on a giant multiheaded serpent named Shesha Naga, who offers divine protection and wisdom.

Damaru drum
As he dances, Shiva bangs the *damaru*, a type of drum, to emphasize the continuous cycle of creation and destruction.

Sacred flame
The flame Shiva holds during his dance is a symbol of purification.

Four arms
Two arms facing forward are in the human realm, while two arms toward the back are in the spiritual realm.

Tiger skin
The strength and power of Shiva can be seen by his wearing of a tiger skin.

Dancing feet
Shiva, the form of his Nataraja avatar (the cosmic dancer), points to his dancing feet to show the continued rhythm of life from destruction to rebirth.

Bhairava
One avatar of Shiva is Bhairava, whose name means "terrifying." When Brahma grew an extra head to watch Shatarupa as she tried to escape from him into the sky, this ferocious deity punished him by chopping it off. Bhairava carried the severed head with him as a warning.

> "Brahman is the one present everywhere and is the great one who is above all."
>
> *Katha Upanishad, verse 5.2*

The ten avatars of Vishnu

According to Hinduism, the god Vishnu came to Earth nine times through forms known as avatars to guide and save humanity. His final avatar will appear in the future.

In the *Puranas*, a set of sacred Hindu texts, Vishnu was said to protect the universe and restore peace in times of crisis, such as when a great flood threatened to end life on Earth. When the world was overcome with evil, he transformed into either a human being or animal and stepped in to help. His wife Lakshmi often joined him in his earthly existence, and could also change herself into an avatar. For example, when Vishnu came to Earth as Rama, she joined him as his wife, Sita.

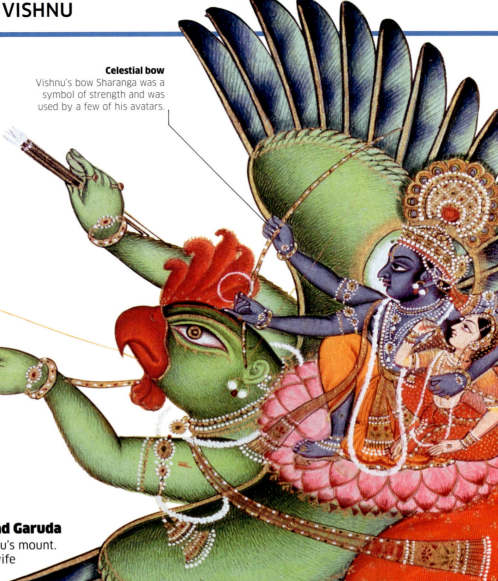

Celestial bow
Vishnu's bow Sharanga was a symbol of strength and was used by a few of his avatars.

Vishnu, Lakshmi, and Garuda
The eagle-like bird Garuda was Vishnu's mount. Vishnu rode on his shoulders with his wife Lakshmi, the goddess of fortune.

King of birds
Part eagle, part human, Garuda was believed to fly swiftly like the wind.

MATSYA
The Fish

Vishnu's first avatar was a fish called Matsya who came to warn Manu, the first man, of a flood. Matsya told Manu to build an ark, and when the flood came, Matsya grew horns to tow the ark, using a sacred snake as a rope. That way, Matsya was able to guide Manu to safety.

KURMA
The Turtle

Kurma was Vishnu's second avatar who appeared as a turtle to help the gods stir an ocean of milk. Kurma positioned himself under a mountain that the gods used as a churning rod. Many treasures emerged from their efforts, including Kamadhenu—a divine cow that grants wishes.

VARAHA
The Wild Boar

Vishnu's third avatar Varaha (left) had the body of a man and the head of a wild boar. When the demon Hiranyaksha hid the Earth under a cosmic ocean, Varaha swam to the bottom and raised it to the surface with his tusks.

Vishnu is often shown with **four arms**, holding a discus, a lotus flower, a conch shell, and a mace.

The asteroid **4034 Vishnu** is named after the **supreme god**.

NARASIMHA
The Man-Lion

The ferocious part-man, part-lion was Vishnu's fourth avatar. When the demon king Hiranyakashipu threatened to kill his own son, Prahlada, for being a devout follower of Vishnu, Narasimha appeared and tore the king to pieces.

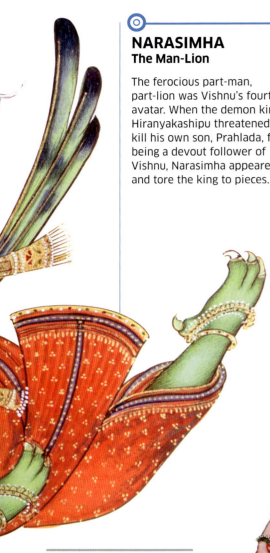

VAMANA
The Dwarf

Vishnu's fifth avatar was the dwarf Vamana who wanted to overthrow the greedy demon king Bali. He tricked Bali by asking him for as much land as he could cover in a few paces. The king laughed and granted his wish, but then Vamana transformed into a giant and covered the three worlds – heaven, Earth, and the underworld – in three steps.

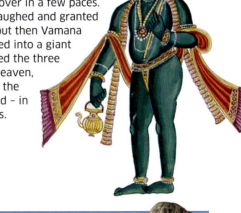

PARASHURAMA
The Axman

In his sixth avatar, Vishnu appeared for the first time as a human being—the wise warrior Parashurama. When a group of warriors, known as Kshatriya, began to terrorize the world, Parashurama led a campaign against them and killed them with his ax. It is said that he filled five great lakes with their blood.

RAMA
The Prince

Lord Rama was Vishnu's seventh avatar. Details of his quest to defeat the powerful demon Ravana are described in the Hindu epic *Ramayana* (see pages 138–139). Rama is still worshipped today and his birthday is celebrated yearly in the festival *Rama Navami*.

> "Glory to the supreme Vishnu, the cause of **the creation, existence, and end of this world.**"
>
> The Vishnu Purana, c.500 BCE

KRISHNA
The Lover

Krishna was Vishnu's eighth avatar, known for his heroic deeds in the war that led the royal family, the Pandavas, to victory (see pages 136–137). Krishna is worshipped alongside his wife was Radha, an avatar of the goddess Lakshmi. Together, the pair are thought to be the perfect couple.

BUDDHA
The Enlightened One

The Buddha is a historical figure who Hindus believe to be Vishnu's ninth avatar. His teachings on seeking freedom from suffering formed the basis of Buddhism. While meditating under a sacred tree, the Buddha achieved a heightened, spiritual state of mind known as enlightenment.

KALKI
The Knight

Vishnu's tenth and final avatar, Kalki, is predicted to arrive at the end of the world when it is consumed in darkness. Kalki will ride on his white horse Devadatta, defeating the forces of evil with his fiery sword, and will summon a new age of truth and peace.

The Great Goddess

In one Hindu creation story, the universe is created and sustained by a feminine power known as Shakti. This divine energy is represented by Mahadevi, the Great Goddess. She is worshipped in many forms, but one of the most important is Durga, the warrior goddess who brings order by defeating the forces of evil.

Since the beginning of time, the deva (gods) had been at war with the asura (demons). After suffering many defeats, the demon Mahishasura prayed to the creator god Brahma. He demanded that he should not be defeated by any mortal man, by any deva, or by the Trimurti–the supreme Hindu gods Brahma, Vishnu, and Shiva. Brahma granted him this wish, knowing that he would be killed by a woman.

Mahishasura and his troops defeated the devas, but the Trimurti came up with a plan to end Mahishasura's reign of terror. They focused their divine energy to create the goddess Durga. Armed with weapons given to her by the gods, ten-armed Durga rode into battle against the asura army, mounted on her lion.

Fearless Durga destroyed Mahishasura's demons, slaying hundreds of them with her many weapons until only their leader was left standing. In the fierce battle that followed, Mahishasura used all his powers to try and overpower Durga, but she was unbeatable. As a last resort, he used his powers of shape-shifting, turning into different animals.

First, he took the form of a lion, but the goddess strangled him with ease. He then transformed into an elephant, but Durga cut off its trunk with her sword. Finally, he turned into a buffalo, but Durga chopped off its head. As Mahishasura emerged from the buffalo's body, she pinned him down and struck him with her trishula (trident), dealing a fatal blow.

A demon defeated
Depictions of Durga commonly show her victory over Mahishasura, who is pinned underneath Durga's foot. In Hinduism, the battle is a very important symbol of the triumph of good over evil.

MAHISHASURA'S DEFEAT

Durga Puja
Durga's victory over Mahishasura is celebrated in parts of India every year. The goddess is worshipped for ten days during Durga Puja – one of the most important festivals in some Indian states, such as West Bengal, and also in Bangladesh.

Annual ritual
Durga Puja celebrations are marked by the worship of idols of the goddess, created out of clay and lavishly decorated by skilled artisans.

Tridevi
The goddesses Saraswati, Parvati, and Lakshmi make up the powerful trio of goddesses known as the Tridevi. They are all aspects of the great goddess and embodiments of Shakti.

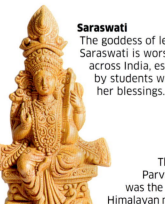

Saraswati
The goddess of learning, Saraswati is worshipped across India, especially by students who seek her blessings.

Parvati
The goddess Parvati's father was the god of the Himalayan mountains. She prayed to Shiva and eventually the two were married.

Lakshmi
The goddess Lakshmi is revered as the deity of wealth and good fortune. She is companion to the god Vishnu.

Kali
The goddess Kali embodies the primal rage of the Great Goddess. A force of destruction and calamity, she slayed an entire asura army, yet her rage could not be subdued. She went on a rampage, killing every living being in her path. Only Shiva could calm her down.

Overcoming her rage
Shiva lay down in Kali's path to stop her rampage. When she stepped on him, she regained her senses and stuck out her tongue in shame.

The name **Mahishasura** means "buffalo demon" in Sanskrit.

The **Santhal, Asur, and Korku** peoples of eastern India revere **Mahishasura** as an ancestor.

135

Trident
Durga used her trishula (trident), a gift from Shiva, to strike the final blow to Mahishasura.

Discus
The spinning *chakra*, or discus, is the weapon of Vishnu.

Sword
The curved sword was a gift from Yama, the god of death.

Thunderbolt
Indra's *vajra*, or thunderbolt, was one of the most powerful weapons in the universe.

Mace
Originally wielded by the god Hanuman, the *gada* (mace) is a weapon symbolizing strength.

Lotus
Bestowed by the god Brahma, Durga's lotus flower symbolizes purity.

Axe
Durga's ax was fashioned by Vishwakarma, the divine architect.

Conch
The conch shell was gifted by Varuna, the god of water.

Spear
Agni, the god of fire, gifted Durga his flaming spear.

Lion
Durga's ferocious mount was a gift from Himavat, the god of the Himalayas.

Warrior goddess
Most depictions of Durga show her draped in a fiery red sari, armed for combat, and mounted on a lion or tiger. Her expression is fierce, indicating her role as the destroyer of evil.

The Mahabharata

Over hundreds of years, many authors contributed to the *Mahabharata*, a Sanskrit epic poem from ancient India. It told of a rivalry between cousins for the throne of Hastinapur, which led to a great, destructive war and ended in bloodshed and grief for all.

Composed between the 8th century BCE and the 4th century CE, the *Mahabharata* chronicled the Kuru family feud between five brothers known as the Pandavas and their 100 cousins known as the Kauravas, culminating in the Battle of Kurukshetra. The tales within the epic poem told of conflicts fought to gain revenge, to protect honor, and to fulfill dharma (the Hindu concept of moral duties). Though the Kauravas had strength in numbers, the Pandavas had dharma on their side. The poem contained lessons on the evils of greed and envy and the triumph of morality over them. The deeds of the characters inspire and teach Hindus to act in just ways.

90,000 With more than **90,000** *shokas* (verses), the *Mahabharata* is the **longest epic poem** in the world.

ORIGINS OF THE COUSINS

When Vichitravirya, the son of Hastinapur's king, died childless, his wives Ambika and Ambalika had children with his stepbrother, Veda Vyasa, a sage. Ambika's son Dhritarashtra and his wife Gandhari had 100 sons, the Kauravas. Ambalika's son Pandu was cursed to never have children, so his wives prayed to the gods, and gave birth to five sons, the Pandavas.

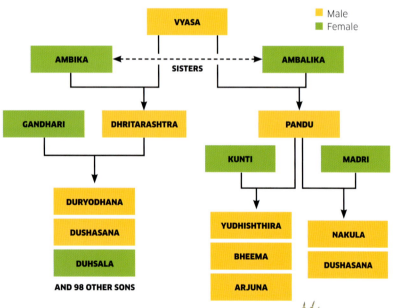

Dhritarashtra and Pandu

Vyasa was a sage with dirty hair and an unwashed smell. Upon first sight of him, Ambika shut her eyes in fear and Ambalika turned pale in fright. And so, Dhritarashtra was born blind, and Pandu was born pale. Dhritarashtra was deemed unfit to rule due to his blindness, so Pandu took the Hastinapur throne.

Equal partners Dhritarashtra's wife Gandhari covered her eyes with a blindfold to forever experience the world as he did.

THE KAURAVAS TAKE CONTROL

After Pandu's death, the Kauravas and Pandavas fought over the Hastinapur throne. Dhritarashtra offered a palace to the Pandavas, but it was set alight by the Kauravas. The Pandavas narrowly escaped with their lives and, after some time in hiding, returned to claim their kingdom. But the eldest Pandava Yudhisthira soon lost everything to the leader of the Kauravas, Duryodhana, in a gambling match. The Pandavas were banished into exile for 13 years.

Winning Draupadi's hand

While in hiding after the burning of their palace, the Pandavas traveled to the Panchala Kingdom. Here, King Drupada held a contest for the hand of his daughter, Draupadi, in marriage. The contestants had to string a special bow and shoot the eye of a fish rotating overhead while looking at its reflection in a pot of oil below. An accomplished archer, the Pandava brother called Arjuna achieved the feat and was married to Draupadi.

When Arjuna returned home with Draupadi, his mother Kunti, without turning to see what Arjuna had won, commanded him to share the "prize" with his brothers. The Pandavas were bound by moral duty to their mother, so Arjuna had to obey her. Thus Draupadi became the wife of all five Pandavas. Her marriage to the Pandava brothers set into motion the events leading up to the great battle.

Born out of fire

King Drupada agreed to split his kingdom with the Kuru princes' teacher Drona. When Drupada went back on his word, Drona asked the Kuru princes to attack Drupada. They defeated him, and he was forced to give half his kingdom to Drona. Drupada built a fire and prayed to Shiva, the god of destruction, for revenge. Draupadi and her brother Dhrishtadyumna were born from the fire. A prophecy told that Draupadi would help destroy the Kauravas and her brother would kill Drona.

A game of dice

On the Pandavas return from hiding, Duryodhana and Yudhishthira played a gambling game of dice. Yudhishthira recklessly bet his kingdom and even Draupadi in the game. But the Kauravas' uncle had enchanted the dice, and the Pandavas lost everything they owned. The Kauravas sent them into exile for 13 years.

Cowrie shell dice The game of dice is often portrayed as a board game played with cowrie shells.

THE BATTLE OF KURUKSHETRA

The Pandavas returned after 13 years of exile, but Duryodhana refused to return the throne. Peace negotiations failed, war became inevitable, and preparations for the Battle of Kurukshetra began. The Kauravas had amassed many allies, but the Pandavas had Krishna, an avatar of the supreme god Vishnu, on their side.

Bhagavad Gita

A dialogue between Arjuna and Krishna, the *Bhagavad Gita* is a sacred Hindu text within the *Mahabharata*. Arjuna realized on the battlefield that he had to fight and kill members of his family. This weakened his resolve, and he wanted to withdraw. Krishna reminded him of his duty (dharma) as a warrior to fight for what is just and maintain order.

Divine charioteer
Although Krishna did not draw weapons, he was Arjuna's charioteer and advised him on ways to counter the Kauravas strategies, enabling the Pandavas to win the war.

Bhishma's Bed of Arrows

Bhishma, the eldest member of the Kuru family, chose to fight alongside the Kauravas in the war. He was a formidable military leader and an unmatched archer, who had been gifted with the ability to choose when he would die. To defeat him, Arjuna fired so many arrows through his body that, when he fell, they formed a bed beneath him.

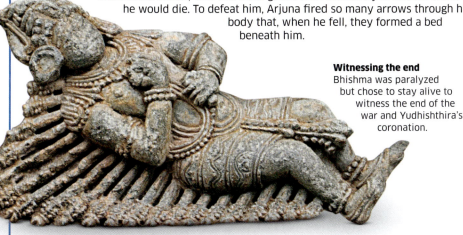

Witnessing the end
Bhishma was paralyzed but chose to stay alive to witness the end of the war and Yudhishthira's coronation.

Battle of the archers

Karna and Arjuna were equally skilled archers. Arjuna had higher status because he was a Kuru prince, while Karna was a charioteer's son. Karna's jealousy soon turned them into enemies and Karna fought against Arjuna and his brothers in the great war. Arjuna killed Karna at the Battle of Kurukshetra with help from Krishna.

BATTLE BETWEEN KARNA AND ARJUNA

AFTER THE WAR

With the Kauravas slain, Yudhishthira was crowned king of Hastinapur. But he could not shake the guilt of killing his family members. To put an end to his ill fate, he renounced the throne and set off to the forest. His brothers and Draupadi accompanied him.

"BUT THIS GREAT GRIEF IS **ALWAYS CIRCULATING IN MY HEART … TO ME THIS VICTORY** SEEMS TO BE **A DEFEAT.**"
The Mahabharata

Journey up the Himalayas

The Pandavas traveled to the Himalayan Mountain range. Yudhishthira suggested climbing the mountains to enter Swargaloka (heaven), which lay at the top. All his brothers and Draupadi died on the treacherous journey.

Canine companion
The group didn't notice that a dog had followed them all the way from Hastinapur to heaven.

Yudhishthira in Swargaloka

The Devas (gods) of Swargaloka welcomed Yudhishthira, but said he must leave the dog behind. As the only constant companion on his arduous journey, Yudhishthira refused to give the dog up. Impressed by Yudhishthira's adoration for all beings, the Devas let him in. He reunited with his brothers and wife who had entered the realm after their deaths.

The Ramayana

A timeless Hindu epic, the *Ramayana* is a tale of duty, heroism, and bravery. It follows the king Rama whose extraordinary strength and determination are tested when he goes on a quest to rescue his wife Sita from the clutches of the Rakshasa leader, King Ravana.

The *Ramayana* is a sacred text that takes the form of an epic tale. It begins with the journey of the young prince Rama, who was the eldest son of King Dasharatha and Queen Kausalya of the city of Ayodhya. He was an avatar of Vishnu (see pages 132–133), sent to Earth to defeat the evil king Ravana. Rama grew up to be a kind but fierce warrior. When he came of age, he won the hand of Sita, the daughter of the king of Mithila, in an archery contest.

Fulfilling a promise to Rama's stepmother, Kaikeyi, Dasharatha crowned his other son Bharata king and banished Rama from his kingdom. Rama's brother Lakshmana and Sita joined him to live in the forest. The trio were faced with many challenges, including fending off attacks from demons. Among them was Ravana's sister Surpanakha, who had fallen in love with Rama, and in her jealousy attacked Sita. Lakshmana came to Sita's defense and wounded Surpanakha. Seeking revenge, she complained to her brother Ravana, a mighty Rakshasa, who sent a golden deer into the forest as a ploy to bewitch Rama and his brother while he abducted Sita. He held her captive in his palace in the realm of Lanka.

Distraught to find Sita gone, Rama went to the king of the Vanaras, a race of humanoid apes, for help. Rama was given the services of the king's Vanara General, Hanuman. His army built a bridge across the sea to Lanka and attacked Ravana's palace.

In the war, Rama slew Ravana and was reunited with his wife Sita. The couple returned to Ayodhya, where Rama was crowned king.

10-headed deity
King Ravana had 10 heads, which represented his vast knowledge. He captured Sita by luring Rama away from her with his servant Maricha, who was disguised as a glowing deer.

RAVANA IN HIS 10-HEADED FORM

The bridge to Lanka
Rama and his army of Vanaras were faced with a vast expanse of sea between them and the island kingdom of Lanka, where Sita was held captive. They constructed a 30-mile (48-km) bridge in just five days to allow their forces to cross.

A safe passage
The Vanaras inscribed the stones that made up the bridge with Rama's name to protect them as they crossed the open sea.

Dangerous illusion
Dazzled by the appearance of a golden deer, which was a demon in disguise, Sita asked Rama to bring it to her, leaving her vulnerable for capture.

Ideal companion
Sita was portrayed as a loyal wife, who was patient, brave, and kind.

Divine being
Rama is usually depicted as having blue skin to reflect his divinity, and carrying his powerful bow—the sharanga.

139

EAST ASIA

China, Japan, and Korea have complex mythologies involving many thousands of gods, goddesses, and spirits. In all three cultures, the narrative told by their myths begins with creation stories and the deeds of gods, but ends with the establishment of an imperial family. This progression gives the rulers of each culture a connection to the gods.

SHARED BELIEFS
China had a great influence over East Asian mythology, spreading their beliefs of Confucianism, Taoism, and Buddhism to their neighboring countries.

Confucianism
Confucius was a highly respected and worshipped figure and his teachings, which became known as Confucianism, had a lasting impact in China and beyond. As he preferred facts over stories, supernatural elements were added in the recording of historical events to create new legends. For example, the mythical Yellow Emperor became a historical figure.

CONFUCIUS

Daoism
The ancient Chinese philosophy of Daoism encourages its followers to live in harmony with the universe. It is believed that dark and light forces known as Yin and Yang are connected and they keep the universe in order. In the manual known as the I Ching, natural forces are shown as trigrams (broken and unbroken lines).

EIGHT TRIGRAMS OF THE I CHING

Buddhism
The founder of Buddhism was the Indian philosopher Siddhartha Gautama. When his teachings were introduced to China during the Han dynasty, they spread across the country and later reached Korea and Japan. Buddhism became a widely practised religion in East Asia and has influenced many of the myths, legends, and stories of heroes in the region.

BUDDHA

IMMORTAL HUMANS
One of the key features in Chinese myths is the belief in immortal humans. These were people who obtained the gift of immortality from the gods by being virtuous on Earth. Heroes, emperors, and priests could become immortal and join the gods in heaven. In Daoism, there are thousands of these divine beings.

The eight immortals
Also known as Ba Xian, the eight immortals are a group of Daoist heroes celebrated across China, often for their colorful personalities. They had a habit of causing mayhem, especially when they were together, but they also acted alone.

Tricksters and deities
The group loved to play tricks on each other and mortals, but they were also serious religious figures.

Bodhisattvas
Another kind of immortal known as a Bodhisattva is found in Buddhism. They are spiritually awakened beings who have delayed their entry into paradise to help people on Earth. In China, the female deity Guanyin is worshipped to provide compassion and unconditional love.

Listening out
Guanyin means "perceiver of sounds" because she is believed to hear the cries of people who are suffering.

TEMPLES AND SHRINES
Religious structures can be found throughout East Asia. Large temples can dominate the architecture of large towns and cities, while shrines might be of any size. Particularly in Japan, they can be found anywhere—at the side of a road, the edge of a lake, or deep within a forest.

Chinese temples
The worship of deities, ancestors, and immortals take place in a Chinese temple. They are also a hub where people gather for festivals.

Shinto shrines
Japan has many Buddhist temples, but the native religion of Shinto makes use of shrines. These structures house the kami, the Shinto deities.

KAMI

In the Shinto religion native to Japan, people worship the kami, which loosely translates as "gods" or "spirits." The Japanese deities are kami, and most things that exist in nature – including people and animals, features of the landscape, and the forces of nature – have a kami.

MOUNT FUJI

IZANAGI AND IZANAMI WITH THEIR CHILDREN

ROCK TIED WITH SHIMENAWA

Kami of place
Kami inhabit particular locations and elements of nature, such as forests, mountains, lakes, and waterfalls. There may be multiple kami found at some places. For example, there are various kami at Mount Fuji, and also a kami of Mount Fuji itself, as well as a kami of mountains in general.

Shinto gods
Some kami that appear in ancient myths have been given names, such as Amaterasu, kami of the sun, and Tsukuyomi, kami of the moon. These are the kami that are most like the gods traditionally found in other religions, and about whom mythical stories are told.

Creatures and objects
Individual plants, animals, and even forged objects such as swords might have a kami. Even the lowliest rock might have a kami. Trees and other natural features with a kami are marked by shimenawa, ropes that signify a sacred place.

SUPERNATURAL CREATURES

East Asian myths and folklore are filled with thousands of gods and immortals, but they also tell stories of many supernatural creatures. These beings might be helpful toward humankind or have malicious intentions.

Chinese dragon
The Chinese version of the dragon is quite different to its European counterpart. It is usually depicted as a snakelike being with four legs and without wings. Dragons are often associated with power.

Fox spirit
Stories of fox spirits are told throughout East Asia. In Japan they are known as kitsune, and are helpful beings that serve the rice god Inari.

Yokai
There are many types of yokai, such as oni, tengu, and kappa, each of which has a different monstrous form. Yokai are dangerous spirits that haunt the Japanese countryside, but they are not necessarily evil.

Dragon turtle
Combining elements of two important animals in Chinese mythology, the dragon turtle has the shell of a turtle but a dragon's body and size. It combines the dragon's power with the turtle's wisdom.

Qilin
The qilin has the head of a Chinese dragon, the body of an ox or goat, and cloven hooves. Its body is covered in scales. Qilin often appear when an important person is about to die.

Dokkaebi
Creatures from Korean folklore, the dokkaebi have a frightening appearance. They like to trick people, but are gullible creatures that are easy to trick themselves. An image of a dokkaebi might be found at the entrance to a home to ward off evil spirits.

asia • PANGU AND NÜWA

18,000 It took **18,000** years for the cosmic egg to **fully form**.

PANGU'S BIRTH
Only the formless substance called chaos existed in the beginning. From it, a cosmic egg emerged, and crammed inside it was Pangu. He remained inside the egg for thousands of years until, one day, tired of being constrained for so long, he smashed his way out. The two opposing forces Yin and Yang were born with him. Pangu separated them by placing the celestial heavens of Yang overhead and the Earth of Yin underfoot.

The first being
Pangu is often described as a beastly giant with two horns on his head.

Earth and sky
Using his ax, the giant god Pangu separated Yin (Earth) from Yang (the sky) and stood between them to make sure they never joined together again.

Pangu's sacred symbols

Hammer and chisel
Pangu is often depicted holding these tools because they helped him create the world.

The Sun
The left eye of Pangu turned into the sun and became his symbol for bringing light on Earth.

The Moon
The right eye of Pangu turned into the moon and became his symbol for lighting the night sky.

Yin and Yang
Pangu separated Yin, the feminine aspect of nature, from Yang, the masculine side of nature.

Shaping the world
Once the sky and the Earth were in their positions, Pangu died. His body parts became the features of the universe. His body formed the hills and mountains, his bones became rock, his blood flowed as rivers, his eyes changed into the sun and the moon, his hair turned into trees, and his sweat fell as rain.

Sacred mountain
According to legend, Mount Tai in China is sacred because it was formed from the head of Pangu. It is also thought to be a dwelling place for immortal deities.

> "HIS BREATH BECAME THE WIND AND CLOUDS; HIS VOICE BECAME PEALS OF THUNDER."
>
> Xu Zheng, *A Chronicle of the Five Cycles of Time*, 3CE

Pangu and Nüwa

The gods Pangu and Nüwa are central to the ancient Chinese creation story. Pangu was responsible for adding structure and order to the universe, while Nüwa created humans and became their protector.

At the beginning of time, two special beings emerged from nothingness—Pangu and Nüwa. They made many sacrifices to bring order and introduce life to the world. Pangu was considered to be the first living being. He used his colossal strength to manipulate the forces of nature. Nüwa was the female goddess of fertility, who became the mother of humanity. Their leading roles in the creation of the world have ensured that they are still revered to this day.

WARRING GODS
Nüwa's human race was thriving until the fire god Zhurong and the water deity Gonggong argued. The pair fought over who should rule the universe. Gonggong was destructive and reckless, and in a rage, he smashed one of the heavenly pillars holding up the sky. Although Gonggong ultimately lost to Zhurong, his actions caused parts of the sky to break away and it was up to Nüwa to fix it.

Nüwa was married to her brother, the benevolent god Fuxi.

Before making humans, Nüwa started off by shaping animals, such as a chicken, out of clay.

In one version of the story, Nüwa used the legs of Ao, a divine turtle, to replace the broken pillars in the sky.

CREATING HUMANS

Once Pangu had sacrificed his body to create the world, the goddess of humanity, Nüwa, appeared. She went to work making and shaping people out of clay. She based the people on the gods to give them the finest qualities and the best chance of survival.

Mother goddess
Nüwa was depicted as half-serpent and half-human. In Chinese culture, serpents symbolized fertility and creation.

Fierce creature
Although the goddess had the body of a serpent, she was thought to have the spirit of a tigress.

Nüwa's sacred symbols

Five colored crystals
The blue, yellow, red, white, and black crystals that Nüwa carried corresponded with the five Chinese elements.

The Earth
The goddess healed the Earth after floods had wreaked havoc across the land.

Mud and water
All the people created by Nüwa were made by mixing mud and water together to make clay.

Mount Kunlun
This mountain in western China was thought to be the home of the goddess.

The Dark Lady

In another version of the creation story, the goddess Jiu Tian Xuannü, better known as the Dark Lady, created a second generation of humans because Nüwa's humans were wiped out in a terrible flood. The Dark Lady married and had children to help populate the planet again.

Warrior and protector
The Dark Lady was a powerful figure, regarded as both a fierce warrior goddess and a fearless protector of the heavens.

Catastrophic flood

When the sky collapsed, there was a gaping hole overhead. Water flowing down from the heavens leaked onto Earth, swamping the land in a disastrous flood. The hole let in dangerous meteorites from space, which caused raging fires. People struggled to survive and their suffering caught the attention of Nüwa.

God of water
This mural captures Gonggong as a terrifying underwater dragon who would stop at nothing for his own gains.

Fixing the sky

Seeing the impact of the flood on Earth, Nüwa mended the hole in the sky using five colored crystals that represent the Chinese elements. She melted them together to make one giant crystal that blocked the gaping hole. When she was done, she died from exhaustion.

Red crystal
This crystal represents fire.

Black crystal
This crystal represents water.

Yellow crystal
This crystal represents earth.

Green crystal
This crystal represents wood.

White crystal
This crystal represents metal.

ESTABLISHING ORDER

The chief Chinese deity was the Jade Emperor (see pages 148–149), who sent three emperors from the heavens to rule humanity. The first emperor was Tian Guan, who ruled the heavens. The second was Di Guan, who ruled the world and judged people's actions. The third was Shui Guan, who ruled water and banished floods.

TIAN GUAN   **DI GUAN**   **SHUI GUAN**

143

144 asia • YI, THE HEAVENLY ARCHER

For his **heroic deeds**, Yi was referred to as the **"Son of Heaven."**

Fooling around
In some versions of the myth, the suns decided to rise together because they were bored.

Gift from a god
The red bow and white arrows that Yi used to kill the suns were given to him by Di Jun.

Legendary archer
Yi is often portrayed as a strong man dressed in military clothing.

Too many suns
As Yi delivered a shot, the sun exploded, revealing its spirit which took the form of a golden crow. People cheered him on from their huts as the Earth began to cool.

The Mid-Autumn Festival
In Chinese culture, Chang'e is celebrated in the Mid-Autumn Festival. Gathering under a full moon, families pray and leave offerings of pastries for the goddess, as Yi had done when she journeyed to the moon.

Spectacular displays
In China, the festival features street parades, lanterns, and the gifting of pastries known as mooncakes.

One of the **terrifying creatures** that wreaked havoc on Earth was the Windbird, which caused **storms** by flapping its **gigantic wings**.

6 In 2024, the **Chinese Lunar Exploration Program** launched six **Chang'e spacecraft**, named after the moon goddess.

> **The ten suns** all rose at once, **scorching** the sheaves of grain.
>
> *The Huainanzi,* c.139 BCE

Yi, the Heavenly Archer

In ancient China, legends featuring the hero Yi hailed him as a savior of humanity. In this story, he was assigned the task of ending a long period of hardship by shooting down ten playful suns. Today, the divine archer remains a celebrated figure in Chinese culture, along with his wife, the moon goddess Chang'e.

There were originally ten suns shining brightly, created by the sun goddess Xihe and the god of farming, Di Jun. Each sun had the spirit of a golden crow. One day, all ten suns flew into the sky at once, drying up the land and the crops people relied on for food. Adding to the people's misery, horrible monsters emerged, such as a beast with a dragon's head.

Desperate to save Earth from total destruction, the Emperor Yao told Xihe and Di Jun to keep their children in check, but the gods could not get the suns to come down, so they asked Yi for help. The heavenly archer came down to Earth with his wife Chang'e and his apprentice Fenmeng.

First, Yi killed the beasts that roamed the land, then he lifted his bow and shot down nine of the suns. The Earth became cooler. Yi was about to shoot the last sun when Yao stopped him, because the people needed it to survive.

As a reward, Yi was given a pill of immortality, but he decided not to take it because he did not want to outlive his wife. Jealous of Yi's success, Fenmeng broke into Yi's house while he was out hunting, and demanded the pill from Chang'e. She refused his request and swallowed the pill herself so Fenmeng couldn't take it. Her body felt light as a feather and she flew away, but stopped herself at the moon, so she could stay close to the Earth where Yi was. Yi was so upset that his wife was gone that each year he made offerings of her favorite foods at an altar on the day she had departed.

Spirit of the sun
The ten suns had identical spirits, which were golden crows with three legs.

Immortal goddess
As the goddess of the moon, Chang'e featured widely in stories. When she became immortal, a white rabbit followed her to the moon, and kept her company. For eternity, the goddess lived in the Palace of Boundless Cold.

Glowing gracefully
The goddess was a stunning young woman dressed in flowing robes, with radiant skin, black hair, and bright red lips.

The moon-eater
In one story, Tiangou the dog licked what remained of the immortality pill and followed Chang'e to the moon. Tiangou grew much bigger in size, which terrified Chang'e. She hid behind the moon, which the dog swallowed, along with Chang'e. Later, he was captured and forced to spit them out. It was believed that Tiangou ate the moon during an eclipse.

asia • ADVENTURES OF THE MONKEY KING

The forces of **chaos and the sky** created a **stone egg** from which the Monkey King hatched.

Iron staff
In one tale, the Monkey King stole an iron pillar from the underwater palace of the Dragon King, and turned it into an effective weapon.

Hero is he alone who vies with **powers supreme!**

Wu Ch'eng-en, *Monkey King: Journey to the West*, 16th century CE

Agile athlete
The Monkey King was an incredible athlete with superhuman strength who used his martial arts skills to beat any opponent. Even a single somersault saw him leap thousands of miles into the sky. He was always holding his magical staff, which could change shape and size. The Monkey King could even transform into different animals and objects, or make himself invisible, to suit his situation.

Perilous journey
The Monkey King was finally freed from his mountain prison by Buddhist monk Xuanzang. The pair traveled together for many years on the monk's journey to collect Buddhist texts in India. There were plenty of obstacles to overcome on Xuanzang's path to enlightenment, but the Monkey King proved a devoted bodyguard, protecting his new master. When Xuanzang returned with the Buddhist works many years later, he was made a Buddha, or "awakened one."

Traveling companions
The Monkey King joined his rescuer Xuanzang, who was traveling on horseback during his pilgrimage. The pair also picked up a companion, Pigsy, on their journey to India.

Goddess of goodness
In ancient times, Buddhists sought help from enlightened and compassionate beings known as bodhisattvas. Xuanzang sought the assistance of bodhisattva goddess Guanyin. She protected him with the companionship of the Monkey King.

STATUE OF GUANYIN

Journey to the West
A classic Chinese novel emerged in the 16th century, entitled *Monkey King: Journey to the West*, by author Wu Ch'eng-en. This book used traditional folk tales to tell the story of the Monkey King and the Buddhist monk.

Xuanzang
Xuanzang is the lead character who brings back Buddhist works from India for the Tang Dynasty of China.

Adventures of the Monkey King

A magical monkey caused chaos in ancient Chinese mythology by getting into all kinds of mischief. Traveling by cloud and transforming his shape, he was a trickster god who lived a life of adventure until he disturbed the peace in heaven. The legendary tales of the Monkey King were immortalized in a classic Chinese novel that still delights readers to this day.

The legend began in ancient China, when a breeze blew over a sacred rock, creating a stone egg. One day the egg hatched, revealing a very special monkey.

This monkey could walk and talk, and was blessed with magical powers to control the different elements of nature. As more monkeys heard of these impressive powers, he became known as the Monkey King. Soon he was leading his own gang around the forests. He fought off rivals and played harmless tricks on his friends in equal measure.

The Monkey King's unruly behavior caught the attention of the Jade Emperor, the ruler of heaven, who gave him a job in the palace in order to keep a watchful eye on him. But the Monkey King grew even more restless in heaven and ran around causing chaos. When the emperor's soldiers arrived to arrest him, he defeated them single-handedly.

The Buddha came to see the disruptive monkey and, after tricking him, sent him back to Earth. Here the Monkey King was imprisoned beneath a mountain for many years. A Buddhist monk in need of a protector eventually freed the Monkey King, and invited him to travel to India as his bodyguard, battling monsters and demons along the way.

The Monkey King became enlightened by his new friend and stopped his bad habits. As a result, he is known in China as Sun Wukong, which means "the monkey awakened by the emptiness."

| 500 | The number of years the Monkey King was **imprisoned under the mountain**. | 147 |

Under control
The Buddhist monk could tighten a magical golden headband when he wanted to control the monkey's bad behavior.

Miniature monkeys
Hair from the Monkey King could be transformed into other items, including miniatures of himself.

Tiger kilt
A kilt made from tiger fur showed the Monkey King's wild side and love of the forest.

Sky boots
The monkey's tough boots enabled him to walk across the clouds in the sky.

The Jade Emperor's court

From his throne in the heavens, the Jade Emperor ruled the universe assisted by many divine beings. His opulent realm reflected the complex court of the Chinese emperor on Earth.

While the Jade Emperor made decisions about matters affecting the world, he was helped by many gods and goddesses. These deities were often people who were sent to the heavens for their good deeds on Earth. They were assigned an area of expertise, such as weather, nature, or human matters. This is why the court of the Jade Emperor is referred to as the celestial bureaucracy—it was a type of divine government.

DIVINE RULER
As the first emperor of China and its heavenly ruler, the Jade Emperor was highly respected. He was fair and righteous, inspiring others to be like him. His decisions dictated whether the Earth remained harmonious or descended into chaos.

LAOZI

Birth of Yühuang
The Jade Emperor began life as a mortal named Yühuang. He was the child of King Ching Teh and Queen Pao Yüeh. For many years, the royal couple could not have children. One night, Pao Yüeh dreamed that Laozi, the founder of Daoism, came to her with a baby in his arms. Soon after, she became pregnant and gave birth to Yühuang.

Ascending to the throne
Even from birth, it was clear that Yühuang was gifted. He began speaking almost immediately, and was blessed with kindness and patience. He also studied meditation and philosophy, which led to his enlightenment—a heightened state of spiritual awareness. This paved the way for his role as ruler of the universe, the Jade Emperor, when he died.

The Jade Emperor's sacred symbols

Jade
This green gemstone represents power, reflecting the Jade Emperor's position in the universe.

Taoism
In the Chinese religion of Taoism, the Jade Emperor is considered the ruler of heaven and Earth.

Chinese Buddhism
The Jade Emperor was also associated with Buddhism, a popular religion in China.

Heavenly light
According to legend, Yühuang was born emitting a heavenly light to show that he was a divine being.

THE JADE EMPEROR

THE CELESTIAL BUREAUCRACY
Although the Jade Emperor's court was a glowing paradise, it was also a bustling establishment managed to the last detail. The court was organized into different departments, with each one led by a specific god, but the Emperor's orders were final.

Heavenly ministers
The Jade Emperor was one of four heavenly ministers. The Emperor of the North Star governed the seasons. The Emperor of the Curved Array looked after heaven and Earth, while the Empress of the Earth oversaw the natural world.

JADE EMPEROR   **EMPEROR OF THE NORTH STAR**   **EMPEROR OF THE CURVED ARRAY**   **EMPRESS OF THE EARTH**

The Eight Immortals
According to the religion of Daoism, a harmonious life could be achieved by finding balance in all things. The Eight Immortals were devout followers of Daoism, and their dedication earned them the prize of immortality. Each immortal carried their own magical object that gave them special powers. Many legendary Chinese stories featured the Eight Immortals in intrepid adventures that included shape-shifting and destroying evil.

Name	Role
He Xiangu	This immortal was a patron of the home and held a lotus flower to symbolize her ability to make flowers bloom.
Cao Guojiu	Cao Guojiu represented theater and drama and was usually shown holding a set of musical clappers, called paiban.
Li Tieguai	As a caretaker of the sick and vulnerable, Li Tieguai used an iron crutch and carried a calabash bottle.
Lan Caihe	Usually shown carrying a basket of flowers, Lan Caihe was a patron of florists, gardeners, and singing minstrels.
Lü Dongbin	Often regarded as group leader, Lü Dongbin carried a sword to slay monsters and a fly whisk to reflect his ability to fly.
Han Xiangzi	Patron of musicians, Han Xiangzi played the Chinese flute so tunefully that everyone was transfixed by his talent.
Zhang Guolao	Protector of fishermen and seafarers, Zhang Guolao carried a phoenix feather to represent eternal life.
Zhongli Quan	This immortal could make silver and gold on a whim, and held a fan with the power to awaken the dead.

14 The **14th day of the first lunar month** is celebrated in China as the birthday of **Lü Dongbin**, leader of the **Eight Immortals**.

3,000 It took **3,000 years** for a **peach** of **immortality** to ripen.

Protectors of China
One of the key roles of the court was ensuring that the people on Earth were cared for. Three main deities were on hand to support the Emperor in bringing good health, harmony, and happiness for all.

Underwater dweller
Known as the dragon king, the god Longwang resided in the oceans and brought rain for the crops to grow.

Zao Shen
The kitchen god watched over families and reported back to the Emperor on their conduct.

The matchmaker
The god of love Yue Lao lived under the moon and brought couples together using a special red thread.

Smooth sailing
One year, when the Eight Immortals were invited to an annual event in the heavens, they decided to journey there by sea instead of taking to the skies. They each used their objects to help them navigate the waters.

Popular tale
The story of this journey is still told in China to describe an event when people come together to showcase their talents.

EMPRESS OF HEAVEN
The wife of the Jade Emperor was Xi Wangmu, who was among the most powerful of the deities. Better known as the Queen Mother of the West, she took charge of life and death. In her orchard, she grew immortal peaches that remained ripe for an eternity.

Divine queen
In the celestial court, Xi Wangmu sat at the side of the Jade Emperor. She determined how long a person had to live, which is why her followers made offerings and prayed to her for good health.

XI WANGMU

Xi Wangmu's sacred symbols

Mount Kunlun
Xi Wangmu's home was a paradise on a mountain peak in the far west of China.

Peaches
The peaches of immortality gave anyone who ate them eternal life.

Hairpin
Using her decorative hairpin, Xi Wangmu sketched the Milky Way in the sky.

The Big Dipper
Xi Wangmu was in charge of the Big Dipper, a ladle-shaped constellation made up of seven stars.

The gift of immortality
According to legend, the Emperor Wu of Han desired the gift of immortality above all else. Instead, Xi Wangmu gave him seven white deer, which the Emperor looked after with great care. Delighted with his efforts, Xi Wangmu gave him a selection of her divine peaches. The Emperor ate them and was rewarded with eternal life.

WHITE DEER

150 asia • IZANAMI AND IZANAGI   Izanami and Izanagi were tasked to **begin creation** by the **previous generations of gods**.

Izanami and Izanagi

According to Japanese mythology, the seventh generation of deities, brother and sister Izanami and Izanagi, descended from the heavens to Earth. They created the universe and gave birth to the kami, or spirits, of the natural world.

Six generations of deities lived in the heavens before Izanagi (meaning He Who Invites) and Izanami (meaning She Who Invites) came into being. At this time, there was nothing on Earth except for an ocean of chaos. Izanagi and Izanami stood on the Floating Bridge of Heaven and stirred the ocean of chaos below with a giant spear. Salt dropped from the tip of the spear into the sea, forming the very first island, where the two creator deities chose to get married. This union brought about the creation of the world.

However, Izanami and Izanagi performed their marriage ceremony wrong, angering the older generations of deities. Their punishment was to give birth to the monstrous leech-child Hiruko. They repeated their ceremony correctly, and from this point on, Izanami gave birth to new deities, including the world's oceans, rivers, winds, mountains, trees, animals, and all elements of nature.

Tragically, her last child, Kagutsuchi, was a fire god whose sizzling flames killed her as he was born.

Izanagi was grief-stricken, so he followed Izanami down to Yomi, the underworld. When he arrived, Izanami refused to see him. But Izanagi pushed his way in anyway, and saw that his wife's body had already started to decay. Disgusted, he rejected her and ran away, so a furious Izanami chased him with an army of underworld beings. He escaped Yomi, and pushed a great stone across the entrance to prevent them from following him. In doing so, Izanagi trapped Izanami in Yomi for all eternity.

Starry spectacle
The Floating Bridge of Heaven may have been formed of the stars of the Milky Way.

The Wedded Rocks
Two distinctive rocks in the waters off southern Japan are known as Meoto Iwa, or the "Wedded Rocks." They represent the marriage between Izanami and Izanagi, and all marriages on Earth.

Sacred stones
The larger stone symbolizing the male and the smaller stone symbolizing the female are linked by a rope to represent their union.

Kagutsuchi
Fire god Kagutsuchi was the last born of Izanami's children, but his heat ended her life. Izanagi took revenge by killing Kagutsuchi with his sword. Eight volcanoes formed where Kagutsuchi's blood was spilled.

Yomi, the World of Darkness
According to Japanese mythology, all deceased souls entered Yomi, the underworld. The realm of the dead was a miserable place covered in eternal darkness. It was impossible for a soul to leave Yomi, especially if they ate any food in the underworld.

Underworld entrance
Legends say that the area known as Yomotsu Hirasaka in Japan marks an entrance to Yomi.

The Three Noble Children

The most powerful deities of nature were the sun goddess Amaterasu, the storm god Susanoo, and the moon god Tsukuyomi. They were chosen to be the heirs of the creator god Izanagi and were known as the Three Noble Children.

After leaving Izanami in the murky underworld of Yomi (see page 150), the first thing Izanagi did was clean himself. As he washed his face, three of his children came into being. Sun goddess Amaterasu was born as he cleaned his left eye, moon god Tsukuyomi was born as he cleaned his right eye, and storm god Susanoo was born as he cleaned his nose.

Amaterasu's bright light was powerful enough to burn the Earth. Izanagi suggested she move to the sky so she could warm Earth from a safe distance.

When Susanoo found that he was unable to visit his mother Izanami in Yomi, he lost his temper, and caused havoc at Amaterasu's home in the heavens. The sun goddess hid inside a cave, and the world fell into darkness. The crops failed and bad spirits emerged from the shadows.

Many attempts were made by the other deities to draw Amaterasu out from her cave. Eventually, Omoikane, the god of wisdom, came up with a clever plan. The gods hung a beautiful mirror and a string of jewels on a tree outside the cave. The dawn goddess Ame-no-Uzume performed a dance that made the other deities laugh. Amaterasu was curious about all the noise, so she peeked out. The mirror caught her reflection, captivating her, and she moved out of the cave. Quickly, the other gods tied the cave entrance with a sacred rope to stop Amaterasu from retreating back inside.

Many Japanese temples **feature a mirror** to honor the moment Amaterasu **saw her reflection**.

On reflection
The gods hung a great mirror from a tree that they had decorated outside the cave in the hope of luring out the sun goddess.

Roping off the entrance
Ritual god Futodama stood beside the cave with a sacred rope in hand, ready to prevent Amaterasu from ever returning inside.

Master plan
God of wisdom Omoikane devised the plan and watched the gods carry it out.

Tsukuyomi

Amaterasu (the sun) and Tsukuyomi (the moon) once shared space in the sky at the same time. But one day, Amaterasu sent her brother to a feast hosted by food goddess Ukemochi. However, Tsukuyomi was appalled when Ukemochi conjured up the meal by spitting out food from her mouth. In his disgust, he killed his host. Amaterasu vowed to never see him again, leading to the separation of day and night.

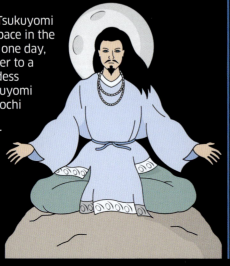

Today, visitors flock to see **Amano Iwato**, the "Heavenly Cave," where Amaterasu is believed to have **hidden herself away**.

It is believed that the **imperial family of Japan are descendants** of Amaterasu.

153

Here comes the Sun
Curious about her own reflection, Amaterasu emerged from the cave.

Shining light
When Amaterasu hid away in the cave, all light left the world. The other gods had to work together to convince Amaterasu to leave the cave and bring light back to the world.

Clearing the way
Ame-no-Tajikarao, the god of strength, pulled aside the giant boulder that Amaterasu had used to block the cave's entrance.

Ise Shrine
Dedicated to the goddess Amaterasu, Ise Shrine in Mie Prefecture is said to hold the Sacred Mirror used to entice Amaterasu from her cave. The mirror is one of three divine treasures given to Japan's imperial family.

Outer Shrine
Members of the public are not allowed inside the holy grounds of Ise's Inner Shrine, but they can visit the wooden buildings of the Outer Shrine.

Morning song
The gods brought cockerels to crow and create the traditional song of sunrise.

Dance the night away
Goddess of dawn Ame-no-Uzume was making merry by dancing outside the cave to make the other gods laugh.

Face the music
Gods of music played instruments, including gongs and flutes, to create a commotion to draw Amaterasu out of the cave.

154 asia • DESCENDANTS OF THE KAMI

The serpent Orochi is sometimes described as an eight-headed dragon.

SUSANOO ON EARTH
Soon after arriving on Earth, Susanoo rescued a princess from an eight-headed serpent. Susanoo then married her, becoming ruler of the lands of Japan.

Princess Kushinade-hime
On his travels across Japan, Susanoo came across a weeping family. They explained that they were gods of the land, and that the great serpent Yamata-no-Orochi would soon arrive to devour their daughter, Princess Kushinade-hime.

Meeting Kushinade-hime
Susanoo met the princess while she was saying goodbye to her parents before Orochi came for her.

Preparing for a fight
Susanoo turned the princess into a comb and placed her in his hair for safekeeping. He then built eight giant platforms and placed a barrel of sake (Japanese rice wine) on each one. Orochi arrived, and seeing the sake began to drink deeply from each barrel at once with its eight heads, soon falling asleep.

Sake barrel
Susanoo planned to get the serpent Orochi drunk.

Comb
Kushinade-hime means "Comb-stroking princess" and Susanoo transformed her into a comb to keep her safe from the serpent.

Susanoo and Orochi
Once Orochi was asleep, Susanoo began to cut of each of the serpent's eight heads and each of its eight tails. As he cut one of the tails, his sword snapped. Investigating, he found a gleaming sword inside the tail, Kusanagi ("Grass Cutter"). After the battle, he presented this sword to Amaterasu to apologize for his previous behavior.

Descendants of the kami

Japanese myths tell of how the rulership of Earth was passed from Susanoo the storm god to his descendant, Ōkuninushi. The great heavenly kami Amaterasu then sent her grandson to take control, leading to the establishment of the Japanese imperial family.

Susanoo was punished by the *amatsukami* (the gods in heaven) after his behavior led to his sister Amaterasu hiding her light away in a cave (see pages 152–153). The *amatsukami* cut off his beard and fingernails, and banished him from heaven.

Susanoo came to Earth, and after some adventures settled down in the Izumo region, becoming a *kunitsukami* (god of the land), and ruling over Japan. His sixth-generation descendant, Ōkuninushi, became his heir. Ōkuninushi gave up control of the land to the descendants of Amaterasu, who brought with them the imperial regalia and set up the imperial family of Japan.

UNITING HEAVEN AND EARTH
The sun goddess Amaterasu decided to unite Earth and heaven by sending her descendants to rule over Earth. Members of her family eventually became the first emperors of Japan.

Heaven takes control
Amaterasu sent her children to Earth to ask Ōkuninushi to give up control to heaven. These messengers ended up siding with the gods of the land. Exasperated, Amaterasu eventually decided to go to war, but Ōkuninushi then gave up control of Earth. Pleased, Amaterasu offered him a great shrine at Izumo where the gods would gather every year.

Izumo Taisha
The gods came to this shrine to Ōkuninushi once a year to decide on a path for humanity.

80,000 Ōkuninushi had a large family, with **80,000 brothers**.

After **giving up control of Japan**, Susanoo moved close to the underworld to be near **his mother Izanami**.

Fearsome Orochi
Orochi was the size of eight hills and eight valleys, and large enough to have cedar trees growing on its back.

ŌKUNINUSHI
Susanoo settled down in the Izumo region with Kushinade-hime. The pair began a family that extended to the sixth generation with the birth of Ōnamuji, who went on to become Ōkuninushi.

Ōnamuji and the rabbit
Once, Ōnamuji and his brothers traveled to Izumo, where there was a beautiful princess they wanted to marry. On the way they came across a rabbit with no skin. The rabbit explained that it had been skinned by crocodiles after it had tricked them. Ōnamuji's brothers laughed at the rabbit, but Ōnamuji told the rabbit how to restore its fur. In gratitude, the rabbit revealed itself to be a kami, and promised Ōnamuji that he would marry the princess.

Ōnamuji's trials
On arriving at Izumo, Ōnamuji fell in love with the princess, Susanoo's daughter Suseribime. With her assistance, and the help of some animals and his own wits, Ōnamuji completed four trials set by Susanoo for her hand in marriage.

Poisonous snakes
Ōnamuji avoided being bitten by snakes using a scarf given to him by Suseribime.

Bees and hornets
Waving the scarf saved Ōnamuji from being stung to death by bees and hornets.

A field of fire
Ōnamuji was able to retrieve an arrow from a field on fire with the help of a mouse.

Centipedes
For the final trial, Ōnamuji pretended to chew up the centipedes living in Susanoo's hair.

Finishing creation
After Ōnamuji's success in the trials, Susanoo handed over rulership of Japan to Ōnamuji, who from that point on became known as Ōkuninushi, the "Master of the Land." His first task as ruler was to finish the work of creation. Ōkuninushi traveled Japan, making the land fertile so it would be a fit place for humanity to live.

Little helper
Ōkuninushi was helped in his task by Sukunabikona ("Little Name Lad"), a mysterious deity with strange powers who had come to Japan from across the ocean.

Ninigi and the Imperial Regalia
Amaterasu's grandson Ninigi, a god of rice growing, came to Earth to be its ruler. Amaterasu gave him three sacred treasures, known as the Imperial Regalia: the sword Kusanagi, and a jewel and a mirror that had been used by the gods to entice Amaterasu to leave the cave she had been hiding in (see pages 152–153).

Yata-no-Kagami
The eight-sided mirror in which Amaterasu saw her reflection as she peeked out of the cave.

Yasakani-no-Magatama
A sparkling jewel that decorated the tree to dazzle Amaterasu when she left the cave.

Kusanagi-no-Tsurugi
The sword given to Amaterasu by Susanoo to atone for his past actions in heaven.

Gods of the sea
Ninigi married a goddess of the land and had many children. Their son Hoderi dived into the ocean to retrieve a lost fish hook one day, and came across a great palace belonging to Watatsumi, the god of the sea. Hoderi fell in love with the god's daughter and married her.

Goddess of treasure
Watatsumi's daughter was called Toyotama-hime, and she was the goddess of ocean treasures.

First emperor
Eventually, Amaterasu's descendant Jimmu became the legendary first emperor of Japan. Due to his lineage, he was descended from the gods of heaven, the gods of the land, and the gods of the sea. Jimmu was given the Imperial Regalia, which remains in the possession of the Japanese imperial family to this day.

Imperial origins
Jimmu became emperor after leading a military force to capture Yamato from the gods of the land.

Kintaro, the golden boy

One of Japan's most famous legends tells of a young hero, Kintaro ("golden boy"). Kintaro embarked on adventures that put his supernatural strength to the test on his way to becoming a samurai warrior.

The story of Kintaro began with a man called Kintoki, a heroic warrior of high standing in the Japanese emperor's court. Kintoki married a young woman, but the pair were unjustly exiled from court after the emperor heard some false rumors about them.

After building a new home in the forest, the couple were soon expecting their first child. Tragically, Kintoki died before the birth of the baby—a boy with incredible strength, named Kintaro. Raised in the forest by his mother, Kintaro could cut down trees with the strength of a grown man by the time he was just eight years old.

Kintaro befriended the wild animals around him, including a monkey, a bear, and a hare. He used his great strength to protect his animal friends from other dangerous creatures, such as the huge earth-spider that poisoned anything it caught in its web.

A legend known throughout East Asia told of a waterfall that could transform a carp into a dragon if it could leap over the top. A carp challenged Kintaro to prove his strength, by catching it before it could reach the top of the waterfall. Although the fish was swift, Kintaro caught up and stopped it by wrapping himself around its back.

A man walking through the forest one day saw Kintaro pull down a huge tree with his bare hands, and challenged him to an arm-wrestle. After the boy beat him, the stranger revealed himself to be a respected samurai and took Kintaro to meet his master, Raiko. Raiko invited Kintaro to join a small group of elite warriors, The Four Braves. From a boy hero protecting the forest, Kintaro had grown into a protector of Japan and all of its people.

> The waterfall that could turn fish into dragons was believed to be at **the source of the Yellow River** in China.

Forest wrestling
As the strongest being in the forest, Kintaro organized wrestling matches among himself and his friends. Demonstrating his fairness, Kintaro gave prizes of rice cakes to both the winners and the losers of the contests.

A fair judge
Kintaro would sometimes also act as the referee of the wrestling matches between the other animals.

The Four Braves
Known across Japan for their skills and bravery, the Four Braves were legendary samurai. Kintaro was the strongest of the team, and led his men into battles against fearsome enemies.

Extra weapon
Some portraits show the brave young hero with a battle-ax in his hand.

King of fish
No other fish was respected in Japanese culture as much as the carp, seen as a strong, heroic species.

Red skin
Kintaro is often pictured with red skin and a cloth around his waist.

A titanic struggle
Kintaro held onto the carp with all his might as it thrashed about and tried to leap up the waterfall. The fish eventually conceded that Kintaro had won the challenge.

Children's Day
The story of Kintaro is celebrated to this day on Children's Day, an annual festival in which Japanese families display miniature Kintaro figures in their homes. Colorful streamers in the shape of carp are also hung outside homes and businesses.

Good luck motif
Kintaro dolls are displayed in the hope that children will become as brave and strong as the young hero.

asia • THE CREATION AND FOUNDATION OF KOREA

Some Buddhists believe that Maitreya will one day return to save the world.

SONGS OF CREATION

Creation stories of the universe, the Earth, and humans were often passed down through the songs of shamans. One tale tells of the god Mireuk, also known as Maitreya, who introduced order to a chaotic universe.

Two suns and two moons

Mireuk appeared at a time when the sky and the Earth were joined together as one. He placed four giant pillars between them to keep them apart. Because there were two suns and two moons, the god took one of each and broke them apart to make the stars.

Holy creator
In Buddhism, Maitreya is believed to be a holy being known as a bodhisattva.

Fire and water

GRASSHOPPER

FROG

MOUSE

The world Mireuk created had no fire or water, so he set off to find them. First, he asked the grasshopper for help, but the insect told him to talk to the frog, who advised Mireuk to seek out the mouse. After some bargaining, the mouse told Mireuk to go to Mount Gumjeong, where he found stone and iron to make fire, and from the top of Mount Sohwa, he could see the ocean.

Caterpillars into humans

After creating the world and finding both fire and water, Mireuk felt lonely. He decided to create humanity. Holding a silver tray in one hand and a golden tray in the other, he offered up a prayer. Caterpillars appeared on each tray—the ones on the silver tray turned into women and the ones on the golden tray became men.

Feeding the monks

A reluctant Mireuk gave up the throne, but cursed Seokga for his trickery. Seokga tried to imprison Mireuk, but the creator god transformed into a deer and escaped. Some monks found the deer and brought it to Seokga, who killed it and cooked it for its meat. Two of the monks refused to eat it, and when they died, they became rocks and pine trees.

PEONY

Seokga's jealousy

Seeing Mireuk's achievements, the god Seokga grew envious. He wanted to replace Mireuk as supreme ruler of the world. Seokga, who was known to be a trickster, challenged Mireuk. He proposed that they fall asleep and whoever made a peony bloom from their body would rule the world. Mireuk agreed, and while he slept, the peony bloomed on him. Seokga pretended to sleep, but seeing the flower, he stole it and put it in his lap.

Standing tall
The two monks, who became rocks and pine trees, are still honored today for their respectful deeds.

The creation and foundation of Korea

North and South Korea share a rich culture that dates back nearly 5,000 years. The myths and legends of their people tell of the creation of Korea and of its first legendary rulers.

Korean mythology is influenced by other Asian traditions, particularly Buddhism, which made its way to Korea from China. The natural world also plays a significant role in Korean stories. The creator god Mireuk, for example, was guided by the wisdom of animals, and the god Hwanung was fascinated with Korea's mountains. Tales from Jeju Island tell a humorous tale of the world's creation, while foundation stories of Korea's early kingdoms tell of heroic deeds by the children of gods.

DIVINE GRANDMOTHER

In an alternative creation story told by the people of Jeju Island, the goddess Grandma Seolmundae caused a chain of explosions by passing wind in her sleep. These explosions created the universe. Then, with her strong hands, she made Jeju Island.

KOREA'S FIRST KING

The prince of heaven, Hwanung, descended to the mountains of Earth to govern humanity. He built a great city and became the father of Dangun, the first ruler of a Korean kingdom.

Heaven King

Accompanied by 3,000 spirits, Hwanung arrived on Baekdu Mountain beneath a sacred sandalwood tree. From there, he founded Shinsi ("City of God") and gave himself the title "Heaven King," ruling over all aspects of life. Each day, a tiger and a bear emerged from their cave to pray to the king.

BAEKDU MOUNTAIN

The tiger and the bear

One day, the two animals begged Hwanung to transform them into human beings. Moved by their pleas, Hwanung gave them each some garlic to eat and told them to stay in a cave for 100 days. The tiger, driven by hunger, soon gave up and left. The bear remained and was transformed into a beautiful woman.

Hwanung's robe
The divine king wore a royal robe while performing his duties.

Human king

The bear woman Ungnyeo gave daily offerings to the king and prayed for a son. Transforming into a human, Hwanung had a child with her, who she named Dangun. Establishing the kingdom of Gojoseon, Dangun became the first king in Korea.

KING DANGUN

Sculpting the land

One day, Grandma Seolmundae was bored and decided to make an island. Equipped with unimaginable strength, she scooped up mud from the sea floor and carried it in her skirt. Then she piled it up to mold Jeju Island. As she went back and forth collecting mud, some of it accidentally fell through a hole in her skirt. This towering heap became Hallasan Mountain—the tallest mountain in South Korea.

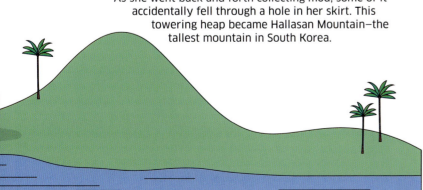

A GREAT KINGDOM

At one time, Korea was split into the kingdoms of Goguryeo, Baekje, and Silla. One story describes the troubled birth of Goguryeo's founding monarch.

Sent from heaven

One day, the god Hae Mosu came down to Earth riding a chariot pulled by divine dragons. He saw Lady Yuhwa bathing in a pond with her sisters, and lured her into his beautiful palace. When Yuhwa's father, the river god Habaek, confronted him, Hae Mosu let her go.

The unbreakable egg

Yuhwa's family exiled her because she had fallen in love with Hae Mosu. One day, the king of Buyeo found her by a river and locked her in a tower to keep her away from the god. But Hae Mosu's rays of sunlight made Yuhwa pregnant when they touched her. She soon gave birth to a large egg, which the king tried hard to break. Eventually, Yuhwa took the egg back and kept it warm.

Narrow escape

A boy hatched out of the egg and was given the name Jumong. He was talented and grew up to be an excellent archer. The king didn't trust Jumong and wanted him dead, so Jumong escaped with his friends. Coming to a river, Jumong cried for help. Fish and turtles assembled to form a bridge for them to cross, and swam away before the king's army could follow. When Jumong reached the Biryu River, he founded the kingdom of Goguryeo there.

THE AMERICAS

Myths and sacred stories from North and South America and the Caribbean often explained features of the natural world. The descendants of the Maya, Inca, and other cultures from throughout the Americas still tell these stories to this day.

NORTH AMERICA

The sacred stories of the Indigenous peoples of what is now mainland United States and Canada are a vital part of their identity to this day. Many of the stories that are still told are at the heart of their diverse belief systems. The land is so vast that there are many different stories and versions of stories, but similar characters appear in the beliefs of particular regions.

NORTHWEST AMERICA

The Indigenous peoples of the northwest traditionally lived in settled villages of wooden houses. Families told stories of their legendary clan founders, who often took the form of supernatural animals.

Totem poles

Expressions of family pride, totem poles trace a clan's ancestors, often back to an animal spirit that represents the clan. Travelers had only to look at the house totem poles when entering an unfamiliar village to see which families shared their clan's totem, and therefore where they would be welcome. Totem poles also tell stories about the foundation of a clan or its history.

Land otter pole
This totem pole in Totem Bight State Historical Park, Alaska, was carved by the Haida people.

Thunderbird

A protective birdlike spirit, the Thunderbird creates thunder and lightning. It is a common character in beliefs across the entire continent, but it frequently features in the art and stories of the Pacific Northwest.

THUNDERBIRD

SOUTHWEST AMERICA

The people of the southwest made buildings from mud bricks. Some of these were temporary, but many people lived together in permanent settlements containing *pueblos*–multi-storied houses. Stories from this region are often concerned with the origins of the people of the area. Also important are rituals in which people put on masks to imitate spirits or create art that tells stories.

Emergence stories

The Diné, Hopi, and Pueblo peoples, among others, tell how humanity had to travel upward through a series of different worlds before arriving in this one, often helped by supernatural figures such as Coyote. This type of tale is known as an emergence story, and is common across many world mythologies and beliefs.

A COYOTE

THE GREAT PLAINS

Running down the center of North America, the Great Plains are flat grasslands once home to nomadic peoples who hunted buffalo. Animal myths were common here, and ceremonies such as the smoking of a sacred pipe and the annual sun dance held in the sun's honor were also important.

Power of the stars

The ceremonies of the Pawnee, such as those performed before a hunt or at the beginning of spring, were timed by observing the movements of the stars. The Pawnee believed that if they carried out their rituals according to the stars, the universe would continue to function and the people would thrive.

Pawnee star chart
This diagram of the night sky was created by the Pawnee on leather made from the skin of a deer.

Sacred pipe

According to the Lakota people, the supernatural figure known as White Buffalo Calf Woman taught them seven sacred rites. She gave the Lakota the *chanunpa*, the sacred pipe, to perform one of these ceremonies. The smoking of the pipe connected people with the world of the divine. Many Lakota have their own personal pipes, but the original pipe has also been handed down through the generations.

A CHANUNPA

Sand painting

Ceremonies are important across the cultures of many Indigenous peoples. In the southwest United States, the Diné people developed a healing ritual that takes the form of dry painting using colored sand and other powders. The temporary art that this creates is destroyed once the ritual is complete.

Sand stories
Medicine men create scenes from sand that often depict characters and stories from their people's beliefs.

The importance of buffalo

The nomads of the Great Plains used every part of the buffalo they hunted, from the meat to the hide. Some believed that buffalo were a gift from the Great Spirit, and that the animals rose up from the earth each spring to give nourishment to humankind. If the people failed to live in tune with nature, the Great Spirit might withhold this great gift.

THE EASTERN WOODLANDS

The beliefs of the people of the northeast United States and eastern Canada reflect local landscapes. Spirits of woods, lakes, and rivers are common features of the region's stories. Their creation tales, including Turtle Island (see pages 164-165), feature many animals.

Cherokee creation

In the story of creation told by the Cherokee, the world began with no land. Water Beetle brought up clay from the bottom of the ocean. The clay spread, forming an island. Then Buzzard flew overhead, carving out high mountains and deep valleys. The animals took the sun to light the Earth. Then they tried to stay awake for seven days and nights. Those who succeeded, such as the owl, were rewarded with better senses at night.

Water beetle
Offering to explore the world below, Water Beetle created the land.

Buzzard
The flight of Buzzard created the mountains as it rose and descended.

Crawfish
At first the sun was too close to the Earth, and it burned the crawfish, turning it red.

Underwater panther

Known as the Mishipeshu ("Great Lynx") to the Ojibwe people, the underwater panther was one of the most important water spirits of the Great Lakes region. Living at the bottom of lakes, they were often unfriendly, and needed to be pacified so that they would grant safe passage across the waters.

A mix of animal parts
The underwater panther had the body, head, and claws of a cat but the horns of a deer or bison. It was covered in scales and had a long tail.

THE ARCTIC

In Alaska, Greenland, and northern Canada, the Inuit people have a very distinct culture from the rest of North America. Their spiritual advisors are known as Angaqquk, and many ceremonies focus on the respectful treatment of animals.

Inua

For the Inuit, all creatures, including humans, share a type of soul called an *inua*. Preparing for a whale hunt, the Inuit perform cleansing ceremonies and use special weapons to honor the whale. It is believed that the animal's *inua* will cooperate in the hunt to ensure success if it is shown the proper respect.

Angaqquk

The equivalent of medicine men and women, Angaqquk perform rituals on behalf of the Inuit people. These ceremonies might involve the wearing of a mask to represent a spirit. One annual rite involves a spirit journey to visit Sedna (see pages 170-171).

INUIT SPIRIT MASK

164 the americas • TURTLE ISLAND

40 There are more than **40 different versions** of the Turtle Island story among **different Indigenous North American communities.**

The fall of Old Woman
When Old Woman fell, she disturbed the water creatures, and Water Fowl, in the form of geese, flew up to slow her descent. There was no dry land to rest on, so Water Fowl placed her on the back of Turtle's shell.

Muskrat saves the day
Many of the water creatures tried to help Old Woman find dirt, but all failed. Finally, Muskrat dived, deeper than ever, and came up with some mud. He spread the mud on Turtle's back, and so created Ga'nowa'geh, Turtle Island.

Muskrat underestimated
The other creatures laughed at Muskrat's offer to help find mud, but he proved he was more capable than all of them.

The forming of Turtle Island
When Muskrat spread the mud he had found at the bottom of the sea on Turtle's back, it spread and grew until it formed the surface of the Earth.

Forming continent
The land was formed from the mud spread on Turtle's back, forming what is now known as the North American continent.

Turtle Island

The Indigenous peoples of northeastern North America tell a creation story of how Old Woman, also sometimes referred to as Sky Woman, fell from the heavens, and a turtle became the land on which she could live.

There are many different versions of this story depending on which group is telling it. Among the Seneca people (part of the Haudenosaunee or Iroquois confederacy), it is said that Old Woman became pregnant when she inhaled the breath of the Earth Holder. Angered, the Earth Holder uprooted the great tree at the center of the sky world, making a hole into which he told Old Woman to look. Then he pushed her in. She tried to grab the tree to stop herself from falling, but she only ended up with some seeds and root. Old Woman then fell all the way to Earth, which at that time was covered in water and inhabited only by water creatures. Old Woman was saved from drowning when she landed on a giant turtle that had come up from the deep.

In order for Old Woman to plant the seeds she had brought with her, she needed soil. With the help of Muskrat, who dived down to the bottom of the water to retrieve some mud, Old Woman made Ga'nowa'geh, or Turtle Island (the continent of North America according to the legends of some Indigenous North Americans). The mud was spread on Turtle's shell, which grew and grew until it formed a large island, where the seeds were able to grow into plants.

Eventually, Old Woman gave birth to a daughter, and her daughter gave birth to two children, the twins Sapling and Flint. Sapling created the moon and stars and made all the good things in the world, including corn, while Flint made all the bad things like weeds and vermin.

1632 The **earliest written version** we know of Turtle Island is from 1632, but the story is **much older**.

6 The **Haudenosaunee (Iroquois) Confederacy** was made up of six tribes, known as the **Six Nations**.

165

Jagged mountains
Old Woman's grandson Sapling created the mountains, but her other grandson Flint made them crooked.

Twisted trees
Sapling made the trees straight, but Flint sent winds to make them gnarled and twisted.

North American lands
Turtle's shell is shaped like North America, and Indigenous peoples often use the term Turtle Island to refer to the continent. This emphasizes the link between American landscape and Indigenous culture and spiritual beliefs. The term is also being used within Indigenous rights activism and environmentalism.

"The Great Spirit ...
pulled up a great tree by the roots, and threw her through the cavity thereby formed."

The Journal of Major John Norton, 1816

166 the americas ○ SPIDER GRANDMOTHER

The dream catcher, a talisman used to get rid of nightmares, was created by Spider Grandmother.

THE WISE WEAVER
Also known as Good Spirit, Spider Grandmother was said to have weaved the four directions—north, south, east, and west—from her silk threads. Her songs were powerful spells that could bring people to life. She didn't keep the secrets of the world to herself, but shared her knowledge, showing people how to weave on a loom and how to grow crops. Acting as advisor and healer, she guided the creatures she had created.

Traditional loom
The Diné loom, which has been used for centuries, is vertical and the frame is usually made from wood.

Working away
Spider Grandmother usually sat beside her loom, working on her cloth while singing her magical song.

Spider's web
She discovered weaving on a loom when her web got stuck to a tree branch by accident.

Spider Grandmother

As an Earth goddess, divine creator, and protector of humans, Spider Grandmother (also known as Spider Woman) has woven her way into the center of Indigenous American stories. Her wisdom is a source of guidance for her people.

Tales of Spider Grandmother are treasured by the Hopi, Diné, Ojibwe, and many other Indigenous American peoples. She is known as Kokyangwuti by the Hopi, Na'ashjé'ii Asdzáá by the Diné, and Asibikaashi by the Ojibwe. Spider Grandmother could change her form, size, and age at will. According to the Hopi, she usually took the form of a spider or an old woman. She features in Indigenous American emergence stories, a type of creation myth in which humans must rise up through a number of realms to reach the world we live in today.

TALES OF THE GRANDMOTHER
Stories about Spider Grandmother have spread far and wide among Indigenous American peoples. There are many variations on her abilities and behavior. However, her supreme wisdom and central role in the creation of the world are present in many cultures.

Giver of totems
Spider Grandmother wove intricate, powerful webs that kept all humans spiritually connected to one another. After she had molded people from clay, she put them into different groups. Each one was gifted a totem animal—a sacred spirit guide to protect them and to provide useful life skills.

Eagle
The eagle was a strong symbol of leadership, offering courage and independence.

Salmon
The salmon promised plentiful food and was thought to be extremely determined.

Beaver
As a resourceful creature, the beaver was a skilled hunter and gatherer.

Dragonfly
A person represented by the dragonfly was naturally creative and easily adaptable.

According to legend, **foxes have black mouths** because the first fox **burned his mouth trying to steal the sun**.

Changing Woman, who is thought to have created the **Diné people**, is the **mother of the Hero Twins**.

THE FOUR WORLDS

Indigenous American emergence stories describe four stages of creation, the last one being the current world we know today. The First World offered only darkness. Spider Grandmother appeared and took all creatures into the Second World and eventually the Third World, where she shared her abilities with humans, then led them to settle in the Fourth World.

The sun god

In the beginning, before the existence of Spider Grandmother and everything else, was Tawa the sun god. He took what he could from the endless space around him and put together the First World. The only life was tiny, insect-like creatures. Tawa then created Spider Grandmother to help these creatures develop. She took them to the Second World, where they grew fur and transformed into bears and wolves. But the animals weren't very smart, so Tawa created a Third World for them to evolve further.

Supreme deity
According to the Hopi, Tawa was a powerful being who had control over all aspects of life.

The helpful hummingbird

When Spider Grandmother took the animals to the Third World, they became humans. They struggled in this new world, unable to live peacefully with one another. A hummingbird arrived and told them about the existence of a better place above the sky – the Fourth World.

Little teacher
The hummingbird gave people fire and showed them how to use it.

Through the sky

Spider Grandmother agreed with the hummingbird that the Fourth World was a better place for them. There was an opening in the sky to access it, but strong winds made it impossible to get there. Spider Grandmother enlisted the help of Chipmunk, who planted a seed that grew into a bamboo reed. Everyone climbed up the bamboo stalk into the Fourth World.

Marked forever
In one story, the chipmunk's stripes are the paw marks of a bear that tried to catch it.

Grandmother steals the sun

In one version of the creation myth, Spider Grandmother brought light to the First World, where everything was consumed by darkness. Rumors about the existence of the sun began to spread. Fox found it first and bit off a piece of the sun. He spat it out instantly because it was too hot. Possum tried to take the sun by wrapping it with his tail, but he lost it. Spider Grandmother weaved a bag and successfully carried a piece of the sun back with her.

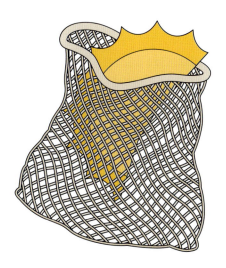

Terrifying kidnapper

In Diné stories, Spider Grandmother had a fearsome side. If children were behaving badly, she would weave a giant web to throw at them like a huge net. She would catch, boil, and devour them. The giant rock where she lived was thought to be covered in white bands from the bones of children that had melted under the sun.

Spider Rock
Considered home of Spider Grandmother, the sandstone Spider Rock in Arizona remains a sacred site for the Diné people.

The Hero Twins

In some Diné creation stories, Spider Grandmother had help from two brothers known as the Hero Twins. Known as the Hero Twins, they assisted her in creating the world and destroying the forces of evil that threatened the future of Earth. They were armed with strong bows and arrows. Spider Grandmother shielded the twins from an attack from monsters by giving them a set of magical hoops made from eagle feathers.

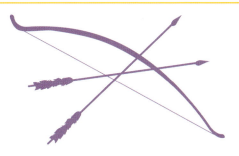

the americas • STORIES OF RAVEN

There are **two separate Raven characters** in Tlingit mythology—**Creator Raven**, who brought light to the world, and the **sly, trickster Raven**.

Ball of light
With the ball of sunlight in his beak, Raven brought light to the universe.

Shriveled claws
Being so close to the sun's heat caused Raven's claws to shrivel and curl up.

Stories of Raven

For many Indigenous peoples of northwestern North America, the raven is a magical, heroic bird with a mythological history. Many creation tales involving Raven have been passed down through generations.

The raven holds a special place in the sacred stories that form the cultural history of the First Nations people who inhabit the northwest Pacific coastal region of North America. These stories portray the bird as clever, playful, and possessing supernatural powers. Raven is credited with such feats as discovering the first humans and bringing fire and light to the world.

The story of Raven stealing the sun has many variations. One version tells of a time when the world was in total darkness, because all the light was hoarded by the Sky Chief in boxes in his home.

When Raven heard about this, he hatched a plan to take the light. Traveling to the sky world, he transformed into a cedar leaf that fell into a pail of water. This water was drunk by the Sky Chief's daughter, who became pregnant and had a baby boy, who was really Raven in disguise.

The boy cried endlessly, so the Sky Chief handed him a box containing the stars to play with. Before the Sky Chief could stop him, the boy opened the box and the stars flew out of a hole in the roof, where they stuck in the sky.

Raven cried again, so the Sky Chief gave him another box, which contained the moon. Raven bounced it like a ball until it bounced out of the house and flew into the sky.

The Sky Chief then gave the crying boy a final box, which contained the sun. Raven quickly transformed back into a bird, took the sun in his beak, and flew away up into the sky, finally illuminating the dark world with daylight.

The first humans
The Haida people of British Columbia, Canada, tell a story of creation in which Raven and Butterfly were playing with a giant clam shell on the beach. All of a sudden, they discovered that humans were hiding inside the shell. Raven assured the people that it was safe to emerge, and they became the first people to populate the land.

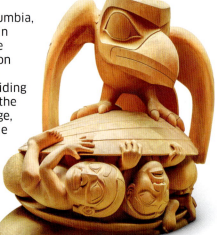

Raven's discovery
In 1980, Haida artist Bill Reid carved Raven's discovery of humans in the clam shell.

Raven was also known as **Txamsem** by the **Tsimshian people**.

169

Blackened feathers
Raven's feathers were burned black from carrying the sun for so long.

Stealing the sun
Raven stole the sun for humankind and brought light to the world, but this generous act didn't come without consequences. Being so close to the sun's heat burned his once-white feathers black and caused his claws to shrivel.

Raven brings fire
According to a Haida creation story, Raven stole the moon, sun, stars, and fire from a shaman, releasing them all from the sky. When Raven dropped fire, it was in the form of a burning piece of wood that landed between two rocks. This is why sparks fly when rocks are struck together.

Raven and Seagull
In the beliefs of the Tlingit people, the Great Spirit gave Seagull a box containing all the world's light. Raven asked Seagull to open the box, but he refused. Raven tried everything to make Seagull change his mind, but nothing worked. So Raven decided to stick a thorn into Seagull's foot. In pain, Seagull dropped the box, causing it to break open and release the sun, moon, and stars.

Sedna, Mother of the Deep

The goddess of the sea, Sedna is an important spirit being in the mythology of the Inuit peoples, who inhabit the frozen north of the Americas and Greenland. Half human, half sea creature, she is an unpredictable goddess whose influence can mean the difference between a successful and an unsuccessful hunt.

Sedna's story is a creation tale that explained the birth of all sea mammals, a main source of food for the Inuit peoples. The story had several versions—in some Sedna was cast out from her village in her father's kayak; in others she was kidnapped by a bird spirit and rescued by her father; and in others she married a mysterious lover and angered her father.

But in all of these versions, Sedna and her father ended up in a kayak in the middle of the sea. In this part of the story, Sedna either fell out of the boat or was pushed overboard by her father. When she tried to cling onto the kayak, he cut off her fingers, which transformed into the first seals, walruses, whales, and narwhals.

No longer able to climb back into the boat, Sedna sank to the bottom of the ocean, where she transformed into a goddess. She became ruler of the Adlivun (which means "those who live beneath us"), residents of the watery underworld of the same name that lay below the land and the ocean.

As the powerful mother of the sea beasts, Sedna guided them to the Inuit's hunting grounds. But if Sedna observed the humans treating them badly, she would become angry and keep the animals in the sea so they could not be hunted. Sedna's temper was unpredictable, and she might also hold back the sea creatures out of ill-temper.

When this happened, Sedna could only be calmed by an *angakkuq*, or shaman, who had to go to the watery underworld and brush and clean Sedna's hair. This was a task she was unable to perform herself without fingers. Once the shaman had tended to her hair, she would free the sea creatures so humans once again had a steady supply to hunt.

The fulmar bride
Some accounts of the story describe how Sedna met a handsome young man who promised her many comforts, and married him. When they were out on a remote island, the man revealed that he was actually a spirit that had taken the form of a fulmar, a type of bird similar to a seagull. He treated her very poorly, and eventually, Sedna's father came to rescue her. The spirit bird raised a destructive storm, and fearful that the storm would only get worse, Sedna's father threw her into the sea.

A FULMAR

Many Inuit legends were **cautionary tales** that reflected the **dangers** of living in the **harsh Arctic environment**.

171

Balance in nature
As the mother and steward of all sea creatures, Sedna is central to the Inuit idea of the need to respect all animals and the environments that they live in. She was often depicted with the upper half of a human and the bottom half of a sea creature.

Tangled hair
Sedna's hair would get tangled and dirty, but as she lacked fingers, she needed a shaman to help her tame her locks.

Fingerless hands
Sedna's hands had no fingers, so she was unable to brush or clean her hair.

Creatures of the deep
Seals were one of the sea creatures that Sedna's fingers became after they were cut off and fell into the sea.

Appeasing Sedna
Before going on a hunt, the Inuit will say prayers to Sedna and ask her to release the animals from the deep so they can capture them for food. Offerings of knives, bones, and morsels of food are also thrown into the sea before the hunters set out on the water.

Bladed offerings
Old Inuit harpoon blades are ceremoniously released into the ocean.

Poor hunting
The shaman figure in the story—*angakkuq* in Inuit—operates as a link between the human and spirit worlds. When the numbers of fish and sea creatures are low, he travels to see Sedna and combs her hair so she will release animals for the hunters.

MESOAMERICA

The name Mesoamerica is now given to a historical region and cultural area made up of parts of Mexico and Central America. Before the arrival of European conquerors in the 16th century, these lands were home to a series of highly developed civilizations, including the Maya and the Aztecs. The people of Mesoamerica worshipped many deities at their pyramid-shaped temples, particularly gods of weather and farming.

SOURCES

Many of the myths of Mesoamerican cultures were first written down on paper by European colonizers. But some of what we know about Mesoamerican religion comes from the illustrations and glyphs (or symbols) found in codices and temple architecture.

Codices
A Mesoamerican codex is an illustrated manuscript, sometimes containing writing. Codices (the plural of codex) might contain images of sacrifice to the gods or calendar calculations used in rituals. Only a small number of codices from before the arrival of Europeans have survived.

THE MADRID CODEX

THE EVOLUTION OF MESOAMERICAN MYTH

The Maya and the Aztec had very complex and sophisticated mythologies, but features of their stories and rituals were taken from the many other cultures that existed over time in the region. Some gods had multiple identities, because they were known by different names in different cultures.

Olmec
The earliest Mesoamerican civilization, the Olmec flourished between c.1500 BCE and c.400 BCE. They lived in southern Mexico, and were the first culture in Mesoamerica who were known to have worshipped a feathered serpent deity.

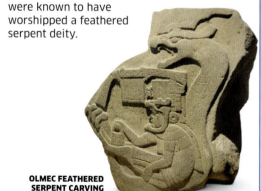

OLMEC FEATHERED SERPENT CARVING

Zapotec
Based in southern Mexico, the Zapotec thrived from around 300 CE to 600 CE. Their most important god was Cocijo, a lightning god who was responsible for rainfall. Many later civilizations had similar rain deities.

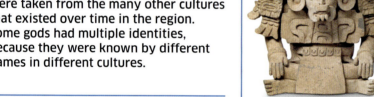

COCIJO

Toltec
Many gods of the Aztecs were borrowed from the Toltec, whose civilization was most powerful between 900 and 1180 CE. Gods such as Quetzalcoatl, Tlaloc, and Tezcatlipoca were originally worshipped by the Toltec.

TOLTEC CUP SHOWING QUETZALCOATL

Teotihuacan
The ruins at Teotihuacan show the importance of temples in Mesoamerican urban life. The heart of the city was a religious center containing two of the largest pyramids in Mesoamerica, the Pyramid of the Moon and the Pyramid of the Sun.

View from Pyramid of the Moon
The Pyramid of the Moon rose above stepped pyramids in Teotihuacan's central plaza. In the distance stood the huge Pyramid of the Sun.

MAJOR GODS

The Mesoamericans worshipped hundreds of gods, but some feature more prominently than others in the stories of the Maya and the Aztecs. Itzamná was a Maya creator deity, while Quetzalcoatl, Tezcatlipoca, and Huitzilopotchli were particularly important in the pantheon of Aztec gods.

Itzamná
Not much is known about Itzamná, except that he was the greatest of the Maya god, and ruled over heaven, day, and night. Sometimes he is depicted as four gods, each of which faces a different direction: north, east, south, and west.

Maya glyphs
The Maya were the only civilization in the Americas to develop a fully formed writing system. Maya glyphs can be found in codices and inscribed in stone at temples.

Temple carvings
Scenes and characters from Mesoamerican myths were carved into the elaborate decorations that can be found on Mesoamerican temples.

WORSHIP OF THE GODS
The gods of Mesoamerica required offerings in rituals that were performed on a regular basis. Many civilizations used a ritual calendar to keep track of these events. Ceremonies would take place on top of huge stepped pyramids that were dedicated to the gods.

Calendars
Mesoamerican calendars were all based on a single system created by the Maya. A 260-day calendar noted important religious days, and was combined with a 365-day solar calendar similar to those we use today. This gave a cycle of days that repeated every 52 years. The festivals that were held at the end of this cycle were particularly important.

Aztec 260-day calendar
Around the central image of the five suns on this Aztec calendar is a ring of 20 days, named after animals and concepts.

Quetzalcoatl
The Aztec god Quetzalcoatl was also known as the Feathered Serpent, because he was half *quetzal*, or bird, and half *coatl*, or snake. He was often a helpful figure, teaching humans to grow corn and measure time. When he took the form of Ehecatl, he became the god of the wind.

Pyramid temples
Temples often dominated Mesoamerican cities. These structures were usually found in large plazas, and their steps were carved with scenes of gods and creatures.

Temple of Kukulcán
The most famous Maya temple, also known as El Castillo, lay at the center of the city of Chichén Itzá.

Tezcatlipoca
The first Aztec sun god, Tezcatlipoca ("Smoking Mirror"), later became a god of the night sky. A dark god, in stories he is often in conflict with Quetzalcoatl, and was responsible for the introduction of human sacrifice to Mesoamerica.

SACRIFICE
Blood sacrifice was a common feature of many Mesoamerican civilizations. Because the gods had spent their own blood to create humanity, a debt was owed to the gods to pay this blood back. The Toltecs and Aztecs in particular used to capture rather than kill their enemies, so they could sacrifice prisoners to the gods.

Feeding the gods
Much of Mesoamerican religious art shows the practice of human sacrifice. In this page from an Aztec codex, the god at the center of the image is being fed blood from various sacrifices.

Huitzilopotchli
The patron of the Aztecs, Huitzilopotchli guided the people to their home in the Valley of Mexico and ordered the building of the Aztec capital city. He was sometimes shown as a hummingbird, a creature that was believed to be the soul of a warrior.

174 the americas • THE HERO TWINS

9 There were **9 gods** of the **underworld**.

The Hero Twins

In Mayan mythology, Hunahpu and Xbalanque were known as the Hero Twins. To avenge their father's death in Xibalba (the underworld), they tricked the gods for an invitation to play a deadly game of ball.

The Hero Twins were skilled at playing ball, much like their father and uncle who were sacrificed by the gods in Xibalba. The twins wanted revenge for their deaths and played a noisy ball game to get the attention of the gods.

The twins were summoned to Xibalba and forced to spend each day playing ball. At night, they stayed in a series of dangerous houses. On the final night, Hunahpu's head was bitten off by a bat and it rolled onto the court.

To keep the gods from finding out, Xbalanque carved a head for Hunahpu from a gourd, and started playing, using Hunahpu's real head as the ball. Xbalanque hit the head right out of the court to make the gods search for it.

While they were distracted, a rabbit returned the head to Xbalanque, who replaced Hunahpu's head. The twins continued playing, and won.

The gods of Xibalba killed the twins for tricking them, but they returned after six days. The twins claimed that they could bring the dead back to life. When the gods asked for proof, the twins sliced their heads off but refused to bring them back to life. From now on, there were no more sacrifices made in Xibalba. The Hero Twins drifted into the sky, and took their place as the sun and the moon.

The First Twins
The father of the Hero Twins was Hun Hunahpu who also loved playing ball games with his twin brother Vucub Hunahpu. They were invited to play ball with the gods of Xibalba, but in the night the gods tricked them and they were sacrificed.

The Mayan god Hun Hunahpu

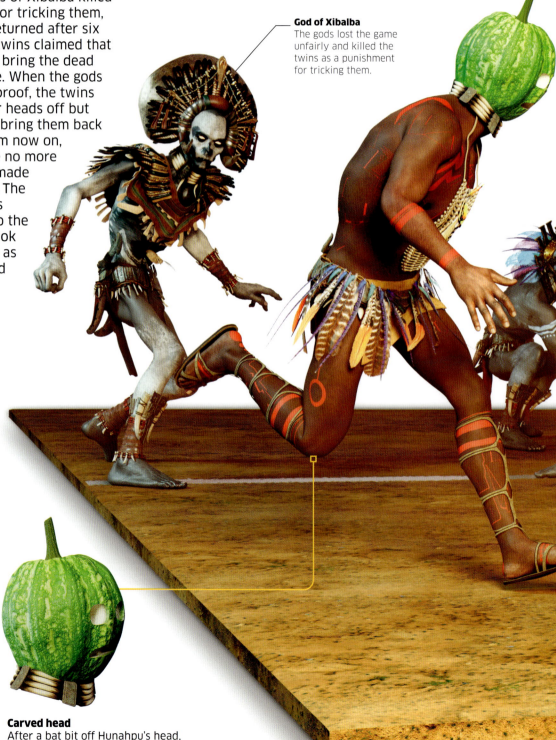

God of Xibalba
The gods lost the game unfairly and killed the twins as a punishment for tricking them.

Carved head
After a bat bit off Hunahpu's head, Xbalanque made him a new one from a calabash gourd to wear temporarily.

Nights in Xibalba
The Hero Twins were put to the test in Xibalba. The gods of the underworld placed them in different houses every night, each with its own kind of horror. They survived the ordeal using their wit and strength.

The Dark House
In total darkness, the twins used fireflies to light their way.

The Razor House
Sharp knives and razors moved around unpredictably, but the twins persuaded them to stay still.

The Cold House
Despite the chill, the twins persevered until morning.

The Jaguar House
The twins distracted the hungry jaguars with bones to gnaw.

The Fire House
The twins were only lightly singed in the burning house.

The House of Bats
A ferocious bat bit off Hunahpu's head in this house.

The ball game **Pok-ta-Pok** dates back thousands of years and is still played today.

The Hero Twins later brought their father **back to life** and made him the **god of maize** (corn).

175

Playing ball
The game that the Hero Twins played against the underworld gods was called Pok-ta-Pok. To score a goal, players had to pass the ball through a circular ring using nothing but their hips, elbows, or knees.

Scoring ring
The aim of the game was to strike a ball, or in this case a head, through a ring.

Hunahpu's head
For part of the game, Hunahpu's head was used instead of the ball.

Rabbit to the rescue
A helpful rabbit later returned Hunahpu's head to Xbalanque.

Stone court
The game of Pok-ta-Pok took place on a huge stone court with high walls at either end.

THE LEGEND OF THE FIVE SUNS

Earth Sun — After his Earth Sun was knocked from the sky, Tezcatlipoca reappeared from the ocean as a giant jaguar.

Giant meal — The race of giants then inhabiting the Earth were all devoured by jaguars.

Wind Sun — When the Wind Sun fell, hurricane winds blew all the people into the trees, where they became monkeys.

Fire Sun — The Fire Sun rained flames down from the sky, scorching the Earth and reducing it to ashes.

Cleansing the Earth — No humans were left on Earth—any that survived the fire were turned into birds.

The Legend of the Five Suns

The Aztecs believed that creation was a cycle. The world had been created and destroyed four times before, and each time a different god had acted as the world's sun. Gods became the sun by stepping into a sacrificial fire—the Aztecs lived in the world of the Fifth Sun.

The First Sun was the Earth Sun of Tezcatlipoca, the war god. Jealous that he himself hadn't been chosen as the Sun, Quetzalcoatl, the wind god, knocked him out of the sky.

Quetzalcoatl took his position as the Second Sun: the Wind Sun. When Tezcatlipoca returned and wrestled Quetzalcoatl from the heavens, the world of the Second Sun ended.

Tlaloc, the rain god, became the Third Sun: the Fire Sun. Mourning the loss of his wife who had been kidnapped by Tezcatlipoca, Tlaloc refused to send rain to nourish the earth. Tired of the requests for rain, he destroyed the world with fire.

Chalchiuhtlicue, the water goddess, became the Fourth Sun: the Water Sun. Tezcatlipoca once again brought ruin to this world, insulting her and making her cry so much that her tears flooded the Earth.

At first, no gods wanted to sacrifice themselves to become the Fifth Sun, but finally Tecciztecatl, a very proud deity, and Nanahuatzin, the poorest god, both volunteered. Tecciztecatl hesitated to walk into the fire, but Nanahuatzin bravely

676 The number of years that the First Sun lasted.

The last time **the New Fire ceremony** was carried out to **keep the Fifth Sun in the sky** was in 1509 CE.

Water Sun
Chalchiuhtlicue cried so much that her tears became a great flood and the sky fell in.

Fifth Sun
The Aztecs believed that Tonatiuh, the Fifth and final Sun, will end in earthquakes.

Rabbit moon
Metztli, with a duller glow, still bears the imprint of the rabbit that was thrown at him.

Underwater life
All of the people were turned into fish as the Earth flooded.

New Fire ceremony
The Aztecs believed that each sun lasted a multiple of 52 years. So, every 52 years, a New Fire ceremony was held to celebrate that the Fifth Sun, and the world, had not ended. It was thought that only acts of blood sacrifice, offered during the ceremony, would ensure that the Fifth Sun remained in the sky.

threw himself into the flames, becoming Tonatiuh, the sun. Tecciztecatl followed Nanahuatzin out of shame. He became a second sun, but as punishment for his reluctance, the gods threw a rabbit at him, forever dimming his light and turning him into Metztli, the moon.

But Tonatiuh refused to move in the sky until he received a blood sacrifice, which the other gods offered to him. The Aztecs offered blood sacrifices to Tonatiuh, to ensure the Fifth Sun kept moving across the sky and that this world was not destroyed.

Remaking humankind
To make the Fifth Sun's people, Quetzalcoatl went to the underworld to gather the bones of humans from previous suns. Although he was initially tricked by Mictlantecuhtli, god of the dead, he eventually took them and ground them to dust. The gods then added their own blood and humans emerged from the mixture.

Lord of the underworld
Mictlantecuhtli told Quetzalcoatl he could take the bones if he blew a conch-shell horn, but it had no holes to blow through.

Aztec gods of nature

The natural elements meant the difference between life and death to the Aztecs. A bountiful harvest was essential for survival, so they made regular offerings and ritual sacrifices to the gods and goddesses of nature.

The Aztecs believed in hundreds of gods. Among the most powerful were the deities who controlled the aspects of the natural world, from the sun and rain to the rivers, seas, and wind. They were in charge of the changing seasons, weather patterns, and food production. It was essential to keep the gods happy for Aztec civilization to thrive.

Tlaloc ruled **four spirits of powerful weather** called the **Tlaloque**, who brewed rain on mountaintops.

Tlaloc
This rain god could choose whether to water the crops or flood the land. The Aztecs were at his mercy, fearing whenever his strong temper would result in terrible thunderstorms and lightning bolts. Some believed Tlaloc to be part-jaguar, and prominent fangs showed his connection to the sacred cat that stalked the forests.

Xipe Totec
The Aztec god of spring symbolized rebirth, as he peeled off his own skin to show the plants and trees how to grow and flower from within. His golden body represented corn, and he was typically shown with a golden shield in hand, while wearing the skin of a human sacrifice. Young men followed his example by wearing the skins from human sacrifices offered to him.

Feathered crown
An impressive crown of heron feathers adorned the head of the god Tlaloc.

Chicomecóatl
Farmers worshipped Chicomecóatl, goddess of sustenance and corn. They believed she had the power to produce a great harvest and spare the people from going hungry. Her name meant "Seven Snakes." Young women made offerings of corn to this goddess in the hope she would bless their harvest.

400 Coatlicue was believed to have given birth to **400 sons who became the stars**.

Centéotl
Corn (maize) was both a main crop and sacred food for the Aztecs. They believed it came from the gods, and the corn god Centéotl was held in high regard. According to some Aztec legends, he was born a goddess before later becoming a male god. In other stories, Centéotl's female counterpart was the corn goddess Chicomecóatl.

Chalchiuhtlicue
The sister of the rain god Tlaloc was the goddess of beauty, Chalchiuhtlicue, who arrived on Earth to protect all the water in the seas, rivers, lakes, and streams. She was said to live in the mountains, where she could start the flow of many rivers to help the harvest. But when she was unhappy, she cut off the water supply, bringing about drought and starvation instead.

Coatlicue
The natural Earth mother of Aztec mythology was the goddess Coatlicue, who symbolized both creation and destruction. She gave birth to the moon and stars, and was a mother figure for both gods and humans, nurturing and protecting them. However, she also devoured the dead, taking their bodies back into the Earth. Most depictions show her wearing a necklace of hands and hearts created from their remains.

Tonatiuh
In Aztec mythology, four worlds existed and ended before a fifth and final world emerged (see pages 176–177). The gods created the last world, then the sun god Tonatiuh climbed into the sky to rule it. Every day he emerged at daybreak, traveled across the sky, and died at sunset. The Aztecs believed this daily journey required the sacrifice of human hearts to sustain him. Tonatiuh took center stage on Aztec stone calendars, and was typically shown with sacrificed hearts in hand.

Sun stone
This stone calendar shows the four worlds surrounding an image of Tonatiuh in the center.

Tepēyōllōtl
The first world (see pages 176–177) had been ruled by the creator god Tepēyōllōtl, whose name means "heart of the mountain." He could be instantly recognized by his skin, which was spotted like a jaguar's and symbolized the starry sky. Other gods borrowed his jaguar skin as a disguise. As well as jaguars, he controlled earthquakes and echoes.

Itztlacoliuhqui
When another deity tried to shoot the sun god Tonatiuh to punish him for his arrogance, they missed and hit Itztlacoliuhqui instead. The dart pierced his skull, and he was immediately transformed into the god of the cold. Frost, ice, and snow all fell under his control. He was usually depicted holding a *tlachpanoni*, a type of straw broom he used to clear the way for new beginnings.

ANDEAN CIVILIZATIONS

The Inca were the most enduring culture of the Andes, and their empire stretched along the west of South America from Ecuador to Chile. However, they were not the only people to found a civilization in the region.

Chavín
Active around 850–200 BCE, the Chavín crafted items that show an icon now called the "staff god."

Early cultures
The cultures that came before the Inca were based in or near Peru. They left many physical remains, but did not develop writing systems, so little is known in detail about their myths.

Paracas
Textiles from this Andean culture that existed around 800–100 BCE feature supernatural creatures and spirits.

Moche
Aipaec is the name given to a mythological character that appears in art from the Moche, who flourished around 100–800 CE.

Huari
The Huari (or Wari) culture was active around 500–1000 CE. Their tombs contained jars in the shape of animals and people.

Tiahuanaco
Lasting from around 600 to 1000 CE, the empire of Tiahuanaco seems to have worshipped many gods, who may have been represented by statues.

Inca sites
The Inca built up an Andean empire between 1230 and 1532. They looked upon Tiahuanaco as one of their places of origin, but also had creation stories that featured Lake Titicaca and the capital of the Inca Empire, Cuzco.

Lake Titicaca
The largest lake in South America, Lake Titicaca is the site of creation in Inca mythology, where the god Viracocha created the world (see pages 182–183).

Cuzco
According to Inca legends, their ancestors first emerged from caves near the site of Cuzco, which became the Inca capital (see page 183). Cuzco was an extremely important religious center, and the site of the Qorikancha ("Golden Temple"), also known as the Temple of the Sun. The temple was dedicated to the sun god Inti, and was the most sacred temple in the whole of the Inca Empire.

Golden star map
This golden tray from the Temple of the Sun in Cuzco shows the Inca understanding of the universe.

SOUTH AMERICA AND THE CARIBBEAN

South America is home to many Indigenous cultures. Each region has its own myths and sacred stories, from the Orinoco River in the north to the Patagonian plains of the south. The Taíno people, originally from South America, spread their stories across the Caribbean. The most well-known myths are those of the Inca, who built an empire in the mountains of the Andes in the west.

PATAGONIAN MYTHS

The Tehuelche people of Patagonia have a creation myth in which the god of the sky creates the Earth. Patagonian folklore also tells the origin story of the guanaco, a close relative of the llama.

Kooch the sky
According to the Tehuelche people, before creation, Kooch lived among dark clouds. Realizing he was alone, Kooch wept for so long that he created the ocean. He sighed, and this became the winds, which blew away the dark clouds. Reaching up into the sky, a bright spark leapt from Kooch's hand and became the sun. Kooch then dragged an island from the bottom of the ocean, and populated it with all types of animals.

Ancient animals
Animals appear in Tehuelche rock art, some of which dates back to around 7000 BCE.

Gentle People
The Gentle People lived in the very south. Their happy lives were free from care, but they were forbidden to travel too far north. One day, one of the Gentle People disobeyed. They came across other humans, who were all violent and selfish. Knowing that one day they would be found, the Gentle People decided to change into guanacos rather than become like other humans.

Guanaco
The guanaco is a wild animal native to Patagonia.

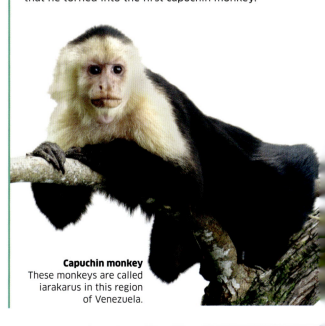

Machu Picchu
The Incas constructed many mountaintop shrines, but the citadel of Machu Picchu contains several well preserved religious structures. Built as a retreat for Emperor Pachacuti in the 15th century, Machu Picchu remained undisturbed by European explorers until the 19th century. The site is based around a central plaza that contains the Temple of the Sun for the worship of Inti the sun god, as well as a ritual stone known as the Intihuatana, which may have functioned as a sundial.

Andean gold
Among the civilizations of the Andes, gold had great religious significance. Among the Inca, gold was believed to be "the sweat of the sun god Inti." All gold was believed to belong to the Inca emperor, who claimed the sun god as an ancestor.

Ritual Object
Many religious objects were crafted from gold, such as this sacrificial knife.

El Dorado
Spanish colonists in South America recorded a legend about a city of gold known as El Dorado that existed somewhere in South America. This legend may have arisen due to the prominent use of gold in Inca ceremonies, such as this gold funeral mask.

THE TAÍNO
Settling in the Caribbean islands in roughly 5000 BCE, the Taíno people honored nature with their sacred stories, believing that the physical world and spiritual world were one and the same. The Taíno believed their civilization to have been built over the span of five eras, which ended with the arrival of European settlers.

The Taíno Petroglyphs
These ancient symbols can be found carved in stone, giving insight into Taíno culture.

TALES FROM THE ORINOCO RIVER
The Indigenous peoples of the Orinoco Basin in Venezuela have many myths and legends. The Warao people tell a story of how the first canoe was made, while the Yekuana people have story about how darkness was released into the world.

The Forest Mother
The hero Haburi created the first canoe so his family could escape from a frog-woman. After the family's escape, the canoe lay unused until it magically changed into a snake-woman. The Warao people called her Daurani, or Forest Mother, and she became the first shaman.

A way of life
Warao means "boat people," and the Warao people spend almost all of their lives in their dugout canoes. Canoes are made from the same wood Haburi used to create the canoe that turned into Daurani.

The coming of the night
The god Wanadi gave his nephew Iarakaru a medicine pouch containing the darkness of the night, and told him not to open it. While Wanadi was hunting, the demon Odosha convinced Iarakaru to open the pouch. Darkness descended on the world, and Iarakaru was so frightened that he turned into the first capuchin monkey.

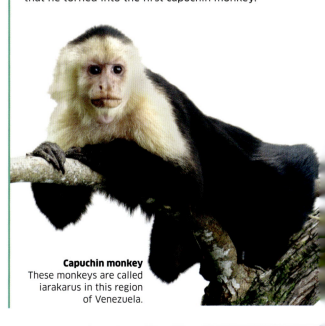

Capuchin monkey
These monkeys are called iarakarus in this region of Venezuela.

Viracocha the creator

Viracocha Pachachayachic was the supreme god of the Incas and the creator of all things. After finishing the work of creation, Viracocha left the world he had made in the care of the other gods. But someday he will return to bring about the end of humankind.

After rising from the dark waters of Lake Titicaca, Viracocha first created the Earth and sky. He then formed the earliest race of humans from huge stones. But these giants were evil and violent and rebelled against him, so he sent a great flood to destroy them.

Viracocha left just two of the giants alive, so they could help him make new creations. He named them Imaymana Viracocha and Tocapo Viracocha and, with their help, summoned the sun and the moon from the lake. Viracocha and his helpers then molded a new race of humans from lumps of clay. The time was not yet right for humans to populate the Earth, so Viracocha concealed them in caves, hollows, and riverbeds throughout the world.

When humanity's time eventually came, Viracocha and his two helpers traveled everywhere to draw the humans out into the world. As they appeared, the trio taught them languages, as well as how to grow food, and how to build houses.

Once the humans were settled, Viracocha traveled the land disguised as an old man to observe the people's behavior. He punished those who treated him badly, and rewarded those who treated him well. When he finally reached the coast, he was saddened by what he had seen and left the world behind, continuing over the ocean. He left the rulership of the world to the sun god Inti and the other Inca deities, promising that one day he would return. But the Inca believed that upon Viracocha's return, his tears at the state of the world would cause a great flood that would drown all of humankind.

Isla del Sol on Lake Titicaca is where Viracocha is believed to have **commanded the sun to rise**.

Viracocha's new creations
Viracocha called up the sun and the moon from Lake Titicaca. Before this there had been no light to illuminate the Earth. He gave the two remaining giants lumps of clay from the lake shore to make new humans.

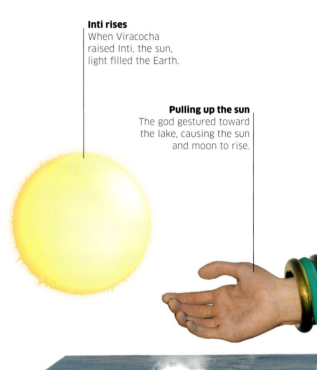

Inti rises
When Viracocha raised Inti, the sun, light filled the Earth.

Pulling up the sun
The god gestured toward the lake, causing the sun and moon to rise.

Isla del Sol
The sun rose from the Isla del Sol (Island of the Sun) at the center of Lake Titicaca.

3,000,000 Lake Titicaca is estimated to be about **three million years old**.

The Inca royal family **descended from Manco Capac**, the leader of the **first human beings** and founder of Cusco.

Royal headdress
Viracocha wears the llautu headband that represents royalty and a headdress of feathers symbolizing the sun and the stars.

Dulling the moon
Some stories say that the sun god Inti was jealous of the moon's brightness, so Viracocha covered the moon with ash.

White beard
Viracocha is often depicted with a long, white beard.

Cave home
Viracocha placed his new human beings in caves, and told them to emerge when the time was right.

Emergence of humans
Another legend tells that it was the sun god Inti who called the first people from the Paqariq Tampu cave. He gave their leader Manco Capac a golden staff, telling him to build a city where it sank into the earth. That city became Cusco, the Inca capital.

MANCO CAPAC

Coniraya Viracocha
The Yauyos people of the Andes have a very different version of Viracocha, who is more of a trickster god than a creator. One story of this Viracocha tells of how he disguised himself as the beggar Coniraya. He tricked Cavillaca, a beautiful woman, into eating a magical fruit that made her pregnant. She ran from Coniraya, who asked the animals to help find her, but it was too late—Cavillaca and her baby had been turned to stone.

Condor
Because the condor helped Coniraya, he gave it great wings and cursed any animal that ate it to die.

Skunk
The skunk did not help Coniraya, so he cursed it with a terrible smell.

Inca gods of earth and sky

From the 13th century, the Incas built an impressive empire high in the mountains of the Andes on the west coast of South America. From here, they worshipped a group of deities who were integral to their everyday lives.

Many Inca gods were associated with the natural world, including the sun, moon, earth, and sky. They had the power to control the weather, dictate the amount of sunlight or rainfall, and bring feast or famine to the people. The Incas made regular offerings to their deities to encourage them to create good conditions for the Inca, so they could live without threat of drought or flood.

INTI

As sun god and ruler of the sky, Inti was more powerful than any other deity. Known as "the leader of the daytime," he kept people warm and helped their crops grow. He also assisted the first Incan ruler, Manco Cápac, in choosing a location for the capital city of Cuzco. When the city was complete, the Incas built many temples to honor Inti.

MAMA KILYA

The sister of Inti was the moon goddess Mama Kilya, who reigned over the sky at night and was also the protector of women. Silver was her metal, so the Incas handcrafted silver offerings and jewelery, which were left as gifts to her at shrines and temples.

Lunar light
Mama Kilya's big, beaming face was believed to be visible in every full moon.

Inca emperors were considered direct **descendants** of the **sun god Inti**.

Glittering gold
The Incas believed that Inti's sweat was made of gold. Many representations of Inti feature his face on a golden disk.

To this day, the **Inca sun god** is honored at the **Inti Raymi festival** in Peru each year.

37566 Illapa is a small asteroid in the Earth's orbit, named after the **Inca thunder god**.

Goddess of nature
Pachamama translates from the Quechua language to Mother Earth, or Mother Nature.

PACHAMAMA

The earth goddess Pachamama presided over the soaring mountains and the fertile soil. Farmers held her in high esteem because she helped their harvests. To provoke her anger could risk unleashing earthquakes that would devastate the land.

ILLAPA

The huge feet of the thunder god Illapa thumped across the sky, casting an enormous shadow that became the Milky Way galaxy. He carried a slingshot from which he fired lightning bolts through the air. Farmers climbed mountains to get closer to Illapa and pray for his rain for their crops.

Sling shooter
Traditional slingshots consisted of a rope sling used to fire small stones at targets.

URCUCHILLAY

Many Incas depended on rearing animals to make a living. Their livestock was protected by the animal god, Urcuchillay. Cattle herders showed their devotion to Urcuchillay by handcrafting gold figurines for him. They also worshipped the constellation Lyra, because its stars created an outline in the shape of a llama.

Prized llama
Gold llama figurines were gifted to Urcuchillay because he usually took the form of a llama.

MAMA COCHA

The mother of Inti and Mama Kilya was Mama Cocha, goddess of the sea and fish. The Incan fisherfolk worshipped her, believing that she could calm troubled waters to bring them home safe and sound. She could also influence the size of their daily catches.

Generous catches
It was believed that Mama Cocha blessed fishermen with nets full of fish, shown here in this Incan ceramic.

CHUICHU

Whenever a rainbow arched across the sky, the Incas believed it was the god Chuichu. They considered him to be a special messenger, bringing news from the supreme sun god Inti to get their attention on Earth. In this way, Chuichu was the link between the celestial deities and the human realm.

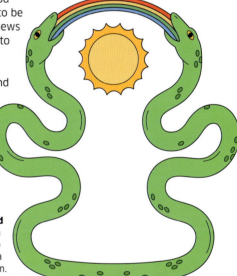

Rainbow god
Chuichu appeared as a dragon deity with two heads, sharing each end of a rainbow between them.

KON

Child of the powerful sun god Inti and moon goddess Mama Kilya, Kon was the god of rain and wind. He provided the Incas with rain to make their crops flourish, in return for their worship. If they forgot to honor him, he could dry out the land so nothing would grow. It was said that Kon was able to carve mountains and valleys by manipulating powerful winds.

Nazca line drawing
One of the line drawings carved into the Nazca Desert in southern Peru possibly shows the god Kon.

Tales of the Taíno

Arriving by boat from South America, the Taíno people settled in the Caribbean islands in roughly 5000 BCE. There, they shared their own creation stories and established a unique pantheon of deities.

The Taíno believed the spiritual and physical worlds were one and the same. They had a deep affinity with nature, recognizing rivers, oceans, mountains, and trees as sacred places. The Taíno calendar honored the changing seasons, the phases of the moon, and the agricultural year. Their deities created the cosmos, kept the world turning, and took care of the people in life and death.

CREATION STORIES

According to Taíno legend, the creation of the universe occurred over five eras, and only ended with the arrival of European settlers in the 15th century. At the very beginning of Taíno time, Yaya was the one supreme deity.

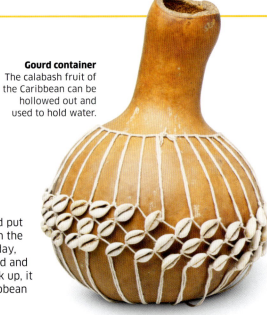

Gourd container
The calabash fruit of the Caribbean can be hollowed out and used to hold water.

Ocean inside a gourd
Following a disagreement, Yaya killed his son and put his bones inside a water-filled gourd that hung on the wall. Soon after, the bones turned into fish. One day, intruders in Yaya's home saw the fish in the gourd and ate them. When they tried to hang the gourd back up, it smashed to the floor. The water became the Caribbean Sea and the first era of creation began.

The watchful sun
The second era of creation started with the sun rising from a cave on the island of Hispaniola. The first men appeared from a neighboring cave and began fishing in the sea. The sun kept a constant watch to ensure the men behaved well. Anyone lazy or selfish was turned into trees or stones, which became part of the landscape. With the start of the third era, women arrived to create families and increase the population of Hispaniola.

Sacred caves
As the birthplace of the sun, caves were considered sacred sites, and the Taíno gathered there to worship.

Cultivating cassava
In the fourth era, the Taíno learned to grow the cassava plant, which became a principal part of their diet.

A new age
The story becomes more historical from the fourth era, when the community on Hispaniola thrived in a golden age. Many villages were built and food grew in abundance. This ended when European settlers arrived, starting the fifth era. The settlers brought diseases with them and ill-treated the Taíno. The fifth era ultimately ended in the destruction of Taíno society.

> The word **Taíno** means "the good people."

ATABEY AND YÚCAHU

In an alternative creation myth, Atabey, goddess of fertility and fresh water, and her son Yúcahu created the cosmos together.

Empty void
At first, Atabey made the heavens, creating a vast, empty void to fill. So Atabey produced two sons: Yúcahu and Guacar. Yúcahu took on the role of creator deity, waking up the world for the first time. He shaped the sun god Boinael and the moon god Maroya.

The work continues
To impress his mother, Yúcahu introduced plants and animals to the world, giving life and color. He transformed four glittering gemstones into a quartet of star beings to help the gods. Yúcahu's work opened a rift in heaven, which released the first human, named Locuo.

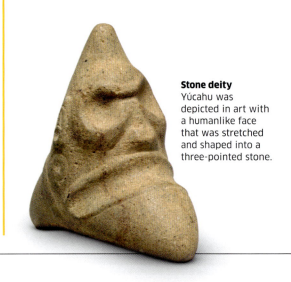

Stone deity
Yúcahu was depicted in art with a humanlike face that was stretched and shaped into a three-pointed stone.

In Taíno tradition, the **goeiza** were spirits of the living and the **hupia** were spirits of the dead.

The Taíno believed that the hurricanes affecting their islands were caused by **the storm goddess Guabancex**.

187

LEGENDS OF THE HUMMINGBIRD

According to Taíno tradition, the first hummingbirds were once flies that were transformed by the sun. The powerful light could turn any creature on Earth into a completely different form.

The story of Alida and Taroo

A young girl named Alida loved a boy named Taroo from another tribe, but her chieftain father refused to let them marry. Alida prayed to the gods, who transformed her into a crimson flower. Taroo searched for Alida, until a god told him what had happened and turned him into a hummingbird to find her. From then on, Taroo flew to every red flower to find his true love.

Lost love
Legend says that Taroo the hummingbird is still flying between red flowers in search of Alida.

THE ZEMIS

The Taíno people honored their gods with sacred carvings and idols known as zemis. They believed that the zemis were divine representations that contained the real spirits of the deities themselves.

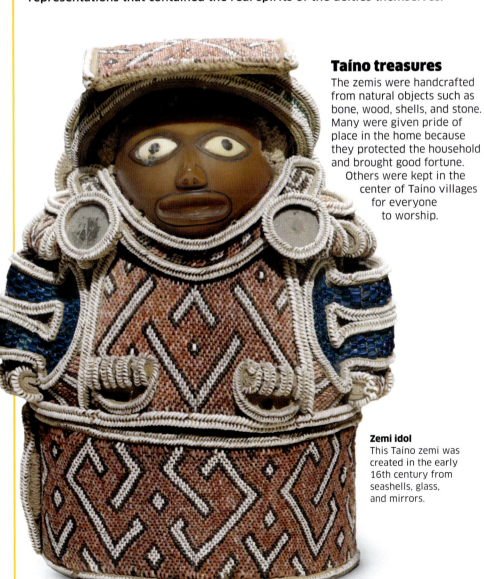

Taíno treasures

The zemis were handcrafted from natural objects such as bone, wood, shells, and stone. Many were given pride of place in the home because they protected the household and brought good fortune. Others were kept in the center of Taíno villages for everyone to worship.

Zemi idol
This Taíno zemi was created in the early 16th century from seashells, glass, and mirrors.

LAND OF THE DEAD

Maketaori Guayaba was the zemi of Coaybay, the mysterious land of the dead. This is where the opías (spirits of the dead) resided.

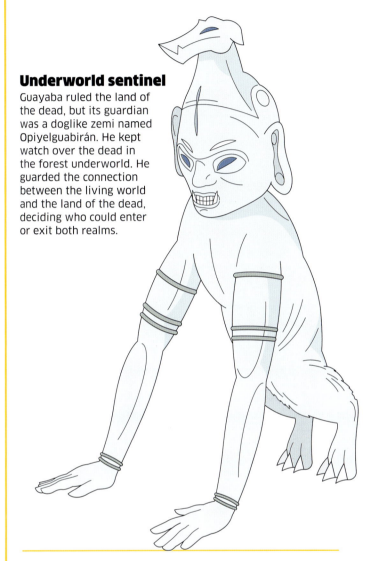

Underworld sentinel

Guayaba ruled the land of the dead, but its guardian was a doglike zemi named Opiyelguabirán. He kept watch over the dead in the forest underworld. He guarded the connection between the living world and the land of the dead, deciding who could enter or exit both realms.

Food of the dead
The guava fruit that the dead were believed to eat has been grown in the Caribbean for more than 5,000 years.

Night feeders

In the land of the dead, the souls slept all day before emerging at night to satisfy their big appetites. Under cover of darkness, they transformed into bats and flew around the forest to feast on sweet guava fruit. The Spanish word for guava is *guayaba*, the name of the zemi of the underworld.

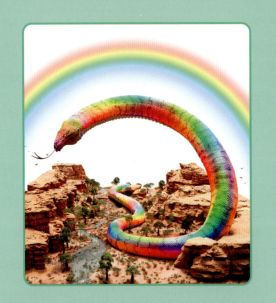

OCEANIA

First Australians have the oldest continuous culture in the world, and their sacred stories have an equally long history. Throughout the Pacific islands, many different cultures share characters and other elements in their myths and folktales.

AUSTRALIA AND THE PACIFIC

Across thousands of miles of ocean, the peoples of Australia and the Pacific islands have developed rich cultures of sacred stories and mythology. Common themes across tales from the region are a deep, spiritual connection to the landscape and elements of nature, as well as paying homage to ancestors.

THE DREAMING

First Australians refer to the creation period as the Dreaming, or Dreamtime. It is believed that the ancestor spirits woke from sleeping in order to bring the land to life, and then returned to their eternal sleep. First Australian groups retell stories of the Dreamtime, a period that is always present and still evolving.

Forming Australia
For each of the First Australian groups, their existence in Australia is told in their individual languages and myths. These stories describe their ancestors' roles in how the land was formed, and differ across peoples. The sacred stories are constantly being retold, continuing the peoples' deep connection with the land.

Creation journeys
Although stories of creation are different across the First Australian groups, they all share similarities. Journeys were made across the country by ancestral beings, who gave life to all living things and brought geographical features into existence. These stories of creation describe how plants and animals came into being, along with the spirits of those that will exist in the future.

MĀORI GODS

The Māori people of New Zealand share their gods with other Polynesian cultures in the Pacific Ocean, although some tellings vary in their origin. Creation gods are worshipped alongside deities of nature, war, and survival skills.

Papa and Rangi
The primal deities of Māori mythology were Papa, the goddess of the Earth, and Rangi, the god of the sky. At the very beginning of time, they held each other tightly, but they were broken apart in order to begin the process of creation. When they separated, Rangi cried so hard that his tears fell from the sky as rain.

Rongo
Rongo was the god of peace, and one of the sons of Papa and Rangi. When his brother Tawhiri sent raging storms to the Earth after their parents' separation, Rongo hid himself in Papa's body for protection.

Tane
In Māori mythology, Tane is the god of trees and forests. He created the first tree, but planted it upside down because he thought the branches were legs and the roots were hair, like a human figure. When the tree didn't grow, he set it upright.

Tawhiri
The god of the weather, Tawhiri was another of Papa and Rangi's sons. When his parents were broken apart, Tawhiri sensed their pain and brought forth many storms to flood the Earth. This created the oceans.

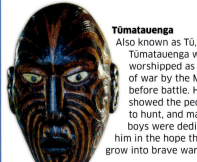

Tūmatauenga
Also known as Tū, Tūmatauenga was worshipped as the god of war by the Māori before battle. He showed the people how to hunt, and many baby boys were dedicated to him in the hope they would grow into brave warriors.

Tangaroa
Tangaroa was the Māori god of the sea, and one of the oldest Polynesian deities. In many island communities, he is regarded as the singular supreme creator of the cosmos.

ANCESTRAL BEINGS

Many Pacific cultures believe their ancestors remain in spirit even after death. Their living descendants find ways to honor them in physical form, and still share their stories.

The dema
The dema were mythical ancestral beings of the Marind-anim people of New Guinea. Geb was a dema who lived in an anthill, where he would lure in children and cut off their heads. The local people attacked Geb and cut off his head, which then escaped up into the sky to become the sun. His body became the land.

Moai
The moai are stone figures carved by the Polynesian people of Rapa Nui (also known as Easter Island). The moai represent the living faces of ancestral chiefs who were descended from the gods.

'Aumakua
In Hawaiian folklore, 'Aumakua were ancestral spirits that were invisible to the living but could also take possession of living creatures. Some people believed that 'Aumakua could take on the body of a shark, to chase fish into their nets or guide their boats to safety.

SUPERNATURAL CREATURES

The region of Oceania offers tales featuring a number of supernatural beings across the many islands—from characters that frighten children, to beings that bridge the link between the natural world and the spirit realm.

Yowie
A creature from the mythology of First Australians, the Yowie had long limbs and was covered in shaggy hair—it was also sometimes referred to as the "hairy man."

Scary figure
The tall and imposing Yowie was believed to steal children away if they were found in the wilderness after dark.

Manaia
In Māori mythology, the Manaia is a creature believed to be a messenger between the living world and the spirit realm. Its form is used in designs and carvings, as well as being a common motif in jewelery.

Bunyip
In the folklore of First Australians, Bunyip was a monster that lived in swamps. It was believed to eat humans, and was used as a cautionary tale to warn children away from water holes.

BUNYIP'S FANGS

Menehune
The Menehune were a mythical race of tiny creatures from Hawaiian folklore. They were said to work throughout the night, farming, fishing, and crafting temples, fishponds, and houses.

Menehune Fishpond
The long wall that separates Menehune Fishpond from the Hulē'ia River is traditionally believed to have been constructed by the Menehune.

STORIES OF THE OCEAN

The island nations in the Pacific Ocean take inspiration for their folklore from their surroundings. Celebrating gods and goddesses of the water, and telling stories of exploration and discovery, Polynesian mythology shares some common themes.

Tales of voyages
The peoples of Polynesia explored the Pacific for more than a thousand years. Many tales from the region share the theme of ocean exploration, from the adventures of the hero Maui (see pages 198–199) to the wandering of the Hawaiian goddess Pele (see page 200).

POLYNESIAN CANOE

Flood myths
A lot of stories from Polynesia included natural disasters such as floods and tsunamis, which were often sent by the gods. Pacific islanders lived close to the ocean and knew its dangers, so these tales were born from respect for the power of the water, and the deities that controlled it.

oceania • THE RAINBOW SERPENT

Rock art
Aboriginal art captures the slithering serpent in various forms and colors, including this example from Arnhem Land in the Northern Territory.

Creator spirit
The movement of the Rainbow Serpent determined the shape of the land and introduced new plants and creatures.

Spectrum of colors
The kaleidoscopic scales of the giant serpent were all the colors of the rainbow.

Serpent shape
The landscape burst into life, following the flow of the serpent's movements.

6,000 The Rainbow Serpent has featured in Aboriginal rock art for more than 6,000 years.

The **super-size serpent** was believed to be more than 20ft (6m) long.

Making rainbows
Some stories claimed that a rainbow appeared when the serpent stood on its tail.

The Rainbow Serpent

The creator deity in the Dreaming stories is the Rainbow Serpent. This colorful character woke from his sleep and began to form the Australian landscape, bringing nature to life and shaping a whole new world.

The Rainbow Serpent lived beneath watering holes in the barren desert, protecting the precious water supply. When it came to the Earth's surface to travel, the rolling movement of its body created features such as rivers, valleys, rocks, and waterfalls. An impressive and inspiring landscape was left behind in the serpent's wake. The presence of the serpent also encouraged plants to grow and animals to thrive.

When the ground became too dry, the Rainbow Serpent would give the gift of rain to help the plants and animals survive.

However, it could also bring a drought or a flood if humans showed a lack of respect toward the natural world around them.

According to First Australian beliefs, the sight of a rainbow spanning the sky is really the Rainbow Serpent making its way between neighboring watering holes. To this day, First Australians pay homage to the serpent before drinking from watering holes. They perform elaborate rituals and ceremonies in honor of this powerful being.

The story of the Rainbow Serpent is passed down through the generations, and encourages Indigenous Australian groups to live in harmony with nature and respect the ground beneath their feet.

Giving color to the world
In some stories, the rainbow colors of the serpent's scaly body were transferred to the surrounding plants and animals, and this is how parts of the world became so vibrant and vivid. Other stories claimed that the Rainbow Serpent could transform into different animals before returning to its serpent form.

Australian parrot
This rainbow lorikeet is a striking example of a colorful creature that could have been touched by the legendary Rainbow Serpent.

Tales from the Dreaming

First Australians have always told stories of the Dreaming, when ancestral figures helped create the land. These stories tell of the deep connection between the First Australians and the natural world.

The tales of the Dreaming are incredibly important to First Australian people, and have been captured in rock paintings for thousands of years. They are still retold and remembered in art, songs, dances, and rituals.

THE WAWILAK SISTERS

Two sisters are the subject of a celebrated story from Arnhem Land in the Northern Territory. The Wawilak Sisters walked the land, shaped the landscape, and shared their knowledge.

Traditional bag
The sisters carried a dilly bag containing all their magic and wisdom.

The sisters' journey

The journey began when the sisters emerged from the ocean. Blessed with magical powers and wisdom, one sister carried a baby while the other was pregnant. They walked the land, giving names to the wonders of nature they saw around them.

GREEDY LUMALUMA

A wise whale lies at the heart of this sacred story from the Yolngu people of northern Australia. Lumaluma was blessed with gifts until his greed got the better of him.

Tale of the whale
Lumaluma was an enormous whale who had learned every sacred rite and ritual. When he swam ashore, he transformed into a giant man and traveled on foot across Australia. He encountered many people and shared his knowledge of rituals with them.

Getting greedy
Lumaluma's appetite remained as big as it was when he was a whale. He devoured everyone's food, claiming it to be sacred so that only he could eat it. When he began trying to eat the people too, they decided that something had to be done.

Killing Lumaluma
The locals decided to kill Lumaluma, but he asked them to kill him slowly so he could finish teaching them his rituals. In some tellings, Lumaluma didn't survive. In others, his body was put back in the ocean, where he turned into a whale again and swam away.

THE BRAM-BRAM-BULT

Yuree and Waniel, better known as the Bram-bram-bult, were creator-warrior brothers of sacred stories from the Gariwerd region of southeast Australia.

Gliding possum
The possum is a sacred symbol of problem-solving and perseverance in the stories of the Dreaming.

Doan hunts a kangaroo
In the Dreaming stories, the brothers had a nephew named Doan, a powerful spirit who appeared as a gliding possum. Doan used his expert hunting skills to follow a kangaroo called Purra. However, Doan was stopped and killed by an echidna spirit named Wembulin before he could catch up with Purra.

The brothers' revenge
As the much-loved nephew of the Bram-bram-bult, Doan was mourned by the brothers. They took their revenge by tracking down Wembulin and killing him in a sudden ambush. Then the pair traveled through Australia, naming all the natural features they came across.

Echidna
The spikes of the echidna symbolize the importance of self-defense.

The Wawilak Sisters are also known as the **Wawalag, Wagilag, Wauwaluk, or Wawalik Sisters**, depending on the dialect.

Watering hole
Scattered across Arnhem Land are watering holes that provide a welcome break for thirsty animals in the hot sun.

Stopping to rest
The sisters used spears to hunt animals along the way. When they grew tired, they stopped to rest by a watering hole. They started cooking the animals in a pot over their campfire, but every animal jumped from the cooking pot straight into the watering hole.

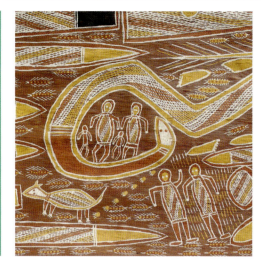

Awakening the snake
The Wawilak Sisters followed the animals into the watering hole. Their splashing disturbed a terrifying snake who inhabited the waters and acted as a protector of animals. He swallowed the women whole, but the other snakes forced him to spit them back out. The sisters landed on an anthill, and the stinging of the ants brought them back to life.

Aboriginal art
This Aboriginal painting on tree bark shows the Wawilak Sisters encircled by the angry snake.

Under attack
This Aboriginal painting shows Lumaluma meeting his doom. Arriving by land and sea, people attacked him armed with spears and sticks.

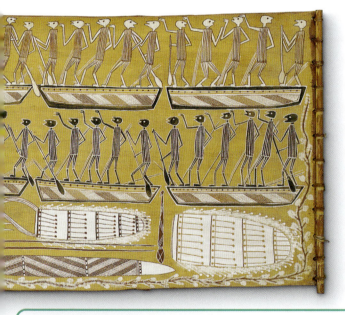

NOBBYS KANGAROO
In this sacred story from southeast Australia, a giant kangaroo is said to hide out in a rocky outcrop known as Nobbys Head.

RED KANGAROO

Kangaroo vs wallaby
According to legend, a giant kangaroo once attacked a wallaby. Fearing punishment for this serious crime, the kangaroo fled to Nobbys Head to avoid capture. He remained there alone, determined to stay isolated from all others.

NOBBYS HEAD

Shaking of Nobbys Head
The kangaroo, frustrated at being stuck among the rocks forever, began to thump his huge tail. Whenever he did this, he created ground-shaking earth tremors. Today, Nobbys Head is still a sacred spot for the local Awabakal people.

TIDDALIK THE FROG
The Dreaming tells of a huge frog named Tiddalik who was much bigger than any others of his kind and who caused a drought from his thirst.

Tiddalik drinks all the water
Tiddalik had a thirst to match his giant size. He began drinking, but couldn't stop. Soon he had drunk all the water there was, from tiny watering holes to great rivers. He was fit to burst with all the water stored inside him.

Water-holding frog
Native to Australia, this frog is named for its ability to store up to half its weight in water.

The animals make a plan
Tiddalik had quenched his thirst, but the other animals were dying without water. They devised a plan to make Tiddalik laugh so the water would be released from him. They tried singing, dancing, and joking, but nothing worked. It was only when an eel tied itself up in knots that Tiddalik burst out laughing and all the water flowed again. The empty water sources filled up and the world was restored.

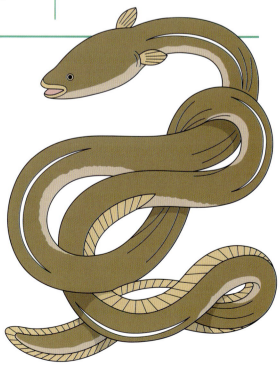

oceania • TA'AROA CREATES THE WORLD

The upper shell
The top half of the cosmic egg's shell formed the sky.

The sun
Ta'aroa placed the sun in the sky to give light for the humans and animals he created.

Land forms
The god Māui helped Ta'aroa by pulling up islands from beneath the ocean.

Tears of Ta'aroa
When Ta'aroa cried, there were so many tears they filled up the previously dry oceans and riverbeds.

The cosmic egg
After he broke apart the cosmic egg, Ta'aroa formed the rest of the world from its pieces, as well as from parts of his own body. He also created more gods to help him continue his acts of creation.

7 Ta'aroa created **seven levels in the world**, all of which were eventually **populated by humans**.

1,000 More than **1,000 islands** make up **Polynesia**, where myths about **different versions of Ta'aroa** exist.

The moon
Ta'aroa hung the moon in the sky to give light at night, and Hina, the moon goddess, made it her home.

Ta'aroa creates the world

Ta'aroa was the supreme creator god of Tahiti and neighboring islands in Polynesia. In the beginning, he was alone inside Rumi, a cosmic egg, which spun around in the endless emptiness before time existed.

All alone within the home of his cosmic egg, Ta'aroa grew bored and lonely, so he broke the egg in two. He swam outside, calling out to see if anyone was there, but he received no answer. Everything was dark and still, so he began the task of creation.

Ta'aroa pushed one half of the broken egg shell upward, which became the dome of the sky, and the other half downward to form the rocks of the Earth. He used his own backbone to form the mountains, his feathers to create the trees and other plants, his intestines to form the clouds, his fingernails for the scales on the fish and the shells of the turtles, and his blood to create the rainbow. Then he cried and his tears filled the oceans, rivers, and lakes.

Once this was done, he called forth the other gods from inside himself, including Tane, Māui, and Hina. Māui helped Ta'aroa pull up Tahiti from the waters and then Ta'aroa created humans to live on it and the other islands. He divided the world into levels, giving the lowest to the humans, but they increased in number so quickly that they soon covered the whole Earth.

Ta'aroa across the Pacific
Equivalents of Ta'aroa appear in other islands across Polynesia and the South Pacific. These gods have different names and stories, but they all play a part in the world's creation.

A'a statue
On this wooden statue of A'a, a local version of Ta'aroa from the island of Rurutu, figures representing gods crawl over the creator deity's body.

Name	Place	Role
Ta'aroa	Society Islands (including Tahiti)	Ta'aroa created everything using pieces of the cosmic egg as well as parts of his own body.
Kanaloa	Hawai'i	Associated with death, when he failed to create humans out of clay, Kanaloa made all poisonous creatures instead.
Tagaloa	Samoa	In the form of a bird, Tagaloa could find no place to land, so he threw rocks from heaven to create the islands.
Tangaloa	Tonga	Tangaloa made humans from the maggots that fed on a creeper vine on the island of 'Ata.
Tangaroa	New Zealand	Tangaroa and his siblings split up their parents, the Earth and the sky, which allowed living things to grow.

198 oceania · **MAUI OF A THOUSAND TRICKS**

Named after the hero, **Maui** is the **second largest** of **Hawaii's** eight main islands.

Casting the fish hook
Maui fished the Polynesian islands from the bottom of the sea. Another version of the story describes Maui catching a giant fish that became the North Island of New Zealand.

"He carried with him a **great fish hook,** which he baited with a star."
Rev. William Wyatt Gill, *Myths and Songs from the South Pacific*, 1876

Looking strong
Maui is usually shown with a muscular body and long hair tied in a bun.

Leafy loincloth
The loincloth worn by the hero is decorated with grass and leaves.

2016 The year the Disney film *Moana*, which includes a character **based on Maui**, was released.

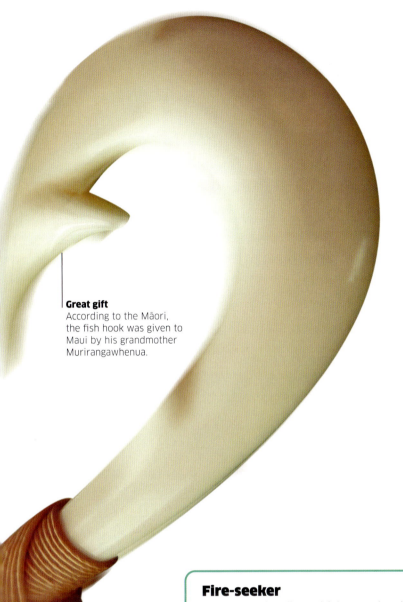

Great gift
According to the Māori, the fish hook was given to Maui by his grandmother Murirangawhenua.

Maui of a Thousand Tricks

The Polynesian hero Maui is revered throughout the islands of the Pacific. Stories of the mischievous warrior include feats of strength and bravery, and a humorous adventure into the underworld.

Maui is a heroic figure from Polynesian legends, but was rarely worshipped as a god. The hero became known as Maui of a Thousand Tricks for his ability to outsmart the gods and use clever strategies.

Although his origins may vary, he is often believed to be the youngest of five brothers. Maui was born very early, and was so small that his mother, the goddess Buataranga, thought he was dead. She cast him into the sea, wrapped in hair that she had cut from her own head. But the gods protected him and he managed to find his way back to his family. The goddess was delighted to see that her fifth son was alive and well, and took him in to live with her. One night, Maui's four brothers went out fishing and left Maui behind. But Maui hid under the boards of his brother's canoe and, to their amazement, revealed himself when they were far from the shore.

Maui took out a giant fish hook, attached it to a line, and threw it into the sea. Soon Maui realized he had caught something huge and told his brothers to row as fast as they could. As they rowed, an island rose up behind them. Maui performed this feat a few times, and this is how many of the Polynesian islands appeared from beneath the sea.

Fire-seeker
Eager to bring fire, which was closely guarded in the underworld, to the world, Maui hid inside a red pigeon and flew into the dark realm. There, Maui took his human form and fought with the god Mauike. When Maui won the battle, the god gave him two fire sticks, but Maui accidentally set the underworld on fire. He made a quick getaway by re-entering the red bird and flying out.

Lifting the sky
In ancient times, the sky was so low that people had to crawl to get around and the trees were tangled up in it. Maui's father kept putting long poles in the ground to keep the sky up, but it kept falling down. Maui decided to solve the problem once and for all. He drank a magic potion from a gourd that made him super strong. He pushed the sky up, which stretched far beyond the mountains to where it is now.

Battling the sun god
Maui's biggest fight was against the sun god Ra (short for Tama-nui-te-ra), who was lazy and used to pass across the sky too quickly. One day, Maui set a trap for the sun god, tying him up with a strong rope. The god could hardly breathe, and so, eager to be released, Ra agreed to appear in the sky longer and Maui set him free.

> "MAUI PULLED **THE ROPE** SO TIGHT AS ALMOST TO **STRANGLE** THE SUN."
>
> Rev. William Wyatt Gill, *Myths and Songs from the South Pacific*, 1876

Myths of the Pacific

The people of the Pacific islands have countless myths and stories, many of which involve the exploration of the ocean itself.

From about 2000 BCE, people first set sail from Southeast Asia to explore the Pacific, relying on natural landmarks for navigation. These historic journeys continued until as recently as the 13th century, and resulted in new communities on thousands of different islands, where they established many belief systems with their own stories.

PELE OF HAWAII

A fire goddess, Pele controls the volcano of Kīlauea on Big Island in Hawaii. She has the power to decide when the volcano will erupt, and commands its lava flow. It is believed her volcanic nature created the rest of the Hawaiian islands.

Hunting for a home
Pele was born on the island of Tahiti to the mother goddess Haumea, and became known for her fiery nature. Unable to settle down, she set sail across the Pacific Ocean to find a new home. Discovering Big Island, she made her home in the Kīlauea volcano. On a nearby island, she noticed a handsome young chief called Lohiau and immediately fell in love.

Big Island
The largest island in Hawaii, Big Island is home to Kīlauea as well as three other active volcanoes.

Volcanic reminders
Legends say that every time the Kīlauea volcano erupts, it is Pele reminding the world of her presence and power.

Pele's jealousy
Pele asked her sister Hi'iaka to bring Lohiau to Big Island. Hi'iaka agreed as long as Pele watched over Hi'iaka's forests. Hi'iaka found Lohiau, but he had died, so she brought him back to life. This took so long that Pele became suspicious of the pair. Unleashing all her volcanic fury, she spewed molten lava and hot rocks in an inferno that reduced Hi'iaka's forests to ash. Hi'iaka returned, and was devastated. Lohiau embraced her, causing Pele's jealousy to erupt once more, turning Lohiau to stone.

TALES FROM RAPA NUI

The remote island of Rapa Nui (also known as Easter Island) has its own local mythology. The supreme creator deity is worshipped along with his wife, the goddess Haua. There is also a legendary founding figure, King Hotu Matu'a.

Haua and the priestess
A story from Rapa Nui tells of how the gods once assigned a priestess to guard a skull on a beach. When a wave swept the skull out to sea, the priestess swam after it until she came ashore on the island of Motiro-hiva. There, Haua appeared and informed her that the skull was actually the creator god Makemake.

Moving to Rapa Nui
Makemake was a bird god as well as a creator, and had come to the island to move all the seabirds to Rapa Nui. Haua agreed to help, and they took the priestess with them to teach the local people about the deities. They created nesting sites for the birds on Rapa Nui, but the local people stole the eggs to eat. Finally, the trio sent the seabirds to the nearby rocky islets, which humans couldn't reach.

Makemake
Known as the Birdman, Makemake is typically depicted with an owllike face.

First ruler
The royal advisor to the legendary King Hotu Matu'a had a dream in which his spirit traveled to the undiscovered island of Rapa Nui. The advisor woke and told the king, who commanded seven men to set sail and explore the Pacific region. When they found Rapa Nui, Hotu Matu'a became its first settler and added the island to his territory. He became the ancestor of Rapa Nui's people.

Settler's statue
This wooden statue of King Hotu Matu'a marks the entrance to his burial site on the south coast of Rapa Nui.

> Kīlauea volcano is **one of the world's most active volcanoes**, erupting on average **every two years**—so Pele must still be angry!

The dwarf planet Makemake was named after the creator god of Rapa Nui.

Ancient Polynesians could navigate across up to 3,000 miles (4,800km) of ocean in a single voyage.

THE INVENTION OF NAVIGATION

Thousands of years ago, explorers had no technology to help them navigate the waters. Instead, they relied on their knowledge of nature. They looked at the position of the sun and stars, the routes of migrating birds, the patterns in the clouds, and the crashing waves and changing tides. They handcrafted basic maps from sticks and shells to help them find their way home after long periods exploring the Pacific.

Coconut milk
The god of navigation Aluluei made his home on the Pacific island of Bwennap. There, there was only a single coconut tree to sustain the many islanders. One day, Aluluei's daughter offered a coconut to some gods in a canoe. Despite it seeming too small, they all drank the milk, and found there was even more left over.

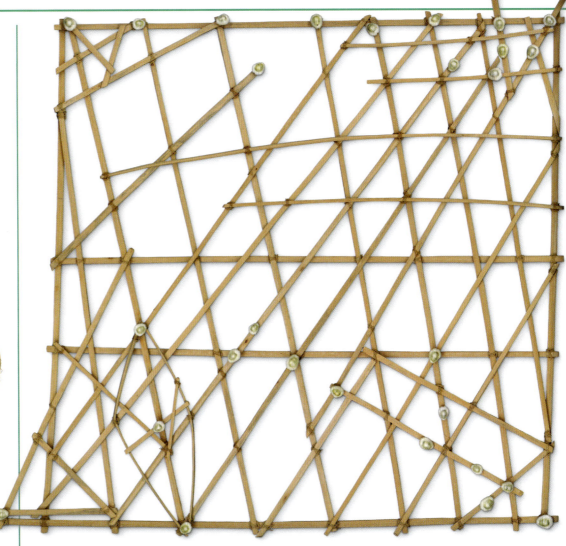

The first sea chart
The gods showed their gratitude for the coconut by giving Aluluei's daughter the first ever sea chart, made by themselves. When the girl showed her father, he was amazed at its precision. Aluluei shared this new knowledge of navigation with all of his people.

Polynesian stick chart
The Polynesians created their own maps by tying sticks together to represent the sea and adding shells to symbolize the islands they passed.

THE FIRST TATTOOS

The ancient Polynesians were the first to use tattoos to decorate their bodies, more than 2,000 years ago. Most people had tattoos, with the signs and symbols representing their individual identity, rank, and tribe.

Tattooing technique
Wolfat's tattooing technique required the man-of-war bird and the breadfruit tree. He handcrafted a sharp needle from the feathered wing of the bird, while the dark, inky pigment came from black soot produced by burning the sap of the tree.

Wolfat
The trickster god Wolfat lived in the sky with the other deities. He was the first god to apply tattoos, and as a powerful deity, he could also remove them at will. He saw a beautiful woman on Earth and pursued her, but she only returned his desire whenever he had his tattoos on. Wolfat then showed other men how to make themselves more attractive with tattoos.

Traditional tattoos
Tattoos varied from island to island, but many shared the same repeated geometric patterns.

Man-of-war bird
Now known as the frigate bird, the man-of-war is a huge seabird that stands out for the bright red throat pouch it displays during mating season.

Glossary

AFTERLIFE
In some myths and religions, the afterlife is the place people go after they die. The kind of afterlife a person enters is often a reflection of the life they led.

ALLY
To side with someone or something in a dispute; also the name for someone or something that does this.

AMBROSIA
The food of the gods in Greek mythology that can make mortals immortal if they eat it.

AMULET
An object, such as a piece of jewelery or a gemstone, that is said to protect its owner from evil spirits, curses, or illness.

AVATAR
In Hindu mythology, a form taken by a god or goddess to appear on Earth. Some gods and goddesses have many different avatars.

BARQUE
A type of boat that the Egyptian sun god Ra used to sail across the sky.

BELIEF SYSTEM
A set of ideas that together form the basis of a religion or a way of living.

BLACKSMITH
A person who makes and repairs metal tools and weapons.

CAUTERIZE
To burn the skin or flesh of a wound, usually to stop bleeding or infection. In the story of Hercules, he cauterizes the stumps of the Hydra to stop its heads from regrowing.

CELESTIAL
Belonging or relating to the sky or heaven.

CHAOS
Complete disorder and confusion.

CHARACTER
A person in a story.

CHARIOT
A two- or four-wheeled vehicle drawn by horses, used in racing and warfare.

CITADEL
A fortress, usually on high ground above a city.

CITY-STATE
A city and its surrounding territory that forms an independent state.

CLAN
A large family, or a group of interrelated families.

COMPASSION
Concern for the sufferings and misfortunes of others.

CREATION STORY
An account of how everything came to be.

CURSE
A magical spell intended to cause harm to other beings.

DEITY
An immortal, powerful being that is worshipped by others.

DEMIGOD
A being that has one parent that is a god or goddess, with the other parent being human.

DEVOTION
Love and loyalty to a person or a god.

DIVINE
Connected with heaven, a god, or a goddess.

ENLIGHTENMENT
The state of attaining or having attained spiritual knowledge or insight.

ENTITY
A thing with a distinct existence, independent of others.

EPIC
A long poem or story that describes an event of great historical and cultural significance.

ETERNITY
Infinite or unending time.

EXPEDITION
A journey undertaken by a group of people for a particular purpose such as exploration or warfare.

FATE
Future events outside a being's control that they cannot avoid. Some gods and goddesses can change the fate of other beings, especially if they feel that it is deserved.

FERTILITY
The ability to grow new life.

FOLKLORE
Traditional beliefs and stories that have been passed on for many years by word of mouth.

FORETOLD
When an event in the present or future has been predicted by someone in the past.

GOD / GODDESS
Male / female supernatural beings, worshipped due to their great powers.

HARMONY
The state of being in agreement, with an absence of conflict.

HERDSMAN
The owner or keeper of a herd of domesticated animals such as sheep or goats.

HERITAGE
Valued traditions that are passed from generation to generation.

HERO
A being who is courageous and triumphs over evil.

HUMANITY
A term for all human beings.

HUMANOID
Having the appearance of or resembling a human being in some way.

IMMORTAL
A being that can live forever.

INDIGENOUS
When applied to people, the word "indigenous" describes the original settlers of a country or region.

JUDGE (PERSON)
A person appointed to decide something.

LEGEND
A traditional story from the past, telling of a famous deed or action. Legends are rarely historically verified.

LYRE
A small, U-shaped harp, popular in ancient Greece.

MEAD
An alcoholic drink made from honey and water. In Viking times, people feasted and drank mead in large single-room buildings called mead halls.

MILITARY
Relating to soldiers or armed forces.

MORTAL
A being who can die.

MOURNING
The expression of sorrow and sadness for someone's death.

MYTH
A traditional story from the past, usually concerning the early history of a people or explaining a natural phenomenon, and typically involving supernatural beings.

NECTAR
The drink of the gods in Greek and Roman mythology.

OBSTACLE
A thing that blocks one's way or hinders progress.

OFFERING
Something that is given as a gift, or as part of a religious sacrifice or devotion.

OLYMPIAN GODS
The 12 major gods of Greek mythology, including Zeus, Athena, and Poseidon.

OMEN
A prophecy or a sign that foretells events, such as a catastrophic flood or a heroic victory.

PANTHEON
All the gods of a people or religion collectively, or a temple dedicated to all of the gods in ancient Greece or Rome.

PARADISE
An ideal and peaceful place where everything is happy.

PATRON / PATRONESS
A being, god, or goddess that protects a particular group of people or a place. A patron may also simply be a supporter of creative arts, crafts, or sciences.

PILGRIMAGE
A journey to a holy place.

PROPHECY
A prediction of what will happen in the future.

REALM
One area or part of the universe. Some myths feature many different realms.

REIGN
The period of rule of a monarch.

REINCARNATION
The process of being born again.

RESURRECT
To restore a dead person to life, or to revive something that is inactive or forgotten.

RITUAL
A series of actions performed in a certain way to please a god or goddess, or to summon an event such as rain for a plentiful harvest.

RUNES
Symbols with mysterious or magical significance, or small pieces of bone or stone that display such symbols.

SACRED STORY
A tale that is deeply rooted in a community's religious or cultural traditions that usually contains a moral message.

SACRIFICE
To kill a person or animal during a ritual, believing that it will please a god or goddess.

SAVIOR
A person who saves someone or something from danger or difficulty.

SCRIBE
Someone who records the details of an event by writing them down.

SHAMAN
A person who is believed to have magical powers, such as the ability to communicate with spirits, heal wounds, or predict the future.

SHAPE-SHIFTER
A person with the ability to change their physical form at will.

SICKLE
A handheld farming tool with a semicircular blade used for cutting crops such as corn or wheat.

SLAY
To kill in a violent way.

SORCERER
A person who has magical powers.

SOUL
The spiritual, nonphysical part of a human or animal. Some cultures believe that souls continue to exist after the body has died.

SPIRIT
A supernatural being. A nature spirit lives inside natural objects or places, such as a tree or in the ocean. Spirit can also refer to a being's soul.

SPIRITUAL
Relating to religion or religious belief, or the human spirit or soul as opposed physical or material things.

STATE OF MIND
A term that refers to someone's mental and emotional state.

SUPREMACY
The state or condition of being superior to others in authority, power, or status.

SUPREME GOD
The highest, most important god in a religion.

SUPERNATURAL
Powers that are beyond what is normal and / or the laws of nature, such as great strength or shape-shifting.

SYMBOL
A thing that represents or stands for something else.

TAPESTRY
A piece of fabric created by weaving threads or embroidering on a canvas.

THRONE
The ceremonial chair that a monarch or religious figure sits on. The word is often used to refer to sovereign power itself.

TOTEM ANIMAL
An animal that is believed by a particular society to have spiritual significance and that is adopted by it as an emblem.

TRAGEDY
An undeserved or unfortunate event that causes pain and suffering. Myths or heroes that are associated with tragedy are described as tragic.

TRAIT
A distinguishing quality or characteristic.

TRICKSTER
A mischievous being that upsets the gods and goddesses and the normal order of things. Some tricksters may be gods or goddesses themselves.

UNDERWORLD
In some myths and religions, the underworld is the realm to which people go after they die. It is also home to evil spirits and demons. It has different names in different cultures, appears in many myths, and is usually ruled by a god or goddess.

VILLAIN
A being that is responsible for causing harm, problems, or damage.

VOID
A place where nothing exists. Beings can be banished to the void.

VOYAGE
A long journey, often involving travel by sea.

WARRIOR
A brave or experienced soldier or fighter.

WISDOM
The quality of having experience, knowledge, and good judgment.

Index

Main topics are shown in **bold** page numbers.

A

Abzu 117
Achilles 36, 37
Acrisius of Argos 22
Acropolis, Athens 21
Actaeon 25
Adonis 35
Aegeus, King 28
Aeneas 19, 37, **40-41**, 42
Aengus 69
Aesir, the 49, 50, 53, 63
Africa **100-113**
  Egypt, ancient **90-99**
Agamemnon, King of Mycenae 36, 37
Agni 128
Ahriman 117, 126-127
Ahura Mazda 117, 126-127
Aido-Hwedo 104-105
Ailill, King 70, 71
Ajax 37
Alfheim 50
Alida 187
Allfather (Odin) **52-53**
Aluluei 201
Amaterasu 152-155
Ame-no-Uzume 152, 153
Ameretat 126
Americas
  Aztecs 172-173, **176-179**
  Caribbean 101, 107, 181, **186-187**
  Maya 172-173, **174-175**
  North **162-171**
  South **180-185**
Amesha Spentas 126
Ammit 98, 99
An 117
Ananse 101, **106-107**
Anat **124-125**
Andean civilizations 180
Andromeda 22
Andvaranaut 63
Andvari 62-63

Angakkuq 163, 170, 171
Angra Mainyu 126-127
Anu 117, 118, 122
Anubis 96, 98, 99
aos si 65
Aphrodite (Venus) 9, **34-35**, 36, 44-45
Apollo **24-25**, 36
Apollodorus 14
Apophis 95
Apsu 117, 118
Arachne 21
Arawn 74
Arctic region 163
Ares 9, 34, 36
Argo 26-27
Argonauts **26-27**
Ariadne 28, 29
Arjuna 136, 137
Armaiti 126
Artemis 9, **24-25**
Arthur, King 65, **76-77**
Asgard 49, 50, 53
Asha 126
Ashanti people 101, 106-107
Ashirat 125
Ashur 116
Asia
  Canaan civilization 117, **124-125**
  China 140-141, **142-149**, 158
  Hinduism 128-129, **130-139**
  Japan 140-141, **150-157**
  Korea 141, **158-159**
  Mesopotamia 116-117, **118-123**
  Persia **126-127**
Ask 48
Assyria 116, 121
Astarte 121
Atabey 186
Atalanta 27, 35
Athena 9, **20-21**, 31, 36
Atum (Ra) 92, **94-95**, 96, 98
'Aumakua 191

Australia 190-191, **192-195**
avatars 132-133
Avesta 126
Aztecs 172-173, **176-179**

B

Baal 117, **124-125**
Bába Yagá **82-83**, 85
Babi 98, 99
Babylonian Empire 117, 118, 121, 123
Badb, the 69
Bag noz 64
Balder 56
Balor of the Evil Eye 66-67
banshees 65
Bastet 90
Basuto people 100
Bataung people 100
Ba Xian (Eight Immortals) 140, 148-149
Bellerophon 31
Benandonner 72-73
Benin 105
Beowulf 46, **60-61**
Bhagavad Gita 137
Bhairava 131
Bhishma 137
black god (En-kai Narok) 108-109
Blodeuwedd 75
Bodhisattvas 140
Book of the Dead 90, 98
Botswana 112
Brahma **130-131**, 132, 134
Brahman 130
Bram-bram-bult 194
Brân 74, 75
Branwen 74-75
Br'er Rabbit 101
Bres, King 66
Brigid 64, 69
Britain 46, **76-77**
brownies 65
Brynhild 63
Buataranga 199

Buddha 129, 133, 146
Buddhism 129, 140, 146, 148, 158
Bull of Heaven 122-123
Bunyip 191

C

calendars 173, 179
Calydonian Boar Hunt 25
Calypso 38
Camelot 76
Cameroon 100
Canaan civilization 117, **124-125**
Cao Guojiu 148
Caribbean Islands 101, 107, 181, **186-187**
Carthage 40, 41
Cattle Raid of Cooley, the 70
celestial bureaucracy 148
Celtic mythology 64-65, **66-75**
centaurs 9, 32
Centéotl 179
Cerberus 18, 41
Ceres 9
Cernunnos 64
Chalchiuhtlicue 176, 177, 179
Chang'e 145
Chango 102
Chaos 10
Charon 18, 40
Charybdis 38
Chavin civilization 180
Cherokee people 163
Chicomecóatl 178
chimeras 31
China 140-141, **142-149**, 158
Chloris 16
Chuichu 185
Circe 38
Coatlicue 179
codices 172
Coeus 10, 11
Conchobar, King 70
Confucianism 140

conga-scepters (flyswatters) 110, 111
Congo 100, 101, 111
Coniraya Viracocha 183
Crius 11
Cronus 9, 14
Cú Chulainn (Hound of Chulainn) **70-71**
Cupid **44-45**
Cuzco 180
Cybele 16, 43
Cyclopes 10-11, 12, 38

D

Dagda, the 66, 68
Dáinn 50, 51
Danaë 22
Daoism 140, 148
Daphne 24
Dark Lady, the 143
Dazhbog 81
Deianira 32
demas 191
Demeter 9, 17
Denmark 61
Deucalion 15
Dhritarashtra 136
Diana 9, 43
Dian Cécht 69
Diarmuid 73
Dido 40
Di Jun 145
Diné people 162, 163, 166, 167
Dionysus 30, 34
Doan 194
Dokkaebi 141
Domovoy 79
Donn Cúailnge 70, 71
Dreaming, stories of the 190, 193, **194-195**
Drupada, King 136
Duat (the Underworld) 94-95, 96, **98-99**
Dumuzi 117, 121
Durga 134-135
Duryodhana 136, 137
dwarves 47, 53, 55, 62-63

E

Ea 117, 118, 122
Earth Holder 164
East Asia **140-141**
  China 140-141, **142-149**, 158
  Japan 140-141, **150-157**
  Korea 141, **158-159**
Easter Island (Rapa Nui) 191, 200
Eastern Europe **78-87**
Efnisien 74
Egypt, ancient **90-99**
Eight Immortals 140, 148-149
El 124
El Dorado 181
elves 47
Embla 48
England 76
Enkai 100
En-kai Narok and En-kai Na-nyokie **108-109**
Enki 117, 120-121
Enkidu 122-123
Ennead 97
Enuma Elish 118
Eos 11
Epic of Gilgamesh **122-123**
Epimetheus 14, 15
Epona 64, 75
Ereshkigal 121
Ériu 68
Erotes 35
Eshu 102
Europe
  Britain 46, **76-77**
  Finland 46, 58-59
  Germanic mythology 46, **60-63**
  Greece, ancient 8-9, **10-39**
  Ireland 64-65, **66-73**
  Norse mythology **46-57**
  Rome, ancient 8-9, 19, 34, **40-44**
  Slavic mythology **78-87**
  Wales 64-65, **74-75**
Eurydice 19
Eurystheus, King 32
Excalibur 76

F

Fafnir **62-63**
Fates, the 11
Fenian Cycle 73
Fenmeng 145
Fenrir 55, 56
Ferdiad 70
Finland 46, 58-59
Fionn mac Cumhaill (Finn MacCool) **72-73**
Fir Bolg 66-67
firebirds 83, **86-87**
First Australians 190-191, **192-195**
First Canadians (Inuit) 163, **170-171**
fish hooks 198-199
Flint 164-165
Floating Bridge of Heaven 150-151
flyswatters 111
Fólkvangr 50, 63
Fomorians, the 66-67, 68
Fon people **104-105**
Four Braves 156
Freyja 46, 49, 55
Frigg 47, 50, 53, 56

G

Gáe Bolg 70, 71
Gaia 10-11, 12
Galahad, Sir 76, 77
Ganesha 128
Ganga 128
Ga'nowa'geh (Turtle Island) 164
Gayomart 126, 127
Geats 61
Geb (Egyptian god) 92-93
Geb (Polynesian dema) 191
Gentle People 180
Germanic mythology 46, **60-63**
Ghana 101, 106-107
Giant's Causeway, Northern Ireland 72-73
Gilgamesh **122-123**
Golden Fleece 26
Golden Mother of the West 149
Gonggong 142-143
Gorgons 22
Gráinne 73
Grandma Seolmundae 158-159
Grandmother, Spider 166-167
Great Ziggurat of Ur 116
Greece, ancient 8-9, **10-39**
Green Knight, the 65
Greenland 163, 170
Grendel 60-61
Grimhild 63
Guayaba 187
Gudrun 63
Gugalanna 117
Guinevere 65, 76
Gunnar 63

H

Hades 9, 13, **16-17**, 18-19, 22
Haiti 101
Hall of Two Truths **98-99**
Hanuman 128, 129, 138
Han Xiangzi 148
harpies 40
Hastinapur 136, 137
Hathor 90, 98
Haua 200
Haurvatat 126
Hawaii 191, 197, 200
Hebe 9
Hecate 18
Hecatoncheires 10, 12
Hector 36, 37
Hel 51, 55
Helen 36
Helios 11, 31
Hephaestus 9, 34-35
Hera 9, 30, 32, 35, 36
Hercules (Heracles) **32-33**
Hermes 9, 34, 36
Hero Twins (Mayan legends) **174-175**
Hero Twins (Diné legends) 167
Hesiod 10, 14
Hestia (Vesta) 12, **42-43**
He Xiangu 148
Hina 197
Hinduism 128-129, **130-139**
hippocampi 9
Hiruko 150
Hittites 117
Hlakanyana 101
Holy Grail **76-77**
Homer 8, 36
Hopi people 166
Horae (Hours), the 16
Horus 96, 97, 98
Hotu Matu'a, King 200
household gods **42-43**
Hrothgar, King 61
Huari civilization 180
Huitzilopotchli 173
Humbaba 122
Hunahpu and Xbalanque **174-175**
Hun Hunahpu 174
Hwanung 159
Hyacinthus 25
Hydra 32-33
Hymir 54
Hyperion 10, 11

I

Iapetus 11
Icarus 31
Iceland 46
Illapa 185
Ilmarinen 58-59
Imaymana Viracocha 182
Inanna 117, **120-121**, 122
Inca Empire 180-181, **182-185**
India 128-129, 136, 146
  see also Hinduism
Indigenous (North) Americans **162-171**
Indra 128
Inis Fáil (the Island of Destiny) **66-67**
Inti 182, 183, 184, 185
Inuit peoples 163, **170-171**
Iolaos 33
Iraq *see* Mesopotamia
Ireland 64-65, **66-73**
Iris 9
Ise Shrine 153
Ishtar 117, 118, 121
Isis 96, 97, 98
Island of Destiny **66-67**
Itztlacoliuhqui 179
Ivan Tsarevich 83, 84-85, 86-87
Ixion 19
Iyangura 111
Izanami and Izanagi **150-151**, 152

J

Jade Emperor 143, 146, **148-149**
Japan 140-141, **150-157**
Jarilo 81
Jason **26-27**
Jeju Island 158-159
Jimmu, Emperor 155
Jiu Tian Xuannü 143
Jörmungandr 54, 55, 56
Jotunheim 51
Jumong 159
Juno 9
Jupiter 9, 41, 42, 45

K

!Kaggen 112
Kagutsuchi 150
Kalevala, the 46, **58-59**
Kali 134
Kalki 133
kami 141, 150, 154
Karna 137
Karnak Temple Complex 91
Kauravas 136-137
kayaks 170
kelpies 65
Kenya 109
Khmer Empire 129
Khonsu 93
Khshathra Vairya 126
Kikimora 79
Kingu 118
Kintaro **156-157**
Kintoki 156
Knights of the Round Table, the 76-77
Kon 185
Kooch 180
Kore (Persephone) **16-17**, 18, 19
Korea 141, **158-159**
Koschei the Deathless **84-85**
Krishna 133, 137
Kronos 10-11, 12, 13, 34
Kuba people 100
Kur 121
Kurma 132

205

Kuru family 136-137
Kurukshetra, Battle of 137
Kushinade-hime, Princess 154, 155
Kvasir 49

L

Labors of Hercules **32-33**
Labyrinth 28-29
Lady of the Lake 76-77
Lakota people 162
Lakshmana 138
Lakshmi 132, 134
Lan Caihe 148
Lancelot du Lac, Sir 65, 76
Lares, the 42, 43
Lemminkäinen 58-59
Leto 24
Lif and Lifthrasir 57
Lisa (Mawu-Lisa) **104-105**
Li Tieguai 148
Little Humpbacked Horse, The 86, 87
Lleu Llaw Gyffes 75
Llŷr 74
loas 101
Locuo 186
Loki 46, **54-57**, 62, 63
Lonkundo 101
Lönnrot, Elias 46, 58
Louhi 58-59
Lü Dongbin 148
Lugh 66-67, 68
Lumaluma 194-195

M

Maasai people 100, **108-109**
Maasinta 109
Maat 92, 95, 98, 99
Mabinogi, the **74-75**
Macha 69
Machu Picchu 180
Mahabharata **136-137**
Mahadevi **134-135**
Mahishasura 134
Maiden Czar, The 83
Maid of the North 58
Maitreya 158
Makemake 200
Malawi 101

Mama Cocha 185
Mama Kilya 184
Manaia 191
Manannán mac Lir 69
Manawydan 74
Manco Capac 183, 184
Mandjet 95
mantises 112-113
Māori people 190, 191, 199
Mara 129
Marduk **118-119**
Mariassa 83
Marind-anim people 191
Mars 9
Marya Morevna 84-85
Mashya 126, 127
Mashyoi 126, 127
Math, King 75
Matholwch, King 74, 75
Mati Syra Zemlya 81
Matsya 132
Maui 197, **198-199**
Mavka 78
Mawu-Lisa **104-105**
Maya 172-173, **174-175**
Mbombo 100
Mead of Poetry 53
Medb, Queen 70, 71
Medea 26, 28
Medusa 20, **22-23**
Mehen 95
Menehune 191
Menelaus, King 36
Meoto Iwa (Wedded Rocks) 150
Mercury 9
Merlin 76-77
Mesektet 94-95
Mesoamerica **172-173**
Aztecs 172-173, **176-179**
Maya 172-173, **174-175**
Mesopotamia 116-117, **118-123**
Midas, King 30
Midgard 50, 51
Milesians, the 66
Mímir 49, 53
Minerva 9
Minos, King 28-29, 31
Minotaur, the **28-29**, 31
Mireuk 158
Mithras 9
Mjölnir 54, 55
Mnemosyne 10

moai 191
Moche civilization 180
Mongo people 101
Monkey King **146-147**
Mordred 76
Morrígan, the 66, 69, 70
Moshanyana 100
Mot 125
Muisa 111
mummification 91, 96
murti 131
Muses, the 11
Muskrat 164
Muspelheim 48, 51, 56
Mwindo **110-111**

N

Namibia 112
Nammu 117
Nanahuatzin 176-177
Nanna 117
Naram-Sin of Akkad 116
Narasimha 133
navigation 201
Nazca people 185
Nemean lion 32, 33
Nephthys 96, 98
Neptune 9
Nergal 117
New Guinea 191
New Zealand 190, 197, 198
Nidhogg 50, 51
Niflheim 48, 50
Ninigi 155
Niobe 24
Nix 79
Nobbys Head, Australia 195
Norns, the 50
Norse mythology **46-57**
North America **162-171**
Northern Europe **46-47**
Finland 46, 58-59
Germanic mythology 46, **60-63**
Norse mythology **46-57**
Ntumba 110-111
Nuada, King 66, 69
Nut 92-93
Nüwa **142-143**
Nyame 106
Nyanga people **110-111**
nymphs 9, 11, 79

O

Obatala 102, 103
Oceania **190-191**
Australia 190-191, **192-195**
Pacific Islands 190-191, **196-201**
Oceanus 10, 11
Odin 46, 48-49, 50, **52-53**, 56
Odysseus 19, 20, 36, 37, **38-39**
Ogun 102
Oisín 64, 72
Ojibwe people 163, 166
Ōkuninushi **154-155**
Old Woman 164-165
Olmec 172
Olokun 103
Olorun 102-103
Olympians 8-9, 11, 12-13
Olympic Games 9
Olympus 8, 15, 31, 35, 45
Omoikane 152
Oonagh 73
Oracle at Delphi 8
orishas 102
Orochi 154-155
Orpheus 19, 27
Orunmila 102, 103
Oshun 102
Osiris 90, 94-95, **96-97**, 98
Ouranos 10-11, 12, 34
Oya 102

P

Pachamama 185
Pacific Islands 190-191, **196-201**
Panathenaia 9
Pandavas 133, 136-137
Pandora 14-15
Pandu 136
Pangu **142-143**
Pantheon, Rome 9
Papa 190
Paracas civilization 180
Parashurama 133
Paris, Prince 36, 37
Parthenon, Athens 21
Parvati 134
Patagonian mythology 180

Pawnee people 162
Pegasus 22, 31
Pele 200
Pelias 26
Penates, the 42
Penelope 39
Penthesilea 37
Persephone **16-17**, 18, 19
Perseus 20, **22-23**
Persia **126-127**
Perun 80
Phaethon 31
pharaohs 90
Phoebe 10
Phoenicia 39, 121
phoenixes 9
Pluto 9
Poetic Edda, the 46
Pohjola 58-59
Pok-ta-Pok 175
Polynesia 190-191, **196-201**
Polyphemus 38
Pomona 16
Poseidon 9, 12, 39
Priapus 43
Prometheus 14-15
Prose Edda 46
Pryderi 74, 75
Psyche **44-45**
Ptah 93
Pueblo people 162
Puranas 132, 133
Pwyll, Prince of Dyfed 74-75
Pygmalion 35
pyramids 90, 172, 173
Pyrrha 15

Q

Qilin 141
Quetzalcoatl 172-173, 176, 177

R

Ra (Egyptian god) 92, **94-95**, 96, 98
Ra (Polynesian god) 199
Ragnarök **56-57**
Raiko 156
Rainbow Serpent **192-193**
see also Aido-Hwedo
rakshasas 138
Rama 133, 138-139

Ramayana, the 129, **138-139**
Rangi 190
Rapa Nui 191, 200
Ratatoskr 51
Ravana, King 138
ravens 24, 53, 70, 84, **168-169**
red god (En-kai Na-nyokie) **108-109**
Regin 62-63
Remus 41
Rhea 10, 12
Rhiannon 64, 74, 75
Rome, ancient 8-9, 19, 34, **40-44**
Romulus 41
Rongo 190
Rusalka 79

S
Sadhbh 72
Sadko 78
sagas 46
Sahara, south of the **100-101**
Salmon of Knowledge 72
Samoa 197
sampo 58, 59
samurai 156
San people **112-113**
Sapling 164, 165
Saraswati 134
Saturn 9
satyrs 9
Scandinavia 61
  Norse mythology **46-57**
Scáthach 70-71
Scotland 64, 70, 72, 73
Scylla 38
Sedna **170-171**
Sekhmet 90
Selene 11
Semele 30
Seneca people 164
Senet 93
Seokga 158
Set 96-97
Sétanta (Cú Chulainn) 70
Shakti **134-135**
shamans 158, 169, 170, 171
Shamash 117, 122, 123
Shamba Bolongongo 101
Shatarupa 130

Shemwindo 110, 111
Shinto 140
Shiva 128, **130-131**, 132, 134
Shu 92-93
Siddhartha Gautama 129
Sif 55
Sigurd 46, **62-63**
Sin 117
Sirens 26, 27, 38
Sisyphus 19
Sita 138-139
Sky Woman 164
Slavic mythology **78-87**
Sleipnir 52-53, 55
South Africa 100, 112
South America **180-185**
South Asia **128-129**, 130-139
Spider Grandmother **166-167**
spiders 21, 106, 166
Sucellos 64
Sumeria 120, 121
Sun Wukong 146
Surpanakha 138
Surya 128
Susanoo 152, **154-155**
Svarog 80
Svartalfheim 51
Svetovid 81
Sybil of Cumae, the 40-41

T
Ta'aroa **196-197**
Tahiti 197, 200
Taíno people 181, **186-187**
Tama-nui-te-ra 199
Tammuz 117
Tane 190, 197
Tangaroa 190, 197
Tantalus 19
Tanzania 109
Taoism (Daoism) 140, 148
Taranis 65
Taroo 187
tattoos 201
Taweret 90
Tawhiri 190
Tefnut 92, 98
Tehuelche people 180
Telemachus 39
Teotihuacan 172
Tepēyōllōtl 179

Tethys 11
Tezcatlipoca 172-173, 176
theater 8
Theia 10
Themis 11
Theseus **28-29**
Thor 46, **54-55**, 56, 57
Thoth 92, 93, 96, 98
Three Noble Children **152-153**
Thunderbird 162
Tiahuanaco civilization 180
Tiamat 117, **118-119**
Tiangou 145
Tiddalik 195
Tiresias 21
Tír na nÓg 64
Titan gods 8, **10-13**
Titicaca, Lake 180, 182
Tlaloc 176, 178
Tocapo Viracocha 182
Toltec 172
Tonatiuh 177, 179
Tonga 197
totems 162, 166
trees of life *see* Yggdrasil
Tridevi, the 134
Trimurti, the 128, **130-131**, 134
Trojan War 8, **36-37**, 39, 41
trolls 47
Tsukuyomi 152
Tuatha Dé Danann 64, 66-67, **68-69**
Tubondo 111
Tūmatauenga 190
Tumbuka people 101
Ture 101
Turtle Island **164-165**
Typhon 12

U
Ugarit 117, 124-125
Ulster Cycle, the 70
Unkulunkulu 100
Urcuchillay 185
Uther Pendragon, King 76
Utnapishtim 122-123
Utu 117

V
Väinämöinen 58-59
Valhalla 50, 63
Valkyries 50, 63
Valmiki 130
Vamana 133
vampirs 79
Vanaheim 49, 50
Vanir, the 49, 53
Varaha 132
Varuna 128
Vasilisa 78, 83, 87
Vayu 128
Ve 48, 49
Vedas 128, 130
Veles 80, 81
Venezuela 181
Venus (Aphrodite) 9, **34-35**, 44-45
Vesta (Hestia) **42-43**
Vestalia 43
Vila 79
Vili 48, 49
Viracocha Pachachayachic **182-183**
Vishnu **130-133**, 134, 138
Vodou 101
Vodyanoi 79
Vohu Manah 126
Völsungs, Saga of the 62
voodoo 101
Vulcan 9

W
Wales 64, 65, **74-75**
Wanadi 181
Warao people 181
Wawilak Sisters 194-195
Wedded Rocks, Japan 150
werewolves 79
West Asia **116-117**
  Canaan civilization 117, **124-125**
  Mesopotamia 116-117, **118-123**
  Persia **126-127**
Western Europe **64-65**
Wolfat 201
Woot 100
World Tree *see* Yggdrasil

X
Xbalanque and Hunahpu (Hero Twins) **174-175**
Xhosa people 101
Xibalba 174
Xihe 145
Xipe Totec 178
Xi Wangmu (Golden Mother of the West) 149
Xuanzang 146

Y
Yamm 124-125
Yao, Emperor 145
Yauyos people 183
Yaya 186
Yelena, Princess 86
Yemaya 102
Yggdrasil **50-51**, 53, 57
Yi **144-145**
Ymir 48-49
yokai 141
Yomi 150, 152
Yoruba people 101, **102-103**
Yowie 191
Yúcahu 186
Yudhishthira 136-137
Yühuang (Jade Emperor) 143, 146, **148-149**
Yuhwa 159

Z
Zande people 101
Zaphon, Mount 124, 125
Zapotec 172
zemis 187
Zeus 9, 12-15, 17, 20, 30
Zhang Guolao 148
Zhongli Quan 148
Zhurong 142
ziggurats 116
Ziva 81
Zoroastrianism 117, 126
Zorya 81
Zulu people 100, 101
Zurvan 126, 127

Acknowledgments

The publisher would like to thank the following people for their assistance in the preparation of this book: Vandana Likhmania, Zarak Rais, Upamanyu Das, and Abi Maxwell for text contributions; Aasha (DK India's Diversity, Equity, and Inclusion team), Professor Nemata Blyden, Dr. Amy Fuller, Leanne Holt, Lauren Keenan, and Tim Topper for authenticity reading; Mik Gates for design assistance; Kelsie Besaw and Steven Carton for editorial assistance; Caroline Hunt for proofreading; Elizabeth Wise for indexing.

The publisher would like to thank the following for their kind permission to reproduce their photographs:

(Key: a-above; b-below/bottom; c-center; f-far; l-left; r-right; t-top)

8 Alamy Stock Photo: SuperStock / Peter Barritt (bl). **Dreamstime.com:** Kmiragaya (c); Kelly Vandellen (cra); Sjankauskas (clb); Mapics (br). **8-9 The Walters Art Museum, Baltimore:** Acquired by Henry Walters, 1913 (c). **9 Adobe Stock:** Kareemov (crb). **Alamy Stock Photo:** Album (tr/Saturnalia); Science History Images (cla); The Picture Art Collection (cr); Science History Images / Photo Researchers (bc). **Dreamstime.com:** Joserpizarro (crb/Hippocampus); Saiko3p (tr); Sborisov (clb). **Getty Images / iStock:** DigitalVision Vectors / Duncan1890 (cla/Iris); Aleksandr Kharitonov (br). **Los Angeles County Museum of Art:** Attributed to Python (Greece, South Italian, Paestan, active mid 4th century B.C.) (cra). **Thorvaldsens Museum:** Bertel Thorvaldsen / Hebe, 1770-1844 / A874 / Jakob Faurvig (tl/hebe). **10 Dreamstime.com:** Biserko (bl/x2). **The Metropolitan Museum of Art:** Rogers Fund, 1941 (c). **11 Alamy Stock Photo:** Zev Radovan / BibleLandPictures (tc); Adam Eastland (tr); Science History Images / Photo Researchers (c/Fates); Ali Kabas (c); Prisma Archivo (cr). **Bridgeman Images:** Photograph © 2025 Museum of Fine Arts, Boston. All rights reserved. / Museum purchase with funds donated in honor of Edward W. Forbes (cl). **Dreamstime.com:** FabioConcetta (tc/Eos). **12 Alamy Stock Photo:** CPA Media Pte Ltd / Pictures From History (bl). **15 Alamy Stock Photo:** Index / Heritage Images (tc); Lebrecht Music & Arts (bl). **Bridgeman Images:** Ghigo Roli (br). **16 Alamy Stock Photo:** Artepics (tl); Pictures Now (clb); The National Trust Photolibrary / Derrick E. Witty (bl). **The Metropolitan Museum of Art:** Gift of Henry G. Marquand, 1897 (cla). **17 Alamy Stock Photo:** Peter Horree (tc). **18 Alamy Stock Photo:** Christian Kober 1 (cr); Lebrecht Music & Arts (tr). **Bridgeman Images:** Photo © AISA (tc). **19 Alamy Stock Photo:** IanDagnall Computing (tl); The Picture Art Collection (b). **Bridgeman Images:** (tr). **Getty Images:** Werner Forman / Universal Images Group (tc). **20 Bridgeman Images:** Photo © Leonard de Selva (crb). **21 Bridgeman Images:** The Stapleton Collection (bc). **Dreamstime.com:** Ivan Bastien (tr). **22 Alamy Stock Photo:** funkyfood London - Paul Williams (bl). **The Metropolitan Museum of Art:** Harris Brisbane Dick Fund, 1939 (clb). **24 Alamy Stock Photo:** ART Collection (bc); Maidun Collection (bl). **The Metropolitan Museum of Art:** Rogers Fund, 1905 (cl). **25 Alamy Stock Photo:** Archivart (bc). The Metropolitan Museum of Art: Gift of Mrs. George S. Amory, in memory of her father and mother, Mr. and Mrs. Amory Sibley Carhart, 1964 (tr). **26 Birmingham Museums Trust licensed under CC0:** (bc). **28 Alamy Stock Photo:** WBC ART (br). **29 Alamy Stock Photo:** Zuri Swimmer (bc). **30 Alamy Stock Photo:** Pictorial Press Ltd (c). **Bridgeman Images:** Raffaello Bencini (bl). **31 Alamy Stock Photo:** Science History Images / Photo Researchers (cla, br). **Bridgeman Images:** Look and Learn / Fortunino Matania (1881-1963) (tr); Look and Learn / Donn P. Crane (1878-1944) (bl). **Dreamstime.com:** Raffaele Amato (bc). **33 Dreamstime.com:** DRpics24 (cr). **The Metropolitan Museum of Art:** Rogers Fund, 1913 (cra). **34 Alamy Stock Photo:** ARTGEN (br). **35 Alamy Stock Photo:** Charles Walker Collection (br); Science History Images / Photo Researchers (tl). **The Metropolitan Museum of Art:** Gift of Waters S. Davis, 1928 (tr). **36 Alamy Stock Photo:** Peter Horree (bc). **36-37 TurboSquid:** 3d_molier International (c). **38 Alamy Stock Photo:** Album (c). **40 Alamy Stock Photo:** Zuri Swimmer (tc). **Shutterstock.com:** Gianni Dagli Orti (tl). **41 Dreamstime.com:** Fedecandoniphoto (br). **42 Bridgeman Images:** © NPL - DeA Picture Library (bc). Shutterstock.com: stoker_1 (ca/Wheat); Techzaka (ca). **43 Alamy Stock Photo:** Art Collection 4 (c); Cormon Francis / Hemis.fr (bl). **Dreamstime.com:** Denise Serra (br). **Shutterstock.com:** Antony McAulay (tl). **44 Dreamstime.com:** Destina156 (bl). **45 Adobe Stock:** Atlas Illustrations (tr); Olena (tr/Collect beauty); Mykola Syvak (ca). **Dreamstime.com:** Carlosvelayos (cb/Jug); Karayuschij (cb). **Shutterstock.com:** a_v_d (cb/Amphora); Vector Export (cra/Eagle aid); Rawpixel.com (br). **46 Adobe Stock:** Archivist (crb). **Alamy Stock Photo:** (cb); Stan Pritchard (tr); Painters (cra); CPA Media Pte Ltd / Pictures From History (cl); Rolf Richardson (clb); Janzig / Europe (bl). **Dreamstime.com:** Onlyfabrizio (cb/Runes). **47 Alamy Stock Photo:** Chronicle (cra); Lebrecht Music & Arts / Music-Images (cr); DE Rocker (bc). **Dreamstime.com:** Jaroslaw Grudzinski (bl); Jojjik (ca). **Getty Images:** Universal Images Group / Werner Forman (c). **48 123RF.com:** smileus (br/ash). **Getty Images:** DEA / A. Dagli Orti / De Agostini (bl). **49 Alamy Stock Photo:** Historic Images (tl); North Wind Picture Archives (bc). **50 Alamy Stock Photo:** Uber Bilder (bl); Ivy Close Images (tc). **53 Alamy Stock Photo:** History and Art Collection (bc). **54 Alamy Stock Photo:** GRANGER Historical Picture Archive (tr). **55 Alamy Stock Photo:** Ivy Close Images (tr). **Dreamstime.com:** Leremy (bc); Maria Nesterova (bc/wolf). **Getty Images:** Werner Forman / Universal Images Group (br). **56 Alamy Stock Photo:** Science History Images / Photo Researchers (tc). **58 Alamy Stock Photo:** ARTGEN (bl); GRANGER Historical Picture Archive (br). **Shutterstock.com:** Matthewshutter (tc). **58-59 Alamy Stock Photo:** ARTGEN (tc). **59 Alamy Stock Photo:** History and Art Collection (clb); Zuri Swimmer (bc); Magite Historic (br). **Dreamstime.com:** Zbyněk Ševčík (cr). **60 Getty Images:** Archive Photos / Transcendental Graphics (br). **62 Alamy Stock Photo:** Ivy Close Images (cla). **63 Alamy Stock Photo:** Penta Springs Limited / Artokoloro (tc). **Dreamstime.com:** Igor Tokalenko (ca). **64 Adobe Stock:** ycharton (c). **Alamy Stock Photo:** GRANGER Historical Picture Archive (tr); The Print Collector / CM Dixon / Heritage Images (tc); Scherl / Süddeutsche Zeitung Photo (tc/Epona). **Dreamstime.com:** MNStudio (cb); Vito Werner (bl). **65 Adobe Stock:** Archivist (br). **Alamy Stock Photo:** Artepics (bl); GRANGER Historical Picture Archive (tc); Keith Corrigan (tr). **Bridgeman Images:** G. Dagli Orti / © NPL - DeA Picture Library (tl). **68 Alamy Stock Photo:** Vincent Lowe (cl). **Shutterstock.com:** Yingna Cai (bl). **69 Alamy Stock Photo:** Menigault Bernard (bc); Ivy Close Images (tl); Reading Room 2020 (tc); Radharc Images / JoeFox Liverpool (tr); Chronicle (bl). **Shutterstock.com:** Simonas Minkevicius (bc/Crow). **71 Alamy Stock Photo:** GL Archive (br); Radharc Images / JoeFoxBerlin (crb). **72 Dreamstime.com:** Anankkml (bc). **73 Alamy Stock Photo:** Janice and Nolan Braud (tr). **74-75 Getty Images:** Universal Images Group / Werner Forman (c). **74 Alamy Stock Photo:** Alan Novelli (bl). **75 Adobe Stock:** Olena (cb). **Alamy Stock Photo:** Album (bc); Charles Walker Collection (tc); Ivy Close Images (cr); Alwyn Jonrs (br). **Dreamstime.com:** Foxyliam (crb/Meadowsweet); Vasyl Helevachuk (cl); Regien Paassen (br/Owl). **77 Alamy Stock Photo:** Josse Christophel (tc). **Bridgeman Images:** (tl). **78 Adobe Stock:** Mariia (cb). **Alamy Stock Photo:** © Fine Art Images / Heritage Images (tr); PAINTING (tc). **79 Alamy Stock Photo:** Album (bc); Heritage Image Partnership Ltd / Fine Art Images (cl); Science History Images / Photo Researchers (c); © Fine Art Images / Heritage Images (bl); The Print Collector (br). **Dreamstime.com:** Roman Sorkin (cr); Alena Yakubouskaya (cra). **80 Dreamstime.com:** Daniela Pelazza (bc); PhotoChur (c). **Shutterstock.com:** Shyjo (r). **81 Adobe Stock:** Nick Edge (bc). **Alamy Stock Photo:** Album (tr). **Dreamstime.com:** Katerina Kovaleva (bl). **Shutterstock.com:** Bissig (tl). **83 Alamy Stock Photo:** © Fine Art Images / Heritage Images (bc). **84 Alamy Stock Photo:** © Fine Art Images / Heritage Images (bc); Zuri Swimmer (cl). **Dreamstime.com:** Punnawich Limparungpatanakij (tc/Falcon); Anastasia Maslova (tl). **Shutterstock.com:** Abdul Fattah19 (tc). **85 Alamy Stock Photo:** EU / BT (cb); Painters (tl). **Depositphotos Inc:** StephanieFrey (cb/silverware). **Dreamstime.com:** Hugolacasse (br). **87 Alamy Stock Photo:** JHU Sheridan Libraries / Gado (crb). **90 Alamy Stock Photo:** Delphotos (bl); Alain Guilleux (cl); Lebrecht Music & Arts (clb); Graham Prentice (br); Index / Heritage Images (bc). **91 Alamy Stock Photo:** Carmen K. Sisson / Cloudybright (cl); Prisma Archivo (tr); funkyfood London - Paul Williams (cr); The Print Collector / CM Dixon / Heritage Images (crb); Kay Ringwood (br). **Dreamstime.com:** Natalia Pavlova (bl). **The Metropolitan Museum of Art:** Rogers Fund and Edward S. Harkness Gift, 1920 (c). **93 Alamy Stock Photo:** Alain Guilleux (br). **The Metropolitan Museum of Art:** Rogers Fund, 1916 (tr). **95 Alamy Stock Photo:** Adam Eastland (crb); The Picture Art Collection (bl). **96 Alamy Stock Photo:** Chronicle (tr); funkyfood London - Paul Williams (bl); GRANGER - Historical Picture Archive (br). **97 Alamy Stock Photo:** Album (c). **Dreamstime.com:** Basphoto (bc). **100 Bridgeman Images:** Lowe Art Museum / Museum purchase through the 2010 Director's Circle (br). **Getty Images / iStock:** E+ / Asbe (cla). **Shutterstock.com:** Andrzej Kubik (cl). **100-101 Dreamstime.com:** Amwu (tc). **101 Adobe Stock:** Anna Lepekha (tr); LiveLove (cra). **Alamy Stock Photo:** Danvis Collection (c); Penta Springs Limited / Artokoloro (crb). **© The Trustees of the British Museum. All rights reserved:** (bl). **Getty Images / iStock:** Coowikie (cr). **102 Getty Images:** SSPL (tr). **103 Alamy Stock Photo:** mauritius images GmbH / David & Micha Sheldon (bl). **The Metropolitan Museum of Art:** Gift of Mr. and Mrs. Klaus G. Perls, 1991 (cr). **naturepl.com:** Bernard Castelein (br). **105 Alamy Stock Photo:** Sarah Dowdall (br). **Getty Images:** The Image Bank / Aldo Pavan (bl). **106 Alamy Stock Photo:** blickwinkel / R. Koenig (bc). **107 Dreamstime.com:** Mykola Ohorodnyk (tr); Natalia Zakharova (tc). **Shutterstock.com:** AfroArt (bl/Pot); iqbaldesigner (tl); Maria Alam Sraboni (bl). **111 Dreamstime.com:** Luckypic (br/tree). **Getty Images / iStock:** Varaponr Nampha (br). **112 Alamy Stock Photo:** AfriPics.com (tl). **Dreamstime.com:** Friedemeier (crb); Dietmar Rauscher (tr); Rahman Malikzade (fcrb); Marc Sailer (bc). **Shutterstock.com:** LaHellen (cb/hare); Save nature and wildlife (cb). **113 Shutterstock.com:** John Ceulemans (tr); Stubblefield Photography (bc); Wirestock Creators (br). **116 Alamy Stock Photo:** Heritage Image Partnership Ltd / © Fine Art Images (c); IanDagnall Computing (cl). **Dreamstime.com:** Dmitrii Moroz (br). **Getty Images / iStock:** Audioworm (cr); Luigi Farrauto (cra). **The Metropolitan Museum of Art:** Rogers Fund, 1987 (bl). **117 Alamy Stock Photo:** BibleLandPictures / Zev Radovan (bc); Zev Radovan (cb). **Dreamstime.com:** Vladimir Melnik (br); Zzvet (cl). **The Metropolitan Museum of Art:** Purchase, 1886 (bl). **118 Shutterstock.com:** Moustafa Tahir (tr). **120 © The Trustees of the British Museum. All rights reserved:** (br). **121 Alamy Stock Photo:** Album (tl); E. Jason Wambsgans / Chicago Tribune / MCT / Sipa USA (bl); The Picture Art Collection (tr). **The Metropolitan Museum of Art:** Dodge Fund, 1933 (bc). **122 Alamy Stock Photo:** Bibleland / Zev Radovan (bl). **123 Alamy Stock Photo:** Ivy Close Images (tr); Science History Images / Photo Researchers (tc). **124 Dreamstime.com:** Brett Critchley (br). **125 Bridgeman Images:** Luisa Ricciarini (cla). **Getty Images / iStock:** Salih Yunus Gundu (cb). **127 Alamy Stock Photo:** GRANGER Historical Picture Archive (br). **128 Adobe Stock:** Rudiernst (fbr). **Alamy Stock Photo:** Louise Batalla Duran (tr); Ephotocorp / Dr. Suresh Vasant (ca); CPA Media Pte Ltd / Pictures From History (tl); Penta Springs Limited / Artokoloro (cr); The Protected Art Archive (cb, bc/Agni); The History Collection (bc). **Dreamstime.com:** Klodien (br). **Los Angeles County Museum of Art:** Gift of the Felix and Helen Juda Foundation (bl). **The Metropolitan Museum of Art:** Samuel Eilenberg Collection, Bequest of Samuel Eilenberg, 1998 (clb). **129 Alamy Stock Photo:** Art Directors & TRIP / ArkReligion.com (bc); FOST (ca); John White Photos (cra); Sabena Jane Blackbird (br). **Dreamstime.com:** Littlewormy (cl). **Getty Images:** Stockbyte / Guido Cozzi / Atlantide Phototravel (bl). **130 Alamy Stock Photo:** The History Collection (tl). **131 Los Angeles County Museum of Art:** Gift of Ramesh and Urmil Kapoor (M.91.293.1) (crb). **132-133 Alamy Stock Photo:** The Print Collector / CM Dixon / Heritage Images (t). **132 Alamy Stock Photo:** Godong (bc); Triangle Travels (bl). **133 Alamy Stock Photo:** Charles Walker Collection (br); Krishna Dev (tc); The Picture Art Collection (tr); The Protected Art Archive (c); FotoFlirt (bl). **Los Angeles County Museum of Art:** Gift of Marilyn Walter Grounds (cr). **The Metropolitan Museum of Art:** Samuel Eilenberg Collection, Ex Coll.: Columbia University, Purchase, Rogers Fund, 1987 (bc). **134 Adobe Stock:** Arup (cl). **Alamy Stock Photo:** Dinodia Photos (cb); PhotosIndia.com LLC (bl). **Dreamstime.com:** Harshit Srivastava (tl). **Getty Images:** Stone / Phillipe Lissac (br). **The Metropolitan Museum of Art:** Bequest of Cora Timken Burnett, 1956 (bc). **135 Adobe Stock:** Krishna / . **TurboSquid:** 3Debuy (durga); PROmax3D (lion). **136 Bridgeman Images:** From the British Library archive (bc). **Shutterstock.com:** Udaya Bhat (br). **137 Alamy Stock Photo:** ePhotocorp (cl); CPA Media Pte Ltd / Pictures From History (tr). **Bridgeman Images:** From the British Library archive (bc); Marshall H. Gould Fund, Frederick L. Jack Fund and / Mary S. and Edward J. Holmes Fund (cr). **138 Alamy Stock Photo:** Dinodia Photos RM (bl). **139 Alamy Stock Photo:** Dinodia Photos RM (tr). **140 Alamy Stock Photo:** maximimages.com (br); The History Collection (cra); Panther Media GmbH / Sorapop (c); CPA Media Pte Ltd / Pictures From History (cr). **Depositphotos Inc:** Daboost (bl). **Dreamstime.com:** Suthee Navakul (clb). **Getty Images / iStock:** Chuyu (bc). **141 Adobe Stock:** Nick (bl). **Alamy Stock Photo:** IanDagnall Computing (tc); Olga Khomyakova (cla); CPA Media Pte Ltd / Pictures From History (crb); Penta Springs Limited / Artokoloro (bl). **Dreamstime.com:** Indigofish (clb); Rozenn Leard (cb). **Getty Images / iStock:** Emmanuel Chansarel-Bourigon (br); PicturePartners (tr). **142 Getty Images / iStock:** daizuoxin (c). **142-143 Dreamstime.com:** Pixattitude (bc). **143 Alamy Stock Photo:** Universal Art Archive (c). **144 Alamy Stock Photo:** myLAM (clb). **145 The Metropolitan Museum of Art:** Gift of Douglas Dillon, 1981 (bc). **146 Alamy Stock Photo:** Ivy Close Images (bc); CPA Media Pte Ltd / Pictures From History (c). **The Metropolitan Museum of Art:** Fletcher Fund, 1928 (cb). **148 Alamy Stock Photo:** CPA Media Pte Ltd / Pictures From History (bl). **The Metropolitan Museum of Art:** Gift of Abby Aldrich Rockefeller, 1942 (c). **149 Alamy Stock Photo:** Farlap (br); GL Archive (ca); Ivy Close Images (tr); The Print Collector (bl). **Dreamstime.com:** Kawisara Kaewprasert (cla); Christopher Rawlins (tc). **150 Adobe Stock:** Koichi Suenaga (bl). **Dreamstime.com:** Robert Van T Hoenderdaal (tl). **153 Dreamstime.com:** Sean Pavone (tr). **154 Adobe Stock:** Kurousagi (c). **Bridgeman Images:** The Stapleton Collection (bc). **Library of Congress, Washington, D.C.:** Sadahide Utagawa (br). **Shutterstock.com:** Glory_Yabe (cl). **154-155 Alamy Stock Photo:** MeijiShowa (ca). **155 Alamy Stock Photo:** CPA Media Pte Ltd / Pictures From History (br); Tibbut Archive (cr); The Print Collector / George G. Harrap (bc). **Bridgeman Images:** 2025 Museum of Fine Arts, Boston. All rights reserved. / William S. and John T. Spaulding Collection / Katsushika Hokusai (1760-1849) (tc). **156 Getty Images:** Hulton Archive / Fine Art Images / Heritage Images (tl). **The Metropolitan Museum of Art:** Gift of Mary L. Cassilly, 1894 (clb). **157 Dreamstime.com:** Meaothai (br). **158 Dreamstime.com:** Irina Filatova (ca); Moomusician (tc). **Shutterstock.com:** ryan7 (crb). **159 Adobe Stock:** YOUSUK (cl). **Alamy Stock Photo:** Album (cb); World History Archive (br). **Dreamstime.com:** Tony Zhao (tc). **162-163 Getty Images:** Universal Images Group / Werner Forman (tc). **162 Alamy Stock Photo:** Matthias Breiter / Minden Pictures (c); Steeve-X-Art (bl). **Dreamstime.com:** Rinus Baak (cra). **163 Alamy Stock Photo:** Penta Springs Limited (cr); World History Archive (br). **Bridgeman Images:** GEO Image Collection / Ted Spiegel (tl). **164 Alamy Stock Photo:** Tom Uhlman (tc). **166 Adobe Stock:** Sergiy (br). **167 123RF.com:** Koji Hirano / Kojihirano (tr). **Bridgeman Images:** Museum of Fine Arts, Houston / Gift of Miss Ima Hogg / Riley "Sunrise" Quoyavema (ca). **Dreamstime.com:** Dimjul (cr); Jaahnlieb (crb). **168 Dreamstime.com:** Peng Ge (br). **170 Alamy Stock Photo:** Dominic Robinson (bc). **171 Alamy Stock Photo:** George Ostertag (cr). **172 Alamy Stock Photo:** Frank Nowikowski (tr); Diana Sanchez (clb); VTR (br). **Bridgeman Images:** © NPL - DeA Picture Library (cb). **Dreamstime.com:** Jesus Eloy Ramos Lara (bc). **The Metropolitan Museum of Art:** Gift of Justin Kerr, in memory of Barbara Kerr, 2014 (ca). **173 Alamy Stock Photo:** Charles Walker Collection (cb, br); Gaetan Mariage (tc); The Picture Art Collection (ca); Peter Horree (tr). **Dreamstime.com:** Agnieszka Murphy (tl). **Getty Images / iStock:** cinoby (cra). **Shutterstock.com:** Peter Hermes Furian (bc). **174 Alamy Stock Photo:** Vidura Luis Barrios / Stockimo (tc). **177 Dreamstime.com:** Gianpierolauretta (br). **178 Alamy Stock Photo:** Classicstock / J. Neubauer (bl); The Picture Art Collection (cl). **Getty Images:** DEA / A. Gregorio / De Agostini (r). **179 Alamy Stock Photo:** Zip Lexing (tl); The Picture Art Collection (bc); Zuri Swimmer (br). **Bridgeman Images:** © Iberfoto (cl). **Dreamstime.com:** Jakub Zajic (tr). **Shutterstock.com:** Mikiko (bl). **180 Alamy Stock Photo:** AP-Photo (bc); The Picture Art Collection (cla); Martin Harvey (br). **Dreamstime.com:** Marktucan (tr); Pytyczech (cr). **Getty Images / iStock:** Ad_Foto (ca); R.M. Nunes (cra). **Getty Images:** Universal Images Group / Werner Forman (c). **The Metropolitan Museum of Art:** Gift of George D. Pratt, 1933 (tc). **181 Alamy Stock Photo:** Peter Horree (c); Prisma Archivo (tc); Marina Movschowitz (bc). **Dreamstime.com:** Sorin Colac (tl); Mark Watson (br). **Shutterstock.com:** Vadim Petrakov (cr). **183 Alamy Stock Photo:** Art Collection 2 (tr). **Dreamstime.com:** Earnfun365 (cr). **184-185 Alamy Stock Photo:** Roy Langstaff. **185 Alamy Stock Photo:** © Fine Art Images / Heritage Images (bl); Jon G. Fuller / VWPics (cl); Jon Arnold Images (br). **Bridgeman Images:** Henri Stierlin / Bildarchiv Steffens (tr). **Getty Images / iStock:** E+ / FernandoPodolski (tl). **186 Dreamstime.com:** Donyanedomam (cb). **Getty Images / iStock:** Lovelyday12 (bl). **The Metropolitan Museum of Art:** Gift of Mr. and Mrs. David Heller, 1983 (br). **187 Dreamstime.com:** Geza Farkas (tc). **Shutterstock.com:** Arnont.tp (br); Dima Moroz (bl). **190 123RF.com:** Stillfx (crb). **Alamy Stock Photo:** Cavan Images (br); One-Image Photography (cra); Paul Mayall Australia (cl); Thierry Grun (bl); JohnBuxton (bc). **Dreamstime.com:** Kevin Oke (c). **Getty Images:** Universal Images Group / Werner Forman (ca). **191 123RF.com:** Stellar001 (br). **Alamy Stock Photo:** Charles Walker Collection (ca, tr); Douglas Peebles Photography / C. Douglas Peebles (bc). **Dreamstime.com:** Manon Van Os (tl); Viktorus (cla); Steveheap (cr). **192 Alamy Stock Photo:** DU Photography (tl). **193 Dreamstime.com:** Isselee (br). **194-195 Bridgeman Images:** National Gallery of Victoria, Melbourne / Gift of Penny Blazey, 1989 / Danny Nolorman Djorlum / © estate of the artist licensed by Aboriginal Artists Agency Lt (c). **194 Alamy Stock Photo:** Auscape International Pty Ltd (bl); Dave Pinson (tr). **Shutterstock.com:** Elena Istomina (cl); Jukka Jantunen (br). **195 Dreamstime.com:** Ken Griffiths (bl). **Getty Images:** Simon McGill / Moment (cra). **naturepl.com:** Jouan & Rius (c). **Photo Scala, Florence:** RMN-Grand Palais / Michel Urtado / Thierry Ollivier / Dist. / Dhawaanygulili Moguu Darrnguwuy / © estate of the artist licensed by Aboriginal Artists Agency Lt (tr). **Shutterstock.com:** Xero9 (tl). **197 Alamy Stock Photo:** The Print Collector / CM Dixon / Heritage Images (crb). **200 Alamy Stock Photo:** Doug Perrine (cl); Graham Prentice (br). **Dreamstime.com:** Kelpfish (bl). **Getty Images:** The Image Bank / James L. Amos (cr). **201 Alamy Stock Photo:** Album (tr); Malcolm Schuyl (br). **Dreamstime.com:** Marina Storm (bl)

Cover images: *Front:* **Alamy Stock Photo:** Juniors Bildarchiv / F368 cb; **Dreamstime.com:** Tirrasa cla; **Getty Images:** Werner Forman / Universal Images Group tc; *Spine:* **Getty Images:** Werner Forman / Universal Images Group t